Pope and Bolingbroke

WITHDRAWN

Henry St. John, Viscount Bolingbroke

Alexander Pope

Brean S. Hammond

Pope and Bolingbroke

A Study of Friendship and Influence

University of Missouri Press

Columbia, 1984

Copyright © 1984 by
The Curators of the University of Missouri
University of Missouri Press, Columbia, Missouri 65211
Library of Congress Catalog Card Number 83–1068
Printed and bound in the United States of America

Library of Congress Cataloging in Publication Data

Hammond, Brean S., 1951–

  Pope and Bolingbroke.

  Includes index.
  1. Pope, Alexander, 1688–1744—Friends and associates.
2. Bolingbroke, Henry St. John, Viscount, 1678–1751.
3. Pope, Alexander, 1688–1744—Criticism and interpretation. 4. Poets, English—18th century—Biography.
5. Politicians—Great Britain—Biography. I. Title.
PR3633.H35   1983   821'.5   83–1068
ISBN 0–8262–0404–X

The etching of Lord Bolingbroke on page ii is unattributed,
probably after a portrait by Jonathan Richardson.
The drawing of Alexander Pope is by Jonathan Richardson.
Both are reproduced courtesy of the National Portrait Gallery.

For
Ann, Adam, and Ruth

Acknowledgments

Early work on this book was aided greatly by Mr. E. G. Midgley of St. Edmund Hall, Oxford, and Miss Rachel Trickett, Principal of St. Hugh's College, Oxford. Professor H. T. Dickinson of Edinburgh University read parts of it in those early days. In addition, I must gratefully acknowledge the help of Mr. Giles Barber, Dr. Howard Erskine-Hill, Dr. James Turner, and my colleagues at Liverpool University, Brian Nellist and John Thompson. In recent years, the manuscript has undergone many sea changes. A version of Chapter 7 appeared in the *British Journal for Eighteenth-Century Studies* 3 (1980), pp. 107–26: I am grateful to the editor, Professor Dennis Fletcher, for permission to reprint. Professor Jack Roberts of the University of Missouri made the happy suggestion that I should publish with his university's press. I owe many debts of gratitude to the various friends who have put up with me and put me up with them when I was working in London: thank you, especially Yasmin and Sky and Aunt Isabel. Mrs. Joan Welford, who typed the manuscript, no expression of thanks can compensate. But my main debt is to my wife, Ann, who must have wished Pope and Bolingbroke at the devil a thousand times, and never said so.

B.S.H.
Liverpool, England
September 1983

Contents

Introduction

Lo! at the Wheels of her Triumphal Car,
Old *England*'s Genius, rough with many a Scar,
Dragg'd in the Dust!

Pope, *Epilogue to the Satires*, 1.151–53

If we needed to supply a catch title for Pope's work, a short tag that would encapsulate the spirit of his poetry, we might call him the poet of friendship. The word *friend* and its cognates are used nearly two hundred times by Pope in his poems, and in many of them, notably the *Epistle to Dr. Arbuthnot* and the *Epilogue to the Satires*, an ostentatious roll call of his major friendships is a potent form of self-justification. From his letters, we get some sense of how friendship functioned as a "Philosophical Principle"— thus designated in a letter to Lyttelton. It was the acorn from which the oak of virtue grew. It implanted in men a sense of duty and responsibility, cultivated sympathetic understanding, and yielded the fruits of hospitality. No one who was not well practiced in the domestic virtues, of which friendship was the chief, could be a worthy servant of the public. Since much of Pope's later poetry is devoted to prescribing and describing how the private virtues can be integrated with the public, friendship was also a source of his poetic inspiration, the spirit of his Muse. The direct impetus behind Pope's greatest work was a feeling of solidarity with a group of like-minded individuals, solidarity greatly strengthened by the hostility of numerous adversaries.

In his early career, his associates in the Scriblerus Club, Swift, Gay, Arbuthnot, and Parnell, provided the sense of a common purpose and of an elite group sharing that purpose that Pope continued to depend on throughout his life. Although the Scriblerus Club formally existed only a few months between 1713 and 1714, it contributed greatly to forming the satiric cast of mind that is a clear hallmark of eighteenth-century literature. The Scriblerians lived in an era of tremendous change. Yet the progress made in science, philosophy, and learning in the age of Locke and Newton also gave rise to much that was useless and absurd, extravagant and fraudulent. To the Scriblerians, there was a danger that accumulation of knowledge was being respected for its own sake, in despite of practical

1

application and more genuine values. Scientific empiricism came to seem to them the highest and most dangerous form of pride. Parody, ridicule, and irony were developed by them as an armory of weapons against this loss of perspective. When Swift returned from Ireland in 1726 to be reunited briefly with Pope, Arbuthnot, and Gay, the spirit of Scriblerus moved again. In *Gulliver's Travels,* in Gay's *Fables,* in Pope's *Essay on Man* and early *Dunciad,* the Scriblerian impulse toward cutting human beings down to size and toward identifying and pillorying the specific enemies of genuine learning is clearly seen. The Indian summer of Scriblerian activity gradually burned itself out, and Pope was without a major project now that the drudgery of Homer translation was over. From this time, Pope's need to belong to an elite group and to be working toward a common purpose drew him more and more into the orbit of Henry St. John, Viscount Bolingbroke.

Bolingbroke first met Pope when Bolingbroke was at the height of his powers as Secretary of State in Queen Anne's Tory ministry and when Pope, by contrast, was a young poet whose London reputation was very much in the making. Drawn together at first, perhaps, by mutual belief in the Stuart cause and certainly by the satiric cast of mind that they both cultivated as well as by similar literary tastes, their friendship was cut short by Bolingbroke's dramatic flight to France in 1715. In France, Bolingbroke watched Pope's career with keen interest; and when Bolingbroke was permitted to return to England in 1723, the peculiar intensity of Pope's delight suggests the strength of the bond that had already been formed. Bolingbroke's friendship with Pope must have been a factor in his choosing to live at Dawley Farm, near Uxbridge, a short ride away from Pope's villa at Twickenham. Thus began a period of intimacy spanning a decade, years in which the first *Dunciad,* the *Essay on Man,* the *Moral Essays,* and some of the *Imitations of Horace* were written, while Bolingbroke composed some of his most significant works of political theory. The Bolingbroke who returned from France in 1723 was much changed from the frantically busy political animal of Queen Anne's last years. He had put his exile to use in extending his learning and deepening his powers of reason, undergoing in the process a personality change that Pope found wholly admirable. The philosophical Bolingbroke became an important influence on Pope's subsequent career, while conversely, Pope played a vital role not merely in the dissemination of Bolingbroke's ideas, but also in the transformation of them into great poetry. Dawley Farm became a cell of organized opposition to the Walpole government. As is only now beginning to be appreciated, the literary struggles of the time were a kind of Eastern Front to the main political war against Walpole, and on this front, Pope was a very active soldier.

On the subject of friendship, on its being the province of the virtuous alone and on the need to distinguish one's friends from one's enemies, Bolingbroke was as sanguine as his friend Pope. Bolingbroke writes in typical fashion to Swift, "Sincerity, constancy, tenderness are rarely to be found, they are so much out of use, that the man of mode imagines them to be out of nature. we meet with few friends. the greatest part of those who pass for such, are properly speaking nothing more than acquaintance, and no wonder, since Tullys maxim is certainly true, that friendship can subsist non nisi inter bonos."[1] He could hardly have wished for a friend more ready to acknowledge his love and gratitude than Alexander Pope. In several important places in his verse, Pope testifies to his debt to Bolingbroke, while the hero worship expressed in the letters was so intense that it cannot be overstated. He thought of Bolingbroke as an otherworldly and superior form of life, scarcely a human being at all. Warburton was not exaggerating when he claimed that to Pope, Bolingbroke "seemed to be sent down hither by Providence, from some higher Sphere, to become the Conservator of the *Rights* and *Reason* of Mankind."[2] This is exactly the way that Pope himself used to speak, on occasion regarding Bolingbroke as actually a god. He said to Spence in 1735, "Lord Bolingbroke is something superior to anything I have seen in human nature. You know I don't deal much in hyperboles: I quite think him what I say"; and in Pope's last year, when death was on his mind, he imagined that an especially bright comet then visible in the sky had come to earth to convey Bolingbroke to another world:

> "I really think there is something in that great man which looks as if he was placed here by mistake" [said Spence].
> There is so, [replied Pope], and when the comet appeared to us a month or two ago I had sometimes an imagination that it might possibly be come to our world to carry him home, as a coach comes to one's door for other visitors.[3]

Despite the importance of Pope's regard for friendship and for his friends and despite the copious testimony to Bolingbroke's place as *primus inter pares,* the relationship between the two men is largely disregarded by modern scholars and readers. Disregard of Bolingbroke has been systematized into the modern reader's experience of Pope by his neglect at the hands of the Twickenham editor of *An Essay on Man,* Maynard Mack. For all too many readers, the only live issue concerning Bolingbroke and Pope is whether the former contributed anything to the shaping of the *Essay on Man,* and on this question, Maynard Mack is discouraging:

> [Bolingbroke's] published *Fragments or Minutes of Essays . . .* cannot be very seriously considered as sources of Pope's work. The chronology is all

against it . . . In the real core of their argument—the approach to the problems of man's life, the kinds of evidence drawn on, the texture of attitudes—Pope's *Essay* and Bolingbroke's philosophy as we know it are sharply at odds . . . Bolingbroke's thought may be said to have transmitted to the poet the outlines of his argument and an unknown number of its subsidiary ideas. It cannot be said to have done more.[4]

Mack's repudiation is certainly one reason for the lack of a thorough investigation of a friendship that was, I believe, crucial to the development of Pope's work and, more generally, to the nature of satiric expression in his lifetime. However, it is not the only reason. There has been the general tendency in recent criticism to regard a poet's life as immaterial to the study of his work, the legacy of New Criticism. Warnings against the "intentional fallacy" and the "affective fallacy," however seriously misplaced in the case of satire, have served to divorce poetry from the conditions of its production. Though many inroads have been made against the hegemony of this view, they have not penetrated far in Pope's case because an authoritative modern biography still remains to be written. The social and cultural milieu in which he wrote is not fully available to the reader as a source of explication of the poetry, so that the scholarly emphasis has perforce been placed on assimilating his work to the tradition of previous practitioners and on examining the conscious artistry of his manipulation of allusion, mode, and convention. Recently, however, literary critics have been regarding their task much less narrowly with respect to Pope, and a number of studies have helped create a climate favorable for reassessing Bolingbroke's friendship with Pope. Oddly, the most important of these is Maynard Mack's *The Garden and the City* (1969), in which he shows how Pope created a personality that is the fictive hero of the traditional confrontation between virtuous simplicity and sophisticated corruption.[5] Mack stresses both the power Pope was able to exert over his own self-image and the use to which that power was put in the political campaign against Walpole. And he places a very different value on Bolingbroke's contribution to Pope's art than in his earlier editorial work. Subsequently, other writers have placed Pope in his sociological or historical milieu, showing that there is nothing incompatible with greatness in an art that derives its muscle and sinew from the observed realities of its own time. In particular, Howard Erskine-Hill in *The Social Milieu of Alexander Pope* (1975) and Bertrand A. Goldgar in *Walpole and the Wits* (1976) have stressed that Pope's poetry is a form of discourse that is continuous with other forms of discourse of the time, notably political discourse, and is not a separate species to be studied in a vacuum with a peculiarly "poetic" attention.[6]

More important still to the genesis of this book are the works of historical revisionism that have emerged in the past decade, for the main stumbling

block to a thorough evaluation of this friendship has certainly been Bolingbroke's reputation. Though there have been many reservations about
Pope's personality and conduct, there have been comparatively few about
his greatness as a poet. Bolingbroke has not been so lucky with his
posterity. He has suffered from the stigma of deism since the posthumous
publication of his *Philosophical Works* in David Mallet's 1754 edition. There
was a widespread sense of outrage that Bolingbroke had silently harbored
such views on metaphysics and revealed religion, most memorably expressed by Dr. Johnson (though, as with *Tom Jones,* he would not read the
work): "He was a scoundrel, and a coward: a scoundrel, for charging a
blunderbuss against religion and morality; a coward, because he had not
resolution to fire it off himself, but left half a crown to a beggarly Scotch-
man [Mallet], to draw the trigger after his death!"[7] In the *Dictionary,*
Johnson gave as a definition of irony, "Bolingbroke was a holy man."
Periodicals like the *Gentleman's Magazine* and the *Monthly Review* for 1755
carried numerous hostile reviews, and the leading experts on philosophy
took up the pen against Bolingbroke. Warburton attacked him in his
scurrilous and inflammatory *A View of Lord Bolingbroke's Philosophy,* while
John Leland ran the entire gamut of objections to Bolingbroke's denial of
the doctrine of an afterlife and the attempt to undermine Mosaic tradition
in *A View of the Principal Deistical Writers of the Last and Present Century.*
These criticisms were reissued by Leslie Stephen in the nineteenth century
and have become definitive in our own:

> The failure was . . . due . . . to the windy and incoherent nature of the
> so-called philosophy. Even the external polish of style repels us, like the
> courtly manner of some palpably insincere diplomatist. And then Boling-
> broke is monstrously diffuse; he is rhetorical where he ought to be logical;
> he repeats himself incessantly, and contradicts himself nearly as often; no
> solid ground of thought can be found in this shifting quagmire of specula-
> tion, where the one genuine ingredient seems to be an indiscriminate
> hatred of all philosophers and divines.[8]

The most recent critique of Bolingbroke's philosophy is D. G. James's *The
Life of Reason,* which preserves the philosophical and logical criticisms of
his predecessors and also the high moral tone. Bolingbroke's religion is
regarded by James as a crime against logic and humanity rather than as a
possibly respectable philosophical position: Bolingbroke, says James,
"was repelled by the spectacle of intellectual enquiry which went beyond
what might be heard in the 'coffee houses and taverns.' "[9] In view of this
reputation, Bolingbroke has not appeared to be the sort of man we want
trifling with one of our most respected poets. It has become difficult to
imagine that Pope regarded Bolingbroke's philosophy more highly than
any other aspect of his work and difficult to reconstitute Bolingbroke's

contemporary standing as a universal genius, who was paid the highest tribute by contemporaries as diverse as Swift, Montesquieu, Voltaire, and Chesterfield.

As a historian and political philosopher, Bolingbroke's reputation has suffered from a process of critical attrition scarcely less damaging. For twenty years, eighteenth-century politics were dominated by Walpole and this dominance was resisted by Bolingbroke. Since those two men came to represent opposite views on the nature of government and on the moral obligations placed on those in power, the student of the period is forced to arbitrate between them, to nail his colors to the mast. Walpole sacrificed purity in government to efficiency, in the belief that the burden of administration had to be diminished by its material advantages. Bolingbroke, on the other hand, feared that manipulating political processes would lead to a weakening of principle and, as government became concentrated in the hands of a narrow oligarchy, would destroy the delicate system of checks and balances that protected the open society. He therefore advocated "virtuous" government of unimpeachable moral probity. Presently, most historians appear to support Walpole on the major issues dividing him from Bolingbroke, so that Bolingbroke's reputation has lost the battle against Walpole's, just as his policies did in life. To some extent, he has been the victim of a particular historical methodology, advocated by Sir Lewis Namier, who has been as influential on his discipline as the New Critics have been on theirs. Bolingbroke's career brings into sharp focus the problematic nature of the relationship between political ideology and political action. Namierite historians have taken the view that political ideas are irrelevant to the determination of action and that the only eighteenth-century reality was the struggle for power. If we consider Bolingbroke's political biography in isolation from his theoretical writings, he can appear to be the ideal exemplar of the Namierite thesis. His career does seem to embody the opportunistic and the instrumental in political action, and his life can be represented as a graveyard of betrayed loyalties—to Marlborough, to Queen Anne, to Harley, to George I, to the Pretender, even to Alexander Pope himself. Embarrassingly, Bolingbroke's life hardly seems to have been lived by the precepts of virtue and moral uprightness that are so central to his ideology. Historians who are disposed to regard all political ideology as hogwash will clearly consider Bolingbroke's ideology to be hogwash of a peculiarly offensive brand.

It is an important advance, therefore, that we now have a biography of Bolingbroke by H. T. Dickinson, which, in trying to represent the political choices that Bolingbroke was forced to make, regards his actions as political calculations and miscalculations rather than as moral outrages. The last few years have also produced historians sympathetic to Bolingbroke, who have argued that his ideology was a sincere and by no means misconceived expression of his fears for English political liberties. The most important of these, and the bedrock supporting this book, is Isaac Kramnick's *Bolingbroke and His Circle*. In this study Kramnick attempts to recreate the historical period as it appeared to the personalities involved. His intention is to see Bolingbroke's political views as "products of his social existence, of his position in the group life of Augustan England, in terms both of economic class and occupational group."[10] Bolingbroke's activities and writings are seen as a response to the socioeconomic results of the financial revolution and the rise of a bourgeois, individualistic middle class that demanded political power in proportion to its wealth. Financial innovations and their impact on political institutions seemed to endanger the time-tested values of the aristocracy and the gentry; the natural leaders of society were being forced to share power with new men, arrivistes whose invisible assets did not represent a genuine stake in the country's well-being. Nostalgia for a purer, more traditional power structure in which men were held together by personal ties of mutual dependence and in which no projectors or innovators threatened established hierarchies with dangerous social mobility is the informing spirit of his writing. This "style of thought" or view of experience is one that Bolingbroke shared with the Tory satirists, Swift, Pope, and Gay. They were all alienated from their age; their England was passing, and they looked to the past to locate their disappearing ideal. What Louis Bredvold called "the gloom of the Tory satirists" is thus no morbid pessimism, no enervating spiritual malaise, but an honest and realistic response to changing social conditions (realistic, that is, according to their observation of them, which Kramnick admits has been belied by history).[11]

Kramnick's work has provided an invaluable framework within which to set the relationship between Bolingbroke and Pope and has created the conditions for a reassessment of it. Nevertheless, his chapters analyzing the literary expression of Bolingbroke's and Walpole's ideas are disappointing, suffering from the historian's tendency to overschematize, to tidy away into convenient pigeonholes. Kramnick treats literary texts as documents in social history, claiming that they "represent" the social attitudes of their authors unambiguously. He thus lines up in one camp Walpole's world view, with its chief literary exponent Defoe and its philosopher-in-residence Mandeville, against, in the other camp, Bolingbroke (who is his own philosopher-in-residence) and his literary exponents Pope, Swift, and Gay. This is far too simple. It makes very little sense of Defoe, an ebullient individualist who identified closely with exactly the class of industrious small tradesmen that Bolingbroke relied on for political support; the *Craftsman* campaigns were frequently intended for this readership, and Bolingbroke never overlooked the importance of trade in creating national prosperity. In respect to the trading class, he was closer to Defoe than to Pope, who frequently satirized the "cit" mentality in terms reminiscent of Restoration comedy, as he could afford to do since he did not depend on them as electors.[12] More generally, Pope's attitude to social mobility was unlikely to have been exactly like Bolingbroke's, since Pope was himself the first conspicuous example of an author who achieved financial independence through exploiting his talents on the open market. Critics are surely justified in detecting in *The Dunciad* Pope's fear of others following where he himself had led. Kramnick's desire to hypostatize a theme in Pope's poems leads him into regarding a complex poem like the *Epistle to Burlington* as "an assault on Mandeville's assumptions" and the *Essay on Man* as an unambiguous articulation of the principle of social hierarchy.[13]

Even if Kramnick has simplified the relationship between Pope's work and Bolingbroke's, he has ensured that the time is now propitious for its revaluation. In the chapters that follow, I shall be examining the interplay of personalities, experience, and ideas in the lives and works of the two men. In the early chapters of the book, I engage with my subject as a biographer and critic, telling the facts of their lives at the significant points of overlap and halting the chronological narrative at times to deal with issues that have a bearing on the relationship though they cannot be resolved entirely factually. Was Pope a Jacobite? How politically committed was he? What mutual interests welded the relationship? Were they compatible in their views of religion? The opening chapter maps out the main lines of the friendship and attempts (perhaps overambitiously) to create its living tissue by considering Bolingbroke's philosophy as a form of conversation. Generally, the first section treats the works of the two men as biographical facts. Despite very great temptation, I have tried to be ascetic in criticizing Pope's poems. The entire study has been undertaken with critical intentions insofar as I wish to claim that knowledge of the friendship will have considerable bearing on our reading of Pope's poems. Usually, this is a question of emphasis, but at times the revisions of accepted readings I am suggesting are substantial. Separate chapters have been assigned, therefore, to the *Essay on Man*, examining Pope's debt to Bolingbroke, and to *Epistle to Bolingbroke (Imit. Hor. Ep. I.1)*, which for obvious reasons occupies a central position in this book.

In the last two chapters, my approach to the subject is that of the historian of ideas, but here also there is a biographical *parti pris*. I have tried to show what there was in Bolingbroke's style of thought that could fascinate a poet with Pope's satirical gifts. Recent work in the field of Augustan studies has already shown that much of the literary activity in this period has an inescapable political cast. Controversies which at this distance may seem to be exclusively literary turn out to be extensions of the political debate on how the nation's happiness is to be secured: opera's status as an art form, Homer translation, the various manifestations of the ancients versus moderns debate, the poet laureateship, even quarrels as specific as Pope's with Theobald over the editing of Shakespeare, need to be placed in the context of affairs of state. My argument will be not only that Pope's poems have political content (which is scarcely new), but also that they were conceived of as a form of political action. Pope's satire and Bolingbroke's political philosophy are two arms of a campaign to arrest a decline in the nation's moral fiber. Because Bolingbroke's philosophy claimed moral reform as its objective and because it applied to public life a model of virtuous conduct that was based on friendship and cultivation of the domestic virtues and that was partly lived out at Dawley and Twickenham, its appeal for Pope was very great. This emphasis on friendship and the domestic virtues gives an identifiable consistency to Pope's poetic voice in the series of *Imitations of Horace* that Bolingbroke urged him to write in the 1730s. They held in common ideals, concepts, a specialized vocabulary containing key words like *liberty, corruption,* and *constitution,* and a myth for the times that derives from their mutual alienation from the direction being taken by progress.

A book of this kind does present difficulties to the reader, and it is as well to be honest about them. The book is interdisciplinary, as it must be since it deals with the attempt made by two men, who themselves stood at the confluence of various forms of knowledge, to come to an understanding of the times in which they lived. It is also eclectic in that it taps various approaches within disciplinary boundaries. Furthermore, there are various contingent but nevertheless constraining factors that operate on the way in which it is written. The biographical section focuses rather more sharply on Pope's career than on Bolingbroke's, because it is in the former's life that the gaps need to be filled at present. The later chapters put a greater burden of exposition on Bolingbroke's ideas. I am aware of one great danger here. Pope's life may appear to the reader as an empty vessel to be filled with Bolingbroke's ideas; or, to change the metaphor, he may be left as a plucked goose, the feathers of his achievement stripped off and stuck in Bolingbroke's cap. While I do not wish to give this impression, I do certainly intend to restore Bolingbroke to his deserved prominence as an influence on Pope's thought and on the direction of his poetic talent, even if this influence was not always beneficial (as perhaps in the *Essay on Man* it was not). It would be impossibly naive to think of Pope as his friend's inferior stooge, though contemporary satires do often image them thus. But Bolingbroke was a dominating personality, and I have no doubt that he had the ascendancy in the power structure that operates even in friendships. The line is a difficult one to draw. But I hope that in the following chapters the reader will sense above all the feeling of mutual participation in what amounted to a crusade against the temper of the times, in Pope's terms to rescue "Old England's Genius" from being dragged in the dust.

Chapter 1

"A Freemasonry of Two"

"Fav'rite of the Skies"

We are fortunate enough to possess a pictorial record of the friendship, bordering on idolatry, that existed between Pope and Bolingbroke. They eagerly collected portraits of each other, portraits which must have hung like icons on the walls of Pope's villa and Bolingbroke's farm at Dawley. Around 1732, Pope received from Jonathan Richardson a commissioned drawing or engraving of his "Guide, Philosopher, and Friend," a visual cue for a typically fulsome tribute:

> Posterity will thro' your means, see the man whom it will for ages honour, vindicate, and applaud, when envy is no more, and when (as I have already said in the Essay to which you are so partial) "The sons shall blush their fathers were his foes."[1]

In the summer of 1738, when Bolingbroke was staying in Pope's villa, both were sitting to Jonathan Richardson for portraits that they were to present to each other. William Kent the landscape gardener describes a trip with Pope to Richardson's studio, which apparently was cluttered with likenesses of the two friends: " . . . three pictures of Lord Baulingbrok one for himself for Pope [sic], another Pope in a mourning gown with a strange view of the garden to show the obelisk as in memory to his mothers Death."[2] One of the pictures that Kent saw on this occasion, the portrait of Pope in a mourning gown, has only recently been rediscovered.[3] It is one of the most personal and intimate representations of Pope that survives. Similarly, it seems reasonable to infer that one of the Bolingbrokes was the picture of him in the National Portrait Gallery "wearing a deep brownish old velvet turban cap . . . and a dark greyish lavender drapery about his shoulders."[4] Appropriately, the likenesses they exchanged were unguarded and informal, paintings that laid bare the soul in a spirit of open friendship. The painting of Pope in mourning attire with the memorial obelisk he erected to commemorate his mother's death forming a mysterious background was also an appropriate gift for Bolingbroke because the latter was admitted to the iconographic pantheon of Pope's beloved parents. In 1772, Horace Walpole bought for Strawberry Hill pencil drawings by Richardson that depict the poet, his dying father, his aging mother, and Bolingbroke all symbolically grouped together in one frame.[5]

These pictures are visual testimony to a relationship that lasted until Pope's death. Shortly after his fiftieth birthday, he wrote to William Fortescue, "I have been very happy these 3 weeks & more, in the Company of one of the oldest & first of my Friends, my Lord Bolingbroke: he has instructed me most, & in many instances proved he loved me the best, of any of a Rank so far above me. But what adds to the obligation is, his being of a Rank in Understanding & Learning more above Others, than any Rank else can make a Man; and That Superiority too he has set aside in my Favour."[6] The strength of feeling on Bolingbroke's side is best seen in Spence's account of Bolingbroke, nine days before Pope died, "leaning against Mr. Pope's chair and crying over him, for a considerable time with more concern than can be expressed," crying, as Spence said, for a "quarter of an hour like a child."[7] Pope was the closest and most loyal friend Bolingbroke ever had.

The circumstances of their lives forced the two men into very similar positions. Pope was always an outsider in his own society, prevented by his religion and his unfortunate appearance from reaping the rewards, social, civil, and romantic, to which his talents seemed to entitle him. Doubtless the deeply malicious thrust of some of his satire is the result of this talent turning inward and, so to speak, septic. But this lack of fulfillment and the insecurity deriving from it also endowed him with a capacity for great loyalty and for the projection that leads to hero worship. Outside his immediate circle of friends, Pope was not well liked, and subsequent biographers have confirmed impressions conveyed by his enemies that he was a hypocrite whose large claims about his virtues were consistently belied by a series of mean and petty acts. A recent biographer-critic, James Reeves, writes:

> . . . One of the chief themes stressed in this book is the chicanery, dishonesty, and frequent downright cruelty by which Pope manipulated his career so as to keep himself constantly in the public eye—a necessity which he realised from the start—and to appear both as a man of moral integrity and as one more sinned against than sinning.[8]

This is much like many eighteenth-century summaries of Pope's character, and it is easy to see why he should seek out the security of Bolingbroke's protection. In this respect, however, Bolingbroke's own needs were precisely reciprocal. Dickinson's biography of Bolingbroke concludes that he "always attracted the attention, but rarely the loyalty, of the majority of his contemporaries in political life. The stark contrast between his undoubted talent and his defects was obvious to all his contemporaries, and this helps to account for his success as a propagandist and his failure as a politician."[9] What he lacked as a politician, in conspicuous contrast to Walpole, was personal popularity. Externally, Bolingbroke seems to have been unscrupulous, devious, and unprincipled. Pope offered him what his abilities were unable to secure—loyalty, friendship, a willingness to be impressed and dominated by him. This latter factor, Pope's quasi-feminine passivity in the relationship, must have had a great deal to do with its capacity to withstand the test of time. Pope was not in any sense a rival to Bolingbroke. He did not regard himself as Bolingbroke's social or intellectual equal. Bolingbroke was cast in the role of glorious elder brother, capable of achieving vicarious satisfactions for Pope. Together they created and acted out a series of roles—rake, retired philosopher, man of action, public servant, patriot, and friend to virtue—and where Bolingbroke could fill these roles more plausibly, Pope was happy to play second fiddle. He conceded superiority in all matters pertaining to the intellect and to politics, practical or theoretical, venerated Bolingbroke's learning and his knowledge of human nature deriving from history, and admired his facility in writing and speech. Only on aesthetic matters and on questions relating to the practice of poetry did Pope presume to assert himself; as he said to Spence, Bolingbroke "is not deep either in pictures, statues, or architecture."[10] Since Bolingbroke was not especially envious of preeminence in poetry, he could enjoy the reputation of his friend Pope in this province with unadulterated pleasure. We may doubt whether the friendship would have been as firm if Pope had consistently harbored political aspirations, as perhaps in the later stages of his life he did.

Similarity of temperament did not make for friction because their egocentricities were in the main compatible. "*Envy* must own, I live among the Great," says Pope in the *Epistle to Fortescue (Imit. Hor. Sat.* II.1), with Bolingbroke and Peterborow in mind; his friendship with the omni-talented Bolingbroke, who combined the accomplishments of the active and the comtemplative man, was a sop to his vanity. Bolingbroke's own sense of what Frederick Keener has aptly described as a "freemasonry of two"[11] is conveyed in the introduction to the *Letters or Essays addressed to Alexander Pope,* where he gives a strong sense of being engaged in a joint project with Pope to combat the ignorance and error of the times:

> But however this may be, pursue your task undauntedly, and whilst so many others convert the noblest employments of human society into sordid trades, let the generous muse resume her ancient dignity, re-assert her ancient prerogative, and instruct and reform as well as amuse the world. Let her give a new turn to the thoughts of men, raise new affections in their minds, and determine in another and better manner the passions of their hearts. Poets, they say, were the first philosophers and divines, in every country; and in ours, perhaps, the first institutions of religion, and civil policy, were owing to our bards. . . .
> Whilst your muse is employed to lash the vicious into repentance, or to laugh the fools of the age into shame, and whilst she rises sometimes to

the noblest subjects of philosophical meditation, I shall throw upon paper, for your satisfaction, and for my own, some part at least of what I have thought and said formerly on the last of these subjects, as well as the reflections that they may suggest to me further in writing on them. The strange situation I am in, and the melancholy state of public affairs take up much of my time, divide or even dissipate my thoughts, and which is worse, drag the mind down by perpetual interruptions, from a philosophical tone, or temper, to the drudgery of private and public business. The last lies nearest my heart; and since I am once more engaged in the service of my country, disarmed, gagged, and almost bound as I am, I will not abandon it as long as the integrity and perseverance of those who are under none of these disadvantages, and with whom I now co-operate, make it reasonable for me to act the same part.[12]

This impression of beleaguered virtue that Bolingbroke cultivated so indefatigably became, for reasons that we will examine, profoundly influential on Pope. He likened Bolingbroke in his imagination to various Roman patriots who had endured their country's neglect with fortitude, just as he saw his own residence in Twickenham as analogous with Horace on the Sabine farm. In public life tirelessly laboring for his country's well-being, in retirement improving his mind and his estate with a Stoic *apatheia*, Bolingbroke was a powerful role model to Pope as the ideal exemplar of Roman civic virtue. Dustin Griffin observes in a recent study of Pope that he possessed an enlarged concept of self that gathered into itself some of his wider concerns, with love of country and service to virtue predominant.[13] To an unusual extent, his friendships with men of merit became part of the fabric of his personality. Under Bolingbroke's tutelage, this apprehension of friendship's importance took on a political dimension; when on 14 April 1741 Pope wrote to Hugh Bethel, "I much better understand the Duties of Friendship & the Merits of Virtue in Private life, than those of Public: and should never love my Country if I did not love the Best Men in it," we can hear an explicit echo of Bolingbroke's charge against Walpole in *The Idea of a Patriot King* that he has corrupted public morals: "I say thus generally, the morals; because he, who abandons or betrays his country, will abandon or betray his friend."[14] *The Idea of a Patriot King* presents the most finished formulation of the concept, among Bolingbroke's major contributions to political theory, that in order to govern well the prince or political leader should make his public moral attributes an extension of his private ones. In saying this, Bolingbroke was arresting a current of thought deriving from Machiavelli that maintained the need for a lamination between the personal, private existence of the prince and the characteristics he must be seen as possessing; and in the early eighteenth century, Mandeville's *The Fable of the Bees* presented one of the most extreme encapsulations of this view in his "Private Vice—Public Virtue" theory of the healthy economy. But Bolingbroke's view, which found expression only in the 1730s, was distilling over a much longer period in his correspondence with Swift when in France and in his intercourse with Pope when he was Pope's near neighbor from 1725 onward. Already in 1719, Bolingbroke was quoting to Swift Cicero's maxim that "friendship can subsist non nisi inter bonos," and since in Bolingbroke's view only good men are fit to govern, friendship becomes the binding force of a governing elite.

Friendship between the two men occupied a middle ground between a purely personal relationship, almost a recreation from the world of public affairs, and a businesslike, organized political partnership. This area of overlap between the domestic and the committed remains to be explored in the chapters that follow. For the moment, let us think of them together at a dinner party at Bolingbroke's, with Bolingbroke pledging the after-dinner toast "Amicitiae et Libertati." Fittingly, since in its juxtaposition of friendship with the political concept of liberty it symbolizes the nature of the poet's bond with his greatest friend, Pope adopted this motto for his doorway at Twickenham.

"From Grave to Gay"

What might their conversation have been like? Although there is comparatively little evidence available to us, especially about Pope's powers of conversation, it is a question worth speculating on because conversation was the main currency of the friendship. Bolingbroke held a widespread reputation as an orator, wit, and conversationalist, recognized not only in panegyrics like this from Thomas Parnell's *Essay on the Different Stiles of Poetry* (1713):

> O Bolingbroke! O Fav'rite of the Skies,
> O born to Gifts by which the Noblest rise,
> Improv'd in Arts by which the Brightest please,
> Intent to Business and polite for Ease,
> Sublime in Eloquence, whose loud *Applause*
> Hath stil'd thee *Patron* of a Nation's Cause,

but also in the more sober estimation of Swift, who thought him "the greatest young man I ever knew; wit, capacity, beauty, quickness of apprehension, good learning, and an excellent taste; the best orator in the house of commons, admirable conversation, good nature, and good manners; generous, and a despiser of money."[15] Chesterfield, recommending him as a model to his son, had no hesitation in ratifying Pope's high opinion: "Lord Bolingbroke . . . joins, to the deepest erudition, the most elegant politeness and good-breeding that ever any courtier and man of the world was adorned with. And Pope very justly called him 'all accomplished St. John,' with regard to his knowledge and his manners.''[16] In the *Essay on Man*, Pope called attention to Bolingbroke's mastery of conversational tone, his ability to manage the transitions of shifting mood, when he steers "From grave to gay, from lively to severe" (4.380). Maynard Mack's introduction to the *Essay on Man* draws attention to the contribution that Bolingbroke's conversation may have made to the poem's genesis, though only to dismiss it.[17] We must return to this issue later because, as I will argue, the poem seems to me to owe a debt to the conversations that Pope and Bolingbroke held in the late 1720s and early 1730s; these were probably recorded by Pope in note form and by Bolingbroke in the form of a prose treatise that is no longer extant. But we can derive some impression of the nature of these philosophical conversations from the writings that do survive, which comprise nearly half of Bolingbroke's oeuvre. His four *Letters or Essays addressed to Alexander Pope Esquire* and the later *Fragments or Minutes of Essays* are recollections in tranquillity of these discussions. They preserve, quite deliberately, the informal, ad hoc structure of oral discourse. Bolingbroke frequently emphasized his obligation to Pope for provoking him to write notes on their conversations:

> In leading me to discourse, as you have done often, and in pressing me to write as you do now, on certain subjects, you may propose to draw me back to those trains of thought, which are, above all others, worthy to employ the human mind, and I thank you for it.[18]

Two suggestions implicit in this are repeated throughout Bolingbroke's philosophical writings: the *Fragments or Minutes* really are, in the business-meeting sense of the term, *minutes* of verbal encounters; and they are the product, as is Pope's *Essay*, of the cross-fertilization of two minds. In the Advertisement to the *Fragments*, we find a similar emphasis:

> The foregoing Essays, if they may deserve even that name, and the Fragments or Minutes that follow, were thrown upon paper in Mr. Pope's lifetime, and at his desire . . . They are all nothing more than repetitions of conversations often interrupted, often renewed, and often carried on a little confusedly.[19]

And indeed Bolingbroke often emphasizes the conversational nature of his writings, the sense in which they are close to the texture of the spoken word, in mitigation of the looseness of their structure:

> . . . You know that I have reserved to myself a right of following the matter as it rises before me, without observing in these essays, any more than I used to do in our conversation, a just proportion in the members of my discourse.[20]

It is in the philosophical writings that the texture of Bolingbroke's thought is most apparent; in them, we have our closest encounter with the living, active intelligence that captivated Pope. As we have observed, history has dealt harshly with Bolingbroke, and nowhere more so than in its verdict on his philosophical ideas, which were always unpopular but are now regarded as prolix and irrelevant. Unlike Berkeley, he was not a problem-solving philosopher, not much interested in language, and the speculative metaphysician who tries to interpret the meaning and purpose of experience is now entirely irrelevant. Pope's considered opinion that "Lord Bolingbroke will be more known to posterity as a writer and philosopher than as a statesman" seems to the modern reader an astonishing error of judgment.[21] Yet it is from his philosophy that we can supply the necessarily missing term in the equation of his friendship with Pope. As a man whose main talents were oral, his writings do not do him full justice. But his philosophical writings convey an impression of the wide sweep of his knowledge and of his ability to handle the straight-faced arguments of staid theologians with a light, ironic touch. There is a certain Renaissance fearlessness about him, a refusal to be subservient to recognized authority.

At first sight, the philosophical writings may not look very promising as a source of enlightenment on the friendship. Much of the time, they seem to reiterate a long tradition of anti-Catholic dicta excoriating "Priestcraft" and accusing Catholic clergy of using religion as a stalking-horse for world domination. Bolingbroke often apostrophized Pope when he had something particularly abusive to say, referring to the Catholic church accusingly as "your church." Here, he blusters in characteristic fashion, comparing the heathen and the Catholic conceptions of purgatory:

> This purgatory your church has borrowed: but the heathen divines applied the belief of it to a very theistical purpose, to justify the providence of God in his dealings with men; and your church has made use of this belief to a very mercenary purpose, to bubble the laity, and to enrich the priesthood.[22]

Much space in the *Essays* and *Fragments* is devoted to analysis of papal stratagem in usurping temporal power. Catholic devotions he regarded as shamelessly utilitarian, mysteries and ceremonies invented to intrigue an ever-gullible public. In the eighteenth century there appears to have been a good deal more tolerance of unorthodox ideas among personal friends; men did not seek out the society of only like-minded individuals. But even allowing for this, Bolingbroke must have trodden on Pope's Catholic sensibilities very often, to judge from the printed word. But this is probably because the ideas that have solidified into prose and now seem so uncompromising were presented to Pope at first in conversation, doubtless fleshed out and made convincing by Bolingbroke's personality. It has often seemed to me when reading these essays that their true achievement is a rhetorical one. The philosophy is at times a triumphant work of the imagination, and in many extended passages, Bolingbroke displays an acute mastery of satire. We can hear in his writings a living voice of flexible tones, and often the switches in tone from invective and irony to a more austere, graver manner are reminiscent of Pope's in the *Essay on Man*. We must not allow the label *philosophical* poem to blind us to the very consider-able number of satirical passages that occur in key positions in the *Essay on Man;* in many respects the poem is as mortifying an attack on human pride as is *Gulliver's Travels*. Bolingbroke's writings also address themselves to this purpose and maintain a tone of oblique aggression. I should like to examine the philosophical writings from the standpoint of satire, in an attempt to show that Pope may have found in their form and content certain elements that coincide with his own poetic interests in the thirties. I believe that they represent the closest approximation to Bolingbroke's idiom in conversation now available to us, including his correspondence. Pope and Bolingbroke were not having high-minded, serious discussions all the time. No doubt they often resorted to satire and enjoyed such iconoclastic tirades as are found in the published works.

Bolingbroke's Philosophy as Satire

In his second *Essay addressed to Mr. Pope*, Bolingbroke begins the vitriolic attack on metaphysics that is characteristic of the substance and tone of much of his philosophy. Metaphysicians are those who presume to de-scribe what lies behind closed doors and is invisible to us, Bolingbroke says. Time and authority have established the incomplete and unclear ideas of the early philosophers and have made them spurious first princi-ples of science. They anthropomorphize the deity:

> They ascribe to the Supreme Being the manner of knowing the ideas, and even the very affections and passions of his creatures. They presume to enter into his councils, and to account for the whole divine economy, as confidently as they would for any of their own paltry affairs. This they call theology. They build intellectual and material worlds on the hypothetical suggestions of imagination. This they call philosophy, metaphysical and physical.[23]

He goes on to propagate and document the view that divines and philos-ophers have been interested, since time immemorial, in preserving a monopoly over their stock-in-trade: to do this, they have evolved doctrine, mystery, and ceremony of such opacity that they have become the sole exegetes of it and have therefore preserved their privileged position in the eyes of the vulgar. Bolingbroke's analysis of the progress of "priestcraft" brings him to a pitch of venom that expresses itself in a sustained passage of satirical prose, brilliant in its unrelentingness. He creates a virtual *Dunciad* of the deceits of the ancients, their allegories, parables, and fables all marshaled in the cause of obscurantism. Plato, a bête noire as infuriating to Bolingbroke as Cibber was to Pope (which reflects adversely on Bolingbroke's philosophical judgment but is the stuff of satire), is castigated roundly:

> Plato, who disgraced philosophy as much as Homer elevated poetry by the use of allegory, declared that this poet, whom he banished in another mood out of his commonwealth, should not be read by any who were not initiated in wisdom: that is, who were not able to draw an hidden sense out of his writings; that is, who were not able to make their own inventions pass for the signification of his fables, and the interpretation of his allegories.[24]

Finally, Bolingbroke can tolerate no longer the folly and moral depravity of the corruption of human reason by false doctrine and vested interest. He issues the classic satiric *pronunciatum* of the *vir bonus*, the plain man to whom truth is his burden, the injured sensibility who must give expression to his feelings of impotent rage at the idiocy of his contemporaries:

> For me who think it much better not to write at all, than to write under any restraint from delivering the whole truth of things as it appears to me; who should think so, if I was able to write and go to the bottom of every subject as well as [Bacon]; and who have no cavils nor invectives to fear, when I confine the communication of my thoughts to you and a very few friends, as I do in writing these essays.[25]

He has reconstructed the genesis of metaphysical and clerical duplicity and created for it a mythology the more potent because it is given the support of a developing technique of historiography.[26] Bolingbroke has the gift of rendering those he is attacking ridiculous merely by letting them speak, by glossing their opinions and including some quotation. In *Essay* 4 section 19, he launches a particular invective against Irenaeus, quoting that early Christian's demonstration of the fact that only four gospels exist as the apogee of spurious logic: "There are four parts of the world. There are four cardinal winds. There have been four covenants, under, Adam, Noah, Moses and Christ. There can be but four gospels therefore."[27] And in the extended footnote following, he renders Cyprian's "confession" and his *De Unitate ecclesiae* ridiculous at the same time. Bolingbroke's scholarship, the dogged earnestness with which he pursues an author who, he has already convinced us, is not worth pursuing, creates an effect similar to the scholarship and annotation of Martinus Scriblerus and makes possible the same kind of bathetic deflation as do Pope's notes to the *Dunciad*. The footnote provides a dialogue between spuriously learned men, with the language trivializing and reducing the whole. What philosophical critics would term his tedious repetitiousness is, when looked at in another way, a luxuriant inventive capacity; there is a brilliance (that of the satirist) in the turns he gives to the screw on the same idea. His devised explanations for the corruption of Christian teaching and the growth of sectarianism, his fundamental conviction that he has unearthed a plot, partly political, partly theological, shows a fecund if simplifying mentality. Plots are unearthed everywhere in Bolingbroke's philosophy; there is a kind of Kafkaesque logic and purpose behind seemingly unconnected and insignificant events. Thus, in *Essay* 4 section 22, he explains how early divines put the church on a sound economic footing by encouraging the view that the selling of worldly pelf by private individuals in the church's interest is a form of piety. The church then uses the money to subsidize the poor—and thereby gains converts. This ascription of motive is idiosyncratic, clearly an example of Bolingbroke's mythmaking, his subjugation of the data to the service of an already formed interpretation. In section 27, when he is well advanced in his argument that the Church of Rome since its institution has usurped the rights and privileges of the temporal monarch, he argues that celibacy is part of the plot to ensure that familial ties do not encourage among clergymen alien loyalties to king and country. Bolingbroke's theory of a plot has clearly become an act of imagination persevered in because it pleases him; his own fertility leads him to make claims of no philosophical value and of little historical or political veracity. But this is far from saying that they are of no value—or that Pope should have found them of no value.

Often, our dissatisfaction with Bolingbroke hinges on the sense that he does not employ the philosopher's mode of discourse. At the opening of the fourth *Essay*, he discusses the habit of mind which teaches men to appropriate to themselves the thought of others and which debars original thought, but the tone here is the unmistakably strident and uncompromising one of the satirist determined to flog the world out of its folly. The characteristic exaggeration is inimical to the logic: if all men think at second hand, how can there be any pool of original ideas for the others to borrow? All thought cannot be derivative any more than all coins can be counterfeit. He goes on to show that this habit of mind is responsible for the growth of distorting prejudice and the ascendancy of spurious authority. Error takes root, and knowledge is more difficult to gain from this position than from a position of ignorance. But again, he is substituting genesis for analysis; he has no coherent theory of error and makes no attempt to discuss the ways in which it is possible to be wrong. The truth is that, as in so many passages, Bolingbroke has no interest in making nice philosophical distinctions. Again the power and the attractiveness of iconoclasm have taken over his critical faculty. Everywhere he sets up stark, black-and-white antitheses, succumbing to the kind of simplification and overstatement which satire demands, but which is often alien to a philosophical methodology of any sophistication. Bolingbroke often grinds axes rather than argues; he rigs the case; he contradicts himself as often as the logic of his position controverts the interpretation supported by his self-interest. But provided he had a moral purpose with which Pope could identify, provided he argued for a view of the world that Pope found congenial, and provided he had a prose style that found room for the well-turned phrase, these weaknesses were not likely to have appeared to the poet as such.

Paragraph 42 of the *Fragments* is a good example of the kind of writing (and, I believe, the kind of conversation) that must have been irresistibly attractive to Pope. Bolingbroke conducts an argument rich in literary allusions that has a strong bearing on the *Essay on Man*. Bolingbroke is attacking the opinion, central to the Newtonian physicotheological view of the universe that he opposed, that this world is a grotesquely uncomfortable environment whose creation is only justified if there is a perfect world beyond the grave. This, Bolingbroke contends, is impiety—God does not owe us anything. Whatever self-important men may think, "The distance between our friend Gay's Fly, in his fables, and the infinite self-existent Being, is not a whit greater than that between this Being and Socrates or St. Paul."[28] In this reference to Gay's *Fable* 49, "The Man and the Flea" (which is itself a source of the famous opening lines of the *Essay on Man* 2.1–2), Bolingbroke shows the same impulse toward deflationary satire as his Scriblerian friends. He goes on to argue, in a wide scholarly sweep that embraces Lucretius, Ovid, Plato, Montaigne, and Pliny, that this world is not such a bad place and that poets have always exaggerated the hopefulness or the hopelessness of the human condition:

> We are apt to carry the judgments we make into extremes, and the characters we give into panegyrics or satyrs. The examples of this kind are without number, but none are so remarkable as those which we find in writers ancient and modern, concerning the human nature. No creature is so miserable, in some descriptions, nor so necessitous as man. He comes into the world bemoaning his state. He grows up, and passes through the human state, exposed to many wants and bodily infirmities, unknown to the brute creation. You remember, no doubt, those fine verses in Lucretius:
>
> *Tum porro puer, at sævis projectus ab undis*
> *Navita, nudus humi jacet infans, indignus omni*
> *Vitali auxilio . . .*

Vagituque locum lugubri complet, ut æquum est
Cui tantum in vita restat transire malorum.
At variæ crescunt pecudes, &c.

No creature is to be compared with man in other descriptions, and in a contrary sense. He was made of earth; but this earth was impregnated with celestial seeds, if you will take Ovid's word for it.

. . . Recens tellus, seductaque nuper ab alto
Æthere, cognati retinebat semina cæli.

He was made in the image of the gods, and his very form denoted his divine original.

Os homini sublime dedit, cælumque tueri
Jussit, &c.

Some of these writers degrade even the human mind, and that intelligence and reason wherein we triumph. Plato, who in one mood raises man up to the contemplation of the abstract forms of all things, sends him in another for instruction to the beasts of the field; and the Hospes in the Politicus reckons their conversation among the means of improvement in philosophy and the knowledge of nature which men enjoyed under the reign of Saturn. Montagne, another prose-poet, deals with man as divines deal with God, and having drawn down human nature as low as he could, he raises that of some other animals so high, that he ascribes a sense of religion to elephants, and represents them deep in meditation and contemplation before the rising sun, and attentive at certain hours of the day to perform certain acts of devotion.[29]

To Bolingbroke—and here he sounds very like Pope indeed—"there is a middle point between these extremes, where the truth lies."[30] Man's faculties are somewhere between God's and those of the higher animals, and though he is the principal inhabitant of this planet, it does not follow that the earth was created for man alone or that God's sole purpose should be the creation of a perfectly happy creature.

All of these ideas are expressed in epistles 1 and 2 of the *Essay on Man*. Not only are the ideas present, but Pope also captures the tone of patient, tolerant long sufferance going ragged at the edges:

VI. What would this Man? Now upward will he soar,
And little less than Angel, would be more;
Now looking downwards, just as griev'd appears
To want the strength of bulls, the fur of bears.
Made for his use all creatures if he call,
Say what their use, had he the pow'rs of all?
Nature to these, without profusion kind,
The proper organs, proper pow'rs assign'd;
Each seeming want compensated of course,

Here with degrees of swiftness, there of force;
All in exact proportion to the state;
Nothing to add, and nothing to abate.
Each beast, each insect, happy in its own;
Is Heav'n unkind to Man, and Man alone?
Shall he alone, whom rational we call,
Be pleas'd with nothing, if not bless'd with all? (1.173–88)

The identifying stylistic feature of Pope's *Essay on Man* is the flexibility with which the poem moves from one tone to another. In virtue of this, modern readers are capable of divorcing form from content and judging that the *Essay* is a great poem, however negligible or even repulsive its philosophy may be. But the poem has always puzzled critics because unlike most of Pope's major poems, it appears to be sui generis; there is no obvious classical referent for it. Precedents most commonly adduced by modern scholars are the Horatian epistle and Lucretius's *De Rerum Natura*, but as I shall argue in the later chapter on the poem, these readings do not entirely convince. In my view, the true model for the poem, the heart of its mystery, is the sort of wide-ranging, witty, frequently satirical conversation that Pope was in the habit of holding with Bolingbroke during the period of its composition and of which Bolingbroke's philosophical writings are transcripts. A claim like this can only be substantiated by proving that the friendship between the two men was so close as to occasion a kind of osmosis. Pope was not working as an amanuensis, as many nineteenth-century critics naively asserted, but rather with the telepathic closeness of a twin brother. Let us examine the facts of their shared experience to see how convincing this idea may be.

Chapter 2

Bolingbroke and Pope, The Early Days

Beginning of the Friendship

Spence rather unhelpfully quotes Pope as having said in August 1735, "Lord Bolingbroke was one of my oldest acquaintances."[1] Most biographers agree that it was through Swift, who had first met Bolingbroke on 11 November 1710 and had become intimate with him in the privileged circles of the Saturday Club and the Brothers Club, that Pope met Bolingbroke.[2] No one is sure exactly when the meeting took place, nor how much of a relationship developed, but there is a general community of opinion that before Bolingbroke's flight to France in 1715 they were not well acquainted. The most common speculation is that they probably first met in the winter of 1713.[3] And certainly, a letter to Swift, dated 8 December 1713, accuses the Doctor of having "brought me into better company than I cared for,"[4] but this is hardly a very exciting hint, since it is quite possible that the Scriblerus Club was meeting by then, and that therefore the web of interrelationships was already woven quite thick. Gay had by this time fallen under Bolingbroke's spell; although *The Shepherd's Week* was not published until April 1714, the same letter to Swift cited above, which refers obliquely to two lines of the Prologue, establishes that it was written before the end of the year 1713. And in *The Shepherd's Week*, Gay makes an explicitly Tory commitment, dedicating the poem to Bolingbroke, who was to him the token of English prosperity, the negotiator of trading benefits with France and Spain. It was at St. John's recommendation that the "joyous madrigals" were published, he suggests in the Prologue; and he describes Bolingbroke thus:

> There saw I St. John, sweet of mien,
> Full stedfast both to Church and Queen.
> With whose fair name I'll deck my strain,
> St. John, right courteous to the swain. (75–78)

I believe, however, that Pope and Bolingbroke were almost certainly acquainted with one another well before that. It has not often been remarked that Pope and Bolingbroke had a common friend, with whom they were both intimate in the first decade of the eighteenth century—a friend, moreover, who exercised considerable formative influence on both their careers. To the young Henry St. John, Sir William Trumbull was a man to be venerated and imitated. St. John's capacity for hero worship was engaged to the full by this man of action who had visited Tangier and Constantinople on government business, who had been a distinguished lawyer and fellow of All Souls College, and who had, in 1695, succeeded Sir John Trenchard as secretary of state, the office his young protégé was later to hold. While visiting Geneva and the Italian cities in his European tour, St. John exchanged views, at Trumbull's request, on the condition of Continental learning, on the state of society and its institutions, and on European men and their morals. This often furnished occasion for broader metaphysical speculation on human nature taken in the round; and Trumbull relished such talk, with the opportunities it presented to make satirical capital out of the diseased state of Italian letters in particular and the shortcomings of mankind in general.

We can already see in this early correspondence the lively, debunking irreverence that characterizes Bolingbroke's later philosophical writings, and it helps to explain why Pope found him such a lively conversationalist. Learning, he affirms, is almost unknown in Italy, and "the nearer one approaches to that place which is the source of light [Rome] the more the mist of ignorance thickens." Of Magliabecchi the Italian scholar, St. John paints this Hogarthian portrait; he is "an old, vain, senseless pedant, a great devourer of books without any method or judgement to digest what he reads, a kind of Bethlem character, one that is always busy without proposing to himself any end." No wonder that Trumbull looks forward to his young friend's return, when they can "be revenged upon the world and use it scurvily, when we are alone."[5] When Bolingbroke returned to England and embarked on his parliamentary career, his letters to Trumbull frankly expressed his political intuitions, thus providing a cogent synopsis of the possibilities for his future. At one stage he was almost persuaded to seek his fortune at the court of Hanover, but was deterred because the Princess Sophia might have been invited to England and the Whigs might have gained ascendancy in his absence.[6] On problems like this, he expected and valued the advice of his patron, as he did also on the personal crisis in his marriage. His first wife, Frances Winchcombe, he treated scandalously, his misconduct nearly jeopardizing his credit with the Queen. There is no reason to doubt the sincerity of his claim to Trumbull that "your indulgence to my faults, your compassion for my misfortunes and a thousand other marks of undeserved kindness have made me yours, and I can with truth assure you that tho' nature has loaded me with numberless imperfections, yet she has given me a grateful heart, a heart wherein you will always have the largest share."[7] The relationship did wane as time passed, but in October 1704, St. John could still plead with Trumbull to make an appearance in the forthcoming parliamentary session: "For God's sake come up yourself and if you will not appear on the

stage, advise, like an old actor, those that do. I expect you with impa-
tience."[8] The Downshire papers mention amicable collaboration between
St. John and Trumbull as late as August 1710, when the former was to use
his influence to secure minor office for a certain de Ste. Croix.[9]

About Pope's relationship with Trumbull we know a great deal more
since the discovery by George Sherburn in 1959 of a collection of manuscripts in the Bodleian Library, which include three letters from Pope to
Trumbull (unpublished in the Sherburn edition of the *Correspondence*) and
fragments of other letters that passed between Trumbull and his nephew,
Ralph Bridges , which were hitherto unknown. Taken in conjunction with
the letters that were deposited by the Marquess of Downshire in the
Berkshire Record Office at Reading, this affords valuable material for the
student of Pope's early career.[10] His friendship with Trumbull was under
way by 1705, rendered possible by the fact that about two years after the
poet's family moved to Binfield, Trumbull retired to Easthampstead Park,
two miles to the south. Pope said to Spence in June 1739, "It was while I
lived in the Forest that I got so well acquainted with Sir William Trumbull,
who loved very much to read and talk of the classics in his retirement. We
used to take a ride out together three or four days in the week, and at last
almost every day."[11] Sherburn suggests that this friendship was of the
same value to Pope as a formal education:

> The literary importance of this friendship has been somewhat neglected.
> Sir William was a bookish man . . . and a man trained in public life,
> especially in diplomacy. The reading Pope did with such aid and supervi-
> sion was easily the equivalent of the university training that his religion
> precluded.[12]

Trumbull, we know, was the stimulus for Pope's translation of Homer,[13]
and the Bodleian manuscripts tell us more about this, about Bridges
having commented on Pope's translation of the "Episode of Sarpedon,"
and about Pope having sent to Sir William the publishing proposals tendered by Joshua Barnes.[14] In return, Pope had dedicated his first *Pastoral* to
Trumbull, later eulogizing his retirement habits in *Windsor Forest*.

At about the same time that Bolingbroke was exhorting Trumbull to
return to the parliamentary fray, more out of respect than expectation,
Pope was formulating the retirement paradox in witty antithetical cou-
plets:

> *You,* that too Wise for Pride, too Good for Pow'r,
> Enjoy the Glory to be Great no more,
> And carrying with you all the World can boast,
> To all the World Illustriously are lost! (*Spring,* 7–10)

It is a tribute to the liberality of Pope's religious views that he could have
struck up a strong relationship with a man of Trumbull's stamp, who was

in his earlier years a strong opponent of Catholicism and a friend to English Protestants in France after the revocation of the Edict of Nantes. Doubtless, politics was a subject that often cropped up between Pope and Trumbull. They must have discussed the question of the Revolution Settlement and the Jacobite cause very often on their rides round Windsor Forest, and there is surely the possibility that Trumbull would have mentioned St. John's name in conversation with Pope. He might have referred to him as another enterprising young man of mettle who would be an advantageous introduction to London society for Pope. However, Pope's relationship with Trumbull was clearly very different from St. John's. Whereas the latter regarded Trumbull as a viable model for his own career and respected him as the elder statesman of English politics, Pope was prepared to make capital out of his youth and the admiration Trumbull felt for the precocity of his "little Pope." There is something unpleasant in Trumbull's fascination with the discrepancy between Pope's physical and intellectual stature. Trumbull found this incongruous; and lying behind this is the tendency to regard Pope as a "zany" or a "prodigy" in the unkind sense, which is encapsulated in the sentiment Trumbull expressed to Bridges in 1707: "The little Creature is my darling more and more."[15]

Certainly, the literary tastes Pope had acquired at this time would have been esoteric enough to interest the philosopher in St. John: on 26 March 1709, Sir William writes to Bridges:

> Little Pope (who is much your Servant) shewed me a Little Book called The Spirit of Christianity, translated out of French by Sir Walter Kirkham Blount, and dedicated to the late K. James, Printed in 1686. Now Pope assuring me It is in French, the work of Monsieur Rapin, & liking it well in English (tho' ill translated) I would beg you to get it for me in French, if you can get the Right. I suppose the French Title is L'Esprit du Christianisme, &c.[16]

To show how close the thought processes of St. John and Pope could be, we might point to a curious coincidence. On 31 July 1698, Trumbull received from St. John a flattering letter, mildly upbraiding him for his retirement from public life; but, St. John comments, at least Trumbull could not be likened to Pomponius Atticus of old, who thought that the negative virtue of doing no harm was sufficient. As Cicero points out: *non nobis solum, sed etiam patriae nati sumus.*[17] And in *Windsor Forest*, when Pope is celebrating the virtues of the secluded life, he concludes thus:

> Such was the Life great *Scipio* once admir'd,
> Thus *Atticus*, and *Trumbal* thus retir'd. (257–58)

At the very least, this shows that Pope and Bolingbroke had a similar range of learning in these early years.

In fact the only documentary evidence we have for the suggestion that Pope met Bolingbroke a good deal earlier than has been supposed, through the agency of Trumbull, is provided in the same collection of Bodleian manuscripts. Tacked on to the Trumbull-Bridges letters is a collection of "anecdotes" that were supposedly dictated by Pope to Jonathan Richardson, Sr., at Twickenham on 5 August 1730, and which are in the hand of Gregson (Richardson's grandson), who has transcribed them for Bishop Percy. They are not accurate enough to be dictations and were probably recollections on Richardson's part, but what they say about Pope's early friendships is worth recording as it consolidates what I suspect is true, that Pope was acquainted with Bolingbroke before the political melee brought them together. His *Pastorals,* says Richardson,

> Occasion'd his being known to Dr. Garth, Mr. Walsh, Mr. Grenville, with whom he both Convers'd & Corresponded, & Sir Wm Trumbal, with whom on his having then resign'd the Office of Secretary of State, he lived Familiarly being his near Neighbour. By some or other of These he was soon Introduc'd into the Acquaintance of the Duke of Shrewsbury Lord Somers Mr. St. John & Ld Halifax . . . The First Works of His that were publish'd were his Pastorals & some pieces of *Homer* & *Chaucer* in 1709. His Windsor Forest in 1710 & the Essay on Criticism in 1711 (1707 & 9) tho written some time before. Mr. Addison to whom he was an utter Stranger, though not to Mr. Steel, published a Spectator on the last of these No 253, which Occasiond their Acquaintance, & he had an Opportunity of returning the Compliment by Writing the Prologue to Cato in the Year 1713. About the same time his Friendship began with Dr. Arbuthnot & Dr. Swift, who brought him into the Familiar Acquantance [sic] of the Lord Oxford, then Lord Treasurer.[18]

This source unequivocally separates, by a period of years, the genesis of Pope's friendship with the Kit-Cats and St. John from that of his friendship with the Scriblerians.[19]

But for anyone who is unconvinced by this evidence, the dating of winter 1713 for the first meeting of Bolingbroke and Pope should still be too late. As one who maintained a lively interest in his surroundings, Bolingbroke would almost certainly have heard of the improving young author who had published the *Essay on Criticism* and several pastorals, who had been named as one of the chief contributors to the *Spectator,* and whom Steele had asked to contribute to the *Guardian.*[20] Indeed, if recent attempts to read political allusions into Pope's very early poems are warranted, Bolingbroke might have read into Pope's translation of *The First Book of Statius his Thebais* an extended reference to English politics.[21] In lines 224–72, it is possible that Thebes represents England under Queen Anne, that Eteocles is an intensely hostile portrait of William III, and that already in 1709 (though the poem was not published until 1712) Pope's poetry was expressing a Stuart or Jacobite sympathy. We cannot say exactly how early Bolingbroke developed the Jacobite hopes that drove him in 1715 to the Pretender's court at St. Germain, but by 1712 he would certainly have been sensitive to any allegory contained in Pope's Statius. When *Windsor Forest* was published in March 1713, Bolingbroke would have had even more reason to notice a reversal of political direction in one whom, it seemed, the Whigs had captured. Since the poem's main intention was to celebrate the conclusion of the Peace of Utrecht (as well as to bring the author to public attention on an important occasion of state), it is very likely that Bolingbroke would have approved of the poem, being a principal negotiator of the treaty. But even assuming that Bolingbroke had not read the unambiguous declaration of "And Peace and Plenty tell, a STUART reigns," there is evidence to suggest that by the time Addison's *Cato* came to be performed in April 1713, Pope and Bolingbroke were certainly well met. The performance and aftermath of *Cato* is a good example of the way in which party polarities could find an avenue of expression in the theatre during Queen Anne's reign and throughout the century. Pope had written the play's prologue; and Addison, assuring him that there was no partisan interest behind it, "pressed [Pope] to shew it to the Lords Oxford and Bolingbroke, and to repeat his assurances to them, that he did not by any means intend it as a party play."[22] Already by April 1713, Addison credited Pope with greater influence on Bolingbroke than his own. On opening night, the audience reacted demonstratively. Parts of the prologue were hissed, since the public expected a highly controversial play and overreacted. The Duke of Wharton applauded furiously any sentiments he considered to redound to the credit of the Whig party, spurring Bolingbroke on to his famous attempt to steal the Whigs' thunder. Pope described the incident in a letter to John Caryll of 30 April 1713:

> The numerous and violent claps of the Whig party on the one side the theatre, were echoed back by the Tories on the other, while the author sweated behind the scenes with concern to find their applause proceeded more [from] the hand than the head. This was the case too of the prologue-writer, who was clapped into a stanch Whig sore against his will, at almost every two lines. I believe you have heard that after all the applauses of the opposite faction, my Lord Bullingbroe sent for Booth who played Cato, into the box, between one of the acts and presented him with 50 guineas; in acknowledgement (as he expressed it) for [his] defending the cause of liberty so well against a *perpetuall dictator.*[23]

Thus, the biter bit, and Marlborough discomfited. (He is the "perpetuall dictator" of the quotation.) Bolingbroke's prompt action captured the play for the Tories. According to John Gay's account of the same incident, the lines of the prologue that read, "These tears shall flow from a more

gen'rous Cause / Such tears as Patriots shed for dying Laws" were applauded by Tory supporters on subsequent nights.[24] "Cato" later came to
be identified with Harley and Bolingbroke; and Pope unwittingly became
associated with a Tory triumph.[25]

Pope was by this time clearly a part of the political ecology. The pam-
phleteers knew him—even such celebrated ones as Dr. Henry
Sacheverell—and they appropriated his name to their causes. Joseph
Trapp, the poet and high Tory apologist, was known to Pope by early 1711
or 1712: in the Downshire papers published by Sherburn is a letter from
Pope to Ralph Bridges of 10 February (?) 1712 in which Pope seeks a
meeting with Bridges "without the Interruption of other Company (unless
Mr. Trapp will oblige us with his, as you seemd to promise he would)."[26]
Pope was presumably interested in Trapp's *Praelectiones Poeticae* (1711), the
first volume of which had been dedicated to Mr. Secretary St. John. Not
long afterward, Swift secured for Trapp the appointment of chaplain to
Henry St. John (now created Viscount Bolingbroke), a position he also held
for Bolingbroke's father: "I have made Trap Chapln to Ld Bullinbroke, and
he is mighty happy & thankfull for it."[27] Bolingbroke's reward was to be
eulogized in Trapp's poem "Peace," which was published in April 1713,
and of which he was the dedicatee. Bridges notes the publication of this
poem in a letter to Trumbull of 21 April 1713:

> I do herewith send you Dr. Sacheverels Sermon presented to You by Him
> and also Mr. Trapp's Poem on the Peace, which I have a duplicate of &
> desire Your acceptance, as being generally reckond a good one. They both
> agree in crying up our Mr. Pope & say that He is one of the greatest
> genius's that this nation has bred. If he were but a Protestant, tho' I can't
> say that wou'd make him a better Poet, yet I can't forbear saying that I
> should like Him better.[28]

Can it reasonably be concluded that, with connections as intricate as
this, Pope had still not met Bolingbroke? I think it more likely that he was
renewing an acquaintance he had made under the auspices of Trumbull
some years earlier—but in a new context, that of party politics. And if it is
the case that Pope knew Bolingbroke this early, we have to challenge the
views with which we opened the chapter, that of the various biographers
who consider that Swift introduced the two men. There is only one
reference to Pope in the *Journal to Stella,* an injunction to the ladies to read
Windsor Forest, dated 9 March 1713, which implies no intimacy. Irvin
Ehrenpreis himself does not know when Pope met Swift, but says non-
committally, "He could easily have met Pope through Lansdowne or else
through his own Irish friend Parnell, who, like the poet, was friendly with
Steele and agreed to write essays for the new periodical the *Guardian.*"[29]
Perhaps, then, Bolingbroke knew Pope before Pope knew Swift. And by

this time Bolingbroke knew Parnell and Arbuthnot. It is therefore possible that Parnell, or Arbuthnot, was the catalyst in developing the relationship between Bolingbroke and Pope, which, I suggest, was instigated earlier by Trumbull.

The extent to which the intimacy between Pope and Bolingbroke grew under the aegis of the Scriblerus Club has often been exaggerated. Adina Forsgren, in her voluminous study of John Gay, makes the common error of supposing that Bolingbroke was actually a member of the club.[30] The source of the error is Pope himself, who said to Spence in 1728, "It was begun by a club of some of the greatest wits of the age: Lord Bolingbroke, Lord Oxford, the Bishop of Rochester, Mr. Pope, Congreve, Arbuthnot, Swift, and others. Gay often held the pen, and Addison liked it very well and was not disinclined to come into it." The statement later recorded by Spence, that "the Scriblerus Club consisted of Pope, Swift, Arbuthnot, Parnell and Gay," is closer to the truth.[31] In fact, there are some very good reasons why Bolingbroke should not have been a member of the Scriblerus Club. The aims of the Scriblerus Club were specifically apolitical; at least, all the blueprints for it were. The scheme mooted by Pope in the *Spectator* 457 for 14 August 1712, to launch *An Account of the Works of the Unlearned*, was certainly intended to be a potent vehicle for satirizing his literary enemies of the moment, but it was still quite closely in line with the literary intentions of the *Proposal*, earlier tendered by Swift, to found an academy for the resuscitation of language on the basis of the Académie française. And in the form in which Pope's plan was seriously forwarded in a letter to Gay of 23 October 1713, the emphasis was still literary-critical.[32] As a literary society, the club would have been of occasional interest to Bolingbroke. But Charles Kerby-Miller makes the point that almost from the instigation of the club, it was dominated by Swift, and this imposed on its business an inescapable political cast.[33] Swift encouraged Oxford to become a kind of honorary member—thus ensuring that Bolingbroke, whose rivalry with and hatred of Oxford at this time was almost fanatical, would never join. Bolingbroke would spend little time under the aegis of any society that extended a sociable welcome to Oxford. And indeed, the duties of office left Bolingbroke very little time to spend on social pursuits. Dickinson says quite rightly that "as Secretary at War, and then as Secretary of State, his industry cannot be questioned by anyone who has consulted his letters in manuscript and his published correspondence."[34] Swift records the effect of overwork on Bolingbroke's constitution once or twice,[35] and in his letters written from 1710 to 1714 while he was secretary of state, Bolingbroke complains periodically to Prior and Shrewsbury of the inequitable burden of affairs.[36]

I should say, then, that when it became expedient for Bolingbroke to leave for France on 27 March 1715, he had already known Pope for some years, but the acquaintance had not ripened into anything more than mutual respect and a recognition of considerable community of interest. Yet the relationship had developed to the extent that Pope passed some days with him at the beginning of January 1715.[37] If Bolingbroke was already involved in Jacobite intrigue before he became an open supporter of the Pretender on arrival in France, he could surely have found a sympathetic listener in Alexander Pope, a Roman Catholic supporter of the Stuart line. The possibility of mutual Jacobite sympathies remains a tantalizing aspect of this friendship. We shall have reason to return to this question later.

Pope's Homer and Bolingbroke in France

Before Bolingbroke went into exile, then, he was not an intimate of Pope's; but Bolingbroke had involved himself sufficiently in the poet's projects to enable Pope to claim, in the 1715 preface to volume 1 of *The Iliad*, that "such a Genius as my Lord *Bolingbroke*, not more distinguished in the great Scenes of Business than in all the useful and entertaining Parts of Learning, has not refus'd to be the Critick of these Sheets, and the Patron of their Writer."[38] And indeed there was little enough advantage to be gained from claiming collaboration with Bolingbroke three months after he had defected from England, leaving those who would have tried him (and executed him as Bolingbroke believed) bitterly frustrated. The boldness of this stroke aroused from Swift his only direct reference to Bolingbroke in his correspondence with Pope during Bolingbroke's exile:

> . . . You talk at your ease, being wholly unconcerned in publick events: for, if your friends the Whigs continue, you may hope for some favour; if the Torys return, you are at least sure of quiet. You know how well I lov'd both Lord Oxford and Bolingbroke . . . do you imagine I can be easy while their enemies are endeavouring to take off their heads? . . . You were pretty bold in mentioning Lord Bolingbroke in that Preface.[39]

Presumably because of the danger of corresponding with a known Jacobite, Bolingbroke and Pope did not communicate at all during the eight years of the former's banishment, and it is often concluded that they lost contact with one another. In fact, they did not. The intellectual and literary worlds of France and England were very close to one another at this time, and a constant shuttle service of news was carried by travelers from both sides of the Channel. In this connection, we could make the same observation that Professor Plumb makes about the small scale of the political world in the eighteenth century: since few individuals took an active part, politics assumed a personal and intimate character. Literary activity in the salons of Paris and the coffeehouses of London was equally incestuous, and we are often surprised to find characters familiar from the French literary stage playing their part also on the English.[40] Pope's reputation, on the ascendant during this period, would filter through to French literary coteries. Dean Audra, in his *Les Traductions françaises de Pope, 1717–1825*, cites three translations of works by Pope that had appeared while he and Bolingbroke were not in epistolary contact. Robethon, the secretary to George I, rendered the *Essai sur la Critique* into French in 1717, Pérelle in 1719 translated the first part of Pope's preface as the *Préface de l'Homère Anglois*, and in 1723, a French translation of the *Guardian* was published at The Hague, entitled *Le Mentor Moderne*. The second item, the translation of Pope's preface to Homer, is extremely important and offers insight into a celebrated literary quarrel of the period, as well as affording evidence that Pope and Bolingbroke were very much aware of one another at this time.

Parisian intellectual society in the 1720s and 1730s centered round L'Hôtel Colbert, where Madame de Lambert had her salon. Habitués included Fénelon, Montesquieu, Mairan, D'Argenson (son of Bolingbroke's best-loved French correspondent, Madame de Ferriol), Fontenelle, and the exiled Bolingbroke. At this salon, the contest between the ancients and the moderns was fought over the issue of Homer translation, by Madame Dacier and Houdard de la Motte. The former had espoused the cause of the ancients in her 1714 *Des Causes de la corruption du goût*, and her veneration for Homer took the form of assuming that nothing in his work could violate the laws of *politesse*. Her assumption that Homer's work was *raissonable*, that Homeric ideals approximated closely to her own, and her sponsorship of the ancients over the moderns provoked Houdard de la Motte's *Discours sur Homère*, which challenged her rigidly authoritarian critical theory.[41] Madame Dacier was therefore sensitive to the charge that she had misrepresented Homer, and it is this accusation that Pope brings in his preface. He argues that either Madame Dacier has not translated Homer faithfully or her partiality for the customs and way of life of the ancients, conceived on the grounds of their civility and manners, cannot be sustained; but he goes on to castigate La Motte for a similarly culpable extremism:

> . . . I must here speak a word of [his *grosser Representations* of the *Gods*, and the vicious and *imperfect Manners* of his *Heroes*], as it is a Point generally carry'd into Extreams both by the Censurers and Defenders of *Homer*. It must be a strange Partiality to Antiquity to think with Madam *Dacier*, "that those Times and Manners are so much the more excellent, as they are more contrary to ours." Who can be so prejudiced in their Favour as to magnify the Felicity of those Ages, when a Spirit of Revenge and Cruelty, join'd with the practice of Rapine and Robbery, reign'd thro' the World, when no Mercy was shown but for the sake of Lucre, when the greatest Princes were put to the Sword, and their Wives and Daughters made

Slaves and Concubines? On the other side I would not be so delicate as
those modern Criticks, who are shock'd at the *servile Offices* and *mean
Employments* in which we sometimes see the Heroes of *Homer* engag'd . . .
When we read *Homer*, we ought to reflect that we are reading the most
ancient Author in the Heathen World.[42]

Bolingbroke was assuredly party to the quarrel between the ancients and
the moderns. Shortly after Houdard de la Motte's *Discours* was published,
Bolingbroke wrote to Madame de Ferriol, protesting that Madame de
Tencin's anger at his failure to ally himself unconditionally with the moderns is unfounded. He admits to certain scruples, but

> Si Madame de T[encin] trouve qu'elle a raison d'estre fâchée contre moy
> sur le rapport qu'on luy a fait de mes sentimens, ce rapport a esté très
> infidel et très malicieux. De dix-neuf propositions que je trouverois dans le
> livre de Monsr. de la Mothe, je souscrirois a dix-huit, et, si j'ay fait quelque
> petite difficulté, cela n'à esté que pour rendre ma conversion plus honor-
> able comme ayant embrassé le parti des modernes avec connoissance de
> cause.[43]

> (If Madame de T[encin] thinks that she is right to be offended with me on
> account of the report that has been made to her of my opinions, the report
> was very inaccurate and very malicious. Of nineteen propositions that I
> could find in Monsr. de la Mothe's book, I would consent to eighteen, and
> if I made any small objection, it was only to render my conversion the
> more honorable for having taken the side of the moderns only after careful
> consideration.)

It would be most interesting to know what the proposition of La Motte's
was to which Bolingbroke would not assent. Did it owe anything to Pope's
strictures in his preface? Certainly, this letter was written to Madame de
Ferriol on 26 June 1715, a mere two days before the letter was written by
Swift to Pope with which we began this section.

At this time Bolingbroke might not have known Mme Dacier and de la
Motte personally. Dennis J. Fletcher argues in an informative thesis that it
was probably in 1717, after St. John had moved to Marcilly near Nogent-
sur-Seine, that he was introduced to the salon of Mme de Lambert.[44] The
Abbé Conti, prominent popularizer of Newtonian principles, was a frequent visitor at L'Hôtel Colbert, and his interest in English literature,
especially in Pope, was stimulated by Bolingbroke. Conti instigated Pérelle's 1719 translation of the *Préface de l'Homère anglois,* which brought
Pope's preface to the notice of Madame Dacier.[45] (She spoke no English
and therefore had not noticed Pope's preface earlier.) She was roused to
fury by Pope's remarks that are quoted above, and she published her
second edition of *The Iliad* in 1719, with annexed to it "quelques reflexions
sur la préface angloise de M. Pope." Pope, she complains, plagiarizes her

work, and the images by which he chooses to represent Homer's work—
"wild Paradise," "a copious Nursery," and "mighty Tree"—are neither
just nor decorous. For her own part, her advocacy of the ancients over the
moderns is based on their simplicity, a virtue which Pope, she points out,
also celebrates, and not on their concubinage and amorality. She finishes
by making political sneers at the poet's expense:

> Un homme si habile ne se bornera pas à perfectionner l'art du poème
> Epique; ce seroit peu de chose; il perfectionnera l'art de la politique . . . un
> homme capable de former des hommes . . . Voila une grande ressource
> pour un Etat![46]

> (A man so useful should not limit himself to perfecting the art of epic
> poetry; that would be too trivial a task; he ought to perfect the art of
> politics . . . a man capable of shaping men . . . That is an immense
> advantage for a country.)

Pope appears not to have seen this squib until 12 February 1723, when he
writes to Buckley thanking him for the gift of a copy which, it seems, came
from Sir Luke Schaub (then ambassador in Paris and well known to
Bolingbroke). Pope says, "Madame Dacier has not done me the honour I
expected as a Critick . . . but has attackd me as a Poet only in two or three of
my Simile's," and he protests that the various errors of which she accuses
him are not in the original and so "if I shou'd be ambitious of recanting my
errors, I could only make satisfaction to my French Readers, which I
apprehend to be very few, if any."[47] But what Pope really objects to are the
political implications, which arrived at a time when Pope's publication of
his edition of Buckingham's *Works* in January 1723 was attracting an
unwelcome degree of attention in the chamberlain's office, and when the
Atterbury trial was close at hand. He finishes by wondering if Tickell is
indeed going to translate the *Odyssey* and by coining a wry conceit:

> I wish you could exhort him hereto, for the honour & safety of the
> Protestant Religion & Establishment, which otherwise (according to M.
> Dacier) a Papist may do much damage to. I did not think I had such
> Talents in Politicks, but I will now begin to look about me, since I am
> thought so capable of great affairs, by the consent of two nations.
>   Pray assure all our Friends of the Office, of my Services & good inten-
> tions toward them all, when I am Premiere Ministre.[48]

Pope was skilled in recognizing cannon fodder for his enemies. In 1724,
Curll published *Madame Dacier's Remarks upon Mr. Pope's Account of Homer
. . . Made English from the French by Mr. Parnell,* and he found it sufficiently
potent to reissue it in the collection of Curlliana called *The Popiad* in 1728.[49]
    We might think that Anne Dacier's barb was harmless enough, but in
fact Pope's translation of Homer had already come under fire from his

literary opponents, especially from Oldmixon in *The Catholick Poet* and from Dennis, who suspected it to have Jacobite and papist intentions, in his *A True Character of Mr. Pope* and the later *Remarks upon Mr. Pope's Translation of Homer.* Bolingbroke, as we have seen, took a close interest in the fortunes of Pope's Homer on both sides of the Channel. Knowing Madame Dacier from the salon, he would certainly have read her censorious remarks on the preface before Pope did. It is conceivable that Bolingbroke monitored Pope's Homer so closely because he himself saw the allegorical possibilities in the work; and if a recent commentator is correct, his attentions would have been well rewarded. John M. Aden finds in Pope's translation a full-scale political suggestiveness. In the *Iliad* book 8, published in 1716, Aden finds the second battle between the Greeks and the Trojans to be an adaptation of the story of the Tory rout at the hands of the Hanoverian Whigs, the fleeing Ulysses standing for Bolingbroke himself.[50] Whether or not he found what he was looking for, it is clear that Bolingbroke searched Pope's Homer keenly and that Pope was at pains to see that the translation reached him. Bolingbroke's main source of information about literary activities during his exile was Swift. Unfortunately, only four letters from Bolingbroke to Swift and two of the doctor's replies are now extant for the period under discussion, but these and other letters provide clues to lost correspondence. Frequently, the go-between in this correspondence is Swift's close friend Charles Ford. He had been closely associated with Bolingbroke's ministry in the position Swift procured for him as editor of the *London Gazette,* and he had many dealings with Bolingbroke in the summer of 1714 regarding the correction and attempted publication of Swift's tract *Some Free Thoughts on the Present State of Affairs.* His correspondence with Swift in the headlong days of the fall of the ministry shows how intimately his fate was connected with Bolingbroke's, and when the secretary fell Ford lost his job. He had been an active participant in the social circle of Parnell, Pope, and Swift, and after Bolingbroke's flight, we next hear of him in Bolingbroke's company in France.[51] Subsequently, Ford went to Paris in mid-October 1716, where he visited Bolingbroke before making the Continental Tour. He proceeded to write to Bolingbroke from various stopping points on the way.[52] It was Swift's practice to ask Ford to forward letters to Bolingbroke, thus saving on postage—and since Ford was a frequent guest of Swift's in Dublin, Bolingbroke would enclose a letter for him when he had occasion to write to Swift. His letters to Ford during this period show that he held Ford in high esteem.

A letter of 29 January 1720 contains definitive evidence that Bolingbroke and Pope were in contact during this period, through Ford, and testifies to the former's continuing interest in the fate of Pope's Homer. On 5 January

1720, Pope wrote to Ford a short note to tell him that he would be joining him (presumably at his London residence) the following week.[53] Bolingbroke's interest in Pope's translation must have been a topic of conversation, because Ford received from Bolingbroke the following sentiments later in the month:

> May I entreat you to assure Mr. Pope of my most humble service &
> inviolable friendship? What Brinsden [his secretary and chargé d'affaires
> in England] means I know not, but he has sent me Priors works which I
> was very indifferent about, & not Mr. Popes which I am impatient to see,
> & which I most earnestly recommended it to him that he should send me
> by the first opportunity. The four volumes of Homer I have not receiv'd. I
> thank Mr. Pope extreamly for his attention, & I write to Brinsden to have a
> little more.[54]

This letter reached Pope very shortly before the publication of volumes 5 and 6 of the *Iliad* in May 1720, where again, in book 24, it is not impossible that some parallels are being drawn between Achilles' merciless obduracy in his dealings with the Trojans and Walpole's refusal to pardon Bolingbroke.[55]

It is clear, then, that Pope's Homer was a constant source of interest to Bolingbroke while he was in France and more than anything else kept him in touch with the poet who had been an acquaintance during his days of power. Two days before Bolingbroke returned to England in 1723, Pope wrote a rhapsodic letter to Harcourt congratulating him on the part he had played in obtaining the reversal of the Act of Attainder. Sentiments like these would be incongruous if they had followed eight years of total silence:

> . . . Ev'ry thing you could hitherto do for me is quite swallowd up & lost in
> what you have now done, for me & for the whole Nation, in restoring to us
> my Lord Bolingbroke. Allow me . . . to say . . . that nothing which could
> have been a mortification to me this year, either as to the loss of any of my
> Fortune, or any of my Friends, could have been so well recompens'd, as
> by this Action of our Government. My personal Esteem for & Obligation
> to, my Lord Bolingbroke, are such, that I could hardly complain of any
> Afflictions, if I saw him at the End of His.[56]

And therefore there was more than graciousness in Bolingbroke's claim to Pope on 18 February 1724 that "I forgot you as little during an absence of several Years, as I have done during another which has now lasted some Months. During both you have be[en] so constantly present to my mind, and the impressions I took of your Character long ago are there so fresh and so strong, that I never did and I think I never shall suspect You of forgetting me."[57]

Chapter 3

Bolingbroke and Pope, 1723–1730

Twickenham and Dawley

From 1723 to 1730, Bolingbroke concentrated most of his efforts on reasserting his public respectability, resuming his political career, and establishing a base from which to work in England. The last of these objectives he achieved when he bought Dawley Farm from the Earl of Tankerville's son in 1725; the proximity of Dawley to Pope's villa at Twickenham ensured that the poet would be a constant visitor to Bolingbroke's home. As for his other aims, Bolingbroke never did achieve full credibility as a public figure, the label *Jacobite* frequently being employed by his enemies to damage him, and his political career had to find other avenues of expression since Walpole's inveterate hatred of him resulted in the government's refusal to reverse all the penalties of his attainder. Stripped of orthodox political influence by being prohibited from resuming his seat in the Lords, Bolingbroke turned Dawley Farm into a gathering place for disaffected and principled opponents of the government; and the result of this collaboration was the *Craftsman*, the influential political journal founded on 5 December 1726 under the editorship of Nicholas Amhurst, but with Bolingbroke and William Pulteney as leading contributors. At the same time Dawley was becoming an organized cell of political opposition, it was also, along with Pope's villa, the major communal resort of the Scriblerians, Arbuthnot, Swift, and Gay, who were able to resume the close intimacy of the last days of Queen Anne since Swift had returned to England in March 1726 and stayed till August. After Swift's return to Ireland, Bolingbroke writes to him of Dawley as "an agreeable Sepulchre" which enables him to "bury my Self from the world": clearly, nothing could be further from the truth.[1]

Meanwhile, Pope was occupied with the drudgery of Homer translation. But he was by no means remote from politics during this period. He had been considerably shaken by the political implications of his edition of the Duke of Buckingham's works, and even more by the insinuations in the popular press that he had played some part in Atterbury's Jacobite plot. Atterbury's banishment was felt as a grave personal loss by Pope, but the arrival of Bolingbroke in England in June 1723 was a compensation: to Swift, he laments a nation that "cannot regain one Great Genius but at the expense of another."[2] Undoubtedly, Pope would have known of Bolingbroke's frenetic attempts to regain his public position, because he was in touch with Lady Bolingbroke (who was in England to rescue her financial investments and, through bribing the Duchess of Kendal, to procure Bolingbroke's restoration) and he was dining, as early as August 1724, with William Pulteney. Already in 1724, Bolingbroke was taking considerable interest in Pope's work, having had his attention drawn to the translation of Homer. This interest was to become increasingly active, even directive, in the years to come. In February 1724, we find him advising Pope to abandon the translation of classical authors in favor of original, philosophical poetry: Pope, he believes, should be performing a service to the English language, which, though it is yet mutable and "unfixed," is now sufficiently mature to adapt to "Poetry . . . Eloquence . . . History." The French have mastered dramatic poetry, and the Italians epic poetry, but the English have as yet no distinctive expertise:

> A Language which is design'd to spread, must recommend it self by Poetry, by Eloquence, by History. I believe England has produced as much Genius first as any Country. Why then is our Poetry so little in request among Strangers? several Reasons may be given, and this certainly as the most considerable, that we have not one Original great Work of that kind wrote near enough to perfection to pique the Curiosity of other Nations . . . Eloquence and History are God knows, at the lowest ebb imaginable among us. The different Stiles are not fix'd, the Bar and the Pulpit have no Standard, and our Historys are Gazettes ill digested, & worse writ. The case is far otherwise in France and Italy . . . In short excellent original writings can alone recommend a Language, and contribute to the spreading of it. No man will learn English to read Homer or Virgil. Whilst you translate therefore you neglect to propagate the English Tongue; and whilst you do so, you neglect to extend your own reputation, for depend upon it your writings will live as long and go as far as the Language, longer or further they cannot.[3]

Partly for reasons of personal reputation and partly because the state of English cultural and linguistic prosperity demands it, Bolingbroke urges Pope to carve out an area of mastery. Can we see in this the genesis of Pope's projected "ethic work," that philosophical leviathan to which, we must never forget, the *Essay on Man* was originally intended to be "what a scale is to a book of maps"?[4]

During this period, Pope was rather unctuously protesting his political nonpartisanship, in a way that provoked the sharp retort from Swift that Pope could afford to be apolitical since "I suppose Virgil and Horace are equally read by Whigs and Toryes you have no more to do with the Constitution of Church and State than a Christian at Constantinople."[5] Yet again the suspicion that Pope's Homer itself was far from apolitical remains. Maynard Mack draws a suggestive analogy between Odysseus and

Bolingbroke in terms of "the knower of men and cities, the exile long prevented from return, the philosopher and man of eloquence," and John M. Aden has improved upon this hint in claiming book 24 of the *Odyssey* to be "almost wholly an allusion to the return and pardon of Bolingbroke."[6] The last two volumes of the *Odyssey* were certainly being prepared for the press in the year after Bolingbroke had moved into Dawley Farm, but doubtless Aden is overstating the case.

At this time, Pope's claim of neutrality was probably justified, whatever it was to become later. He was on fairly good terms with Walpole, from whom he had received visits and to whose good offices he probably owed the £200 he received from court for translating the *Odyssey*, though it is very likely that what he said in Walpole's company did not square with what he said out of it. A letter to Fortescue contains a mysterious and anxious reference to a dinner with Sir Robert, some conversation of which had been reported by another guest: "One of the most innocent words that ever I dropped in my life . . . which might reasonably *seem* odd, if ever it comes to Sir R's ears."[7] After Swift's arrival in England, Pope's social life intensified as he escorted Swift to the various friends and acquaintances who were anxious to see him. There is in the letters a strong sense of a coherent and close circle of acquaintance, comprising, inter alia, the Scriblerians themselves, the Bolingbrokes, Pulteney, Wyndham, Lords Peterborow, Harcourt, Chesterfield, Bathurst, and Oxford, and Mrs. Howard. Equally strong is the sense of heightening literary activity in this period: *Gulliver's Travels* would be published shortly after Swift's return to Ireland in August and would become the talk of the town, Gay is putting the finishing touches to the first series of the *Fables*, Pope himself is presumably still working on the "Progress of Dulness," and Arbuthnot has published his *Table of Ancient Coins*.

The literary and political worlds were impinging on one another in a mutually fructifying way at this time; when Pope complains to Caryll that he is being too much visited—"My house is too like the house of a patriarch in the Old Testament, receiving all comers"—he is referring to the same group of people who visited Dawley.[8] At the latter end of 1726, Pope was at Dawley a good deal. It was on a return trip from Dawley to Twickenham that his coach overturned and he was nearly drowned, injuring two nerves in his right hand. Bolingbroke's account of the accident to Swift is as follows:

> Have you heard of the accident which befel poor Pope in going lately from me? A Bridg was down, the coach forc'd to go thro' the water, the Bank Steep, an hole on one side, a block of timber on the other, the night as dark as pitch, in short he overturned, the fall was broke by the water, but the

glasses were up, & he might have been drownd if one of my men had not broke a glass & pull'd him out thro the window. his right hand was Severely cut; but the surgeon thinks him in no danger of losing the use of his fingers. however he had lately had very great pains in that arm from the shoulder downwards, which might create a Suspicion that some of the glass remain'd still in the flesh.[9]

In view of this close contact between the Scriblerians and the leading opposition politicians, I cannot fully agree with the most recent literary historian of the period, Bertrand A. Goldgar, who argues that there was no organized hostility to the government among literary men until considerably later and that what emerged at this period was the independent expression of hostility toward a government unsympathetic to serious literary endeavor.[10] Goldgar underestimates the scale of involvement in politics of the Scriblerians even at this early stage. His claim that "there is no evidence that Swift, Pope or Gay contributed papers" to the *Craftsman* requires some qualification. Swift did collaborate with Bolingbroke on the *Letter to the Writer of the Occasional Paper*, a would-be *Craftsman* essay that Bolingbroke finally rejected. Furthermore, Simon Varey has shown that Gay did write at least one paper and marshals evidence to suggest that both Pope and Arbuthnot may well have done likewise.[11] The very frequency of Pope's visits to Dawley at this time must have resulted in his becoming familiar with the editorial policy of the *Craftsman*, which was to force the Tories into a homogeneous party and fuse them with opportunist Whigs such as William Pulteney who were in opposition because they had not received their due from the ministry. Perhaps as early as the end of 1726, we can detect in Pope's letters to Swift evidence that he was learning a political language at Dawley. Of Pulteney, Pope observes to Swift in a manner redolent of Dawley gossip, "He would rather be in power, than out";[12] and a letter to Swift of 16 November 1726 seems to present views on party that may have been tutored by Bolingbroke, as well as an animus against government hacks:

> Surely, without flattery, you are now above all parties of men, and it is high time to be so, after twenty or thirty years observation of the great world.
>
> *Nullius addictus jurare in verba magistri.*
>
> I question not, many men would be of your intimacy, that you might be of their interest: But God forbid an honest or witty man should be of any, but that of his country. They have scoundrels enough to write for their passions and their designs; let us write for truth, for honour, and for posterity.[13]

Gardening: A Common Pursuit

Politics aside, the period 1723–1726 must have allowed Bolingbroke and
Pope to develop a mutual interest they shared all their lives: the interest in
gardening. Intelligent readers of Pope's verse and correspondence have
always been aware that gardening was to him no mere hobby. In the
theories that underpropped the design of his garden at Twickenham, Pope
was in many ways ahead of his time.[14] He is not always given full credit for
this, perhaps because the constraints of his "bitt of ground that would
have been but a plate of Sallet to Nebuchadnezzar, the first day he was
turn'd to graze" gave the effect of preciosity—an effect much relished by
the owner.[15] But Pope was in the forefront of developments that pushed
the English garden far beyond the geometric formalisms of Dutch and
French taste, as professional gardeners Charles Bridgeman, Stephen Switzer, and William Kent broke down boundaries between the cultivated
garden and the natural landscape that surrounded the estate. Not only did
Pope combine perimeter areas of "wilderness," interpenetrated by secre-
tive, mysteriously winding paths, with more formal groves planted in
quincunxes, mounts, and a bowling green, but he also manipulated light
and shade in a pictorial way and arranged elevations and plantations to
afford pleasing or tantalizing prospects of the river Thames.

Most important, the garden was also a museum of the poet's personal
iconography. After his mother's death, he erected an obelisk at the western end of the garden which was, as Maynard Mack says, its "visual and
emotional climax."[16] The garden became for him a monument to filial
piety. Pope's grotto, though not part of the garden proper, was his crown-
ing glory, and it was here that he achieved his most successful conflation of
art and nature. Capitalizing on his initial good fortune in discovering an
underground spring on the site, Pope manipulated it to imbue each cham-
ber of the grotto with a characteristic atmosphere calculated to elicit from
the visitor a different psychological response, ranging from melancholy to
a sense of the sublime. Landscape, worked upon by human artifice,
becomes minutely sensitive to changing moods in order to provide an
entirely hospitable environment for the poet and his company. At the
same time that he was husbanding nature with art by balancing and
combining formal and informal elements in his own garden at Twickenham, he was also advising Mrs. Howard on the design of Marble Hill
and corresponding with other large-scale gardeners—Lord Bathurst, who
had entirely renovated the landscape of Cirencester Park, and Lord Peterborow of Bevis Mount. In mid-1724, the poet visited the Digby family of
Sherborne, and his letter to Martha Blount of 22 June 1724, providing an
account of the castle and grounds, is one of the finest that he ever wrote.[17]

The letter is rich in a sense of the dramatic; we are taken on an expert tour of the site and permitted to experience with the poet the effects of the changing landscape on his sensibility. Particularly remarkable is his awe-stricken description of the ruins—"more romantick than Imagination can form them." Digby himself is represented in the letter somewhat as the Man of Ross was to be in the later poem: a type of goodness and benevolence, the happy landlord of fortunate tenants who is modest about his good works and enjoys a fortune not "rais'd upon the Spoils of plunderd nations, or aggrandiz'd by the wealth of the Publick."[18]

What has never been sufficiently stressed is that while Bolingbroke was in France, living at the Château de La Source (a few miles south of Orléans), he also engaged in gardening and landscape architecture, with intentions similar in important respects to those of Pope. A description of the grounds is provided by Sir William Young in his biography of his grandfather Brook Taylor, the mathematician and close friend of the exiled Bolingbroke:

> The place derives its name from the source of the Loirette, which forms a natural fountain springing from the centre of a small lake situate in the gardens. It is of a depth, or rather of a force, which hath resisted all attempts to fathom it; and from its very spring, to where it falls in the Loire, about six miles distant, pours a stream as clear as copious. Lord Bolingbroke turned this great and beautiful feature of nature to due account, adapted the grounds and plantations to the river's course, and gave the whole an effect of improved nature, which is now well understood by the terms of *English Gardening*.[19]

Coincidentally, then, the characteristic impact of La Source, as of Pope's villa, is likewise achieved by the manipulation of a naturally occurring stream. Like Pope, Bolingbroke created in La Source a nourishing environment for retirement and study, a locality remote from the competitive world of the court wherein friendship could flourish and hospitality be afforded to a select group of peers. John Dixon Hunt cites Bolingbroke's apothegm from his *Of the True Use of Retirement and Study*—"Every man's reason is every man's oracle; this oracle is best consulted in the silence of retirement"[20]—though he does not observe that Bolingbroke also designed for himself a landscape appropriate to the consultation.[21] It is clear from St. John's letter to Swift of 28 July 1721 that La Source was an iconographical museum of both a public and private nature:

> You must know that I am as busy about my hermitage, which is between the château and the maison bourgeoise, as if I was to pass my life in it; and if I could see you now & then, I should be willing enough to do so. I have in my wood the biggest & clearest spring perhaps in Europe, which forms before it leaves the park a more beautiful River than any which flows in

greek or latin verse. I have a thousand projects about this spring, and, among others one which will employ some marble.[22]

There follows the text of two Latin inscriptions composed by Bolingbroke and designed for his temple, which reflect on his disappointments in public life, and a request to Swift for "some mottos for groves, & streams, & fine prospects, & retreat, & contempt of grandeur &c. I have one for my green house, & one for an ally which leads to my apartment, which are happy enough. The first is hic ver assiduum, atque alienis mensibus aestas. The other is—fallentis semita vitae."[23] Bolingbroke's use of these publicly available mottoes from Virgil and Horace,[24] combined with his own personal inscriptions, has something in common with Pope's decoration of his garden; indeed, the latter motto in the fuller form "secretum iter et fallentis semita vitae" was used in Pope's grotto later. But La Source became a shrine to the memory of Bolingbroke's murdered political career, rather than to the death of a parent as in Pope's case. It probably did not resemble Twickenham in layout—clearly, there were vast differences in scale—but from Sir William Young's description quoted earlier, where he speaks of "adapting the grounds and plantations to the river's course," it seems that Bolingbroke was already in the 1720s consulting the genius of the place and paying respects to the goddess Nature as recommended by Pope in the *Epistle to Burlington*. Notice has been taken of this very important connection between the two men by Kenneth Woodbridge in an article in *Garden History*, though he does not go far enough in detailing its nature:

> Apart from his influence on the fashion for reinforcing the associations of a scene with inscriptions with a classical allusion, and the contribution which he made to the iconography of Stowe, it is interesting to speculate whether the river at La Source may not have inspired a similar concept in the Elysian Fields; and further, if the inspiration for Pope's lines, engraved on the pavement before the springs at Stourhead, did not begin with Bolingbroke's thoughts on the spring in his French garden. What Pope and Bolingbroke owed to one another is incalculable as is the ramification of their influence.[25]

In his letter to Bolingbroke of 9 April 1724, Pope wrote some lines of verse in which he imagined his spirit leaving his body in his own garden and visiting La Source, where the Bolingbrokes are to be found in an attitude of harmonious cooperation. The lines culminate in a graceful pun:

> I see thy fountains full, thy waters roll
> And breath the Zephyrs that refresh thy Grove
> I hear what ever can delight inspire
> Villette's soft Voice and St. John's silver Lyre.[26]

In a letter written much later to William Fortescue, Pope is explicit about the respect in which his garden and grotto was to provide a nourishing atmosphere for friends: it could be either a pure recreation for the overworked, a source of inspiration to the politically minded, or a consolation to the politically frustrated:

> I see nothing but Mrs. Vernon [his landlady], or [a] Sugar-baker, to succeed to my Plantations. However they will have abundantly recompensed my Care, if they serve to receive, amuse, & shelter a few such friends as you, at your Intervals of leisure, while I live: relieve a laborious Lawyer between the Terms; inspire a Political Acquaintance between a Saturday Evening & Munday, with Schemes for public Good in Parliament; or receive with hospitality a discarded Courtier. *Mihi & Amicis,* would be the proper Motto over my Gate, & indeed, Plus Amicis quam Meipsi.[27]

When Bolingbroke settled at Dawley Park in 1725, he began to transform it from a French design rather like that of the estate at La Source he had recently left to the new English taste for the ornamented villa-farm. Although we cannot say how far he took these improvements, it is certain that in this endeavor of converting Dawley Farm from the outmoded formality of its French design to the *ferme ornée* type, Bolingbroke had Pope's advice. His house at Dawley was remodeled by Pope's architect James Gibbs, and it is likely that Pope put St. John in touch with his own favorite landscape gardener, Charles Bridgeman.[28] In all likelihood, the estate never really operated as a working farm, but became the perfect environment for Bolingbroke and his friends to preserve the appearance of statesmen in retirement while actually using it as a base for guerrilla operations against the government.

Retirement

Clearly, then, when the Earl of Peterborow invited Pope to dine with Harcourt and Bolingbroke in a letter of 1723, we can safely assume that the conversation would turn on landscape gardening, as well as on what interest Lord Harcourt, as a recently appointed privy councellor, could make in restoring Bolingbroke to power. But gardening was only an aspect of the larger concern for retirement that obsessed both men during their lifetimes. Gardens have long been idealized as the instantiation in landscape of a golden age—of the freedom from artifice and irksome toil associated with a purer state of existence. To Pope and Bolingbroke, for whom friendship was a supreme value and almost a cult, the garden was a form of self-expression and its organization a statement about the quality of friendship and hospitality its owner would offer. But a vexing question remains to the biographer of Pope and of Bolingbroke: what role did retirement genuinely play in their lives? Just as the student of Bolingbroke's grandiose ideological edifice must try to determine what purchase his rhetoric had on the realities of the power structure—to be blunt, whether Bolingbroke would have been a Walpole if he governed—his biographer has to decide what *kind* of inconsistency is represented by a man who constantly affirmed that he had turned his back on the world even when his political activity was at its height. The question was thoroughly discussed by the men themselves. It is a perennial topic of their epistolary intercourse, especially in 1725 when Swift was engaged in writing *Gulliver's Travels* and trying very hard to decide what degree of *contemptus mundi* or of misanthropy was being expressed in that work.[29]

Bolingbroke, for his part, was probably only honest about his view of retirement in the early stages of his career. Shortly after his flight to France in 1715, he wrote to Madame de Ferriol a letter in which he refused to speak in the tone of a lofty philosopher on the matter of solitude, frankly confessing that he was not an exile through choice:

> Je ne suis pas, Madame, si avide de gloire que vous pensez; et bien loin de me sentir l'audace d'aspirer au caractère de philosophe, je connais les bornes que la nature m'a prescrites, et je m'y renferme. Le sage serait dans une solitude, telle que la mienne, par son choix. Du haut de ces montagnes, il jeterait des regards de mépris sur le pauvre monde; il le contemplerait, sans se soucier de le pratiquer. Pour moi, je vous avoue que je suis assez fou, pour être ici à contre coeur. La nécessité dans laquelle je me suis trouvé, de me bannir de Londres, m'a paru un commencement de malheur; et celle de quitter Paris, en a eté assurément le comble. Voilà ce qui se passe dans le fonds de mon âme, mais je me garderai bien de donner aux esprits malins, ce triomphe qu'ils attendent. Mon chagrin ne paraîtra pas.[30]

> (I am not, Madame, so eager for glory as you believe; and far from having the temerity to aspire to the temper of a philosopher, I know the limits that nature has set for me, and I contain myself within them. A wise man would live in a solitude like mine by his own choice. From the top of these mountains, he would cast contemptuous glances on the base world; he would contemplate it without desiring to frequent it. For my part, I confess to you that I am mad enough to resent being here. The necessity of exiling myself from London seemed to me the beginning of misfortune; and that of leaving Paris has certainly been its height. That is what is going on in the depths of my soul, but I will be careful not to give to mischievous minds the triumph they expect. My chagrin will not be apparent.)

Just as Bolingbroke promised in this remarkably candid letter, subsequently he never did allow his true feeling about retirement to escape him and provide his numerous political enemies with fuel. The language of retirement served him as a pressure valve for his frustrations accumulated in the world of affairs; he had no genuine use for the conventional comforts afforded by it. Sheila Biddle, in her study of Bolingbroke and Harley, precisely dates his adoption of retirement rhetoric to "the moment [he] left the Pretender's service."[31] In an unpublished letter to Lord Essex of 12 and 23 March 1733, he writes with world-weariness of his unworldly desires:

> I grow old. Imagination is so far from deceiving me on this side of the case, that I contrived to make her delude me on the other as long as I could. I have not passed for young I believe this good while with others, and I cannot pass for such now even with myself, tho' self be the most artful flatterer of self in the whole world. But my Dear Lord I have long learned not to repine at the conditions of human nature; and besides, my life neither has been, nor is, prosperous enough, for me to be much concerned that the term of parting with it approaches, all I desire in the mean while is retreat & Quiet. the false opinion that I desired something else has kept me out of them long, but even that shall keep me so no longer. I have so little concern in the world, that it concerns me little who governs it, or how it is governed.[32]

But this was written at the time of the excise bill crisis, when his "concern in the world" had never been more intense. This is less a matter of insincerity than of sublime sour grapes.

To Pope, retirement was a rather different matter. John Dixon Hunt is right to stress Pope's awareness of the sense in which the role of solitary recluse, indifferent to the lures of the court and of Grub Street, was a partial fiction and depended on being so for its success: "His dreams of making Twickenham his Sabine farm are mediated by his delight, sometimes his annoyance, at the difference between their situations [Horace's and his own]. The traditional rivalry between country and city for which Horace was often a spokesman both sustains and fails to fit Pope's professional predicament. But a large part of his enjoyment of Twickenham was obviously the play it provoked between 'visionary beauties' and the realities of his life."[33] And indeed, Pope himself was frequently puzzled by Bolingbroke's attitude to retirement, a subject on which he was never frank with Pope. Pope's letter to Swift of 15 October 1725 manifests unquestioning conviction; his sentiments are expressed in the cosmic imagery the poet habitually used when referring to Bolingbroke:

> Here is one, who was once a powerful Planet who has now (after long experience of all that comes of shining) learn'd to be content with returning to his First point, without the thought or ambition of shining at all . . . Lord B. is the most *Improv'd Mind* since you saw him, that ever was without shifting into a new body or being Paullo minus ab angelis.[34]

But Pope was very much more skeptical of Bolingbroke's management of
Dawley Farm. Though few contemporaries doubted that Dawley was a
base for journalistic guerrilla warfare, its owner tried to camouflage it as a
working farm and ostentatiously engrossed himself in rustic pursuits. In
1728, he had the hall painted in monochrome with farm implements, and
in some rooms the paintings combined mythological figures with georgic
and sylvan scenes of cupids guiding the plough.[35] Bolingbroke has de-
ceived at least one modern writer into taking him seriously about his
attempts to turn Dawley into a working farm. David Jacques notes that
Stephen Switzer, the royal gardener, lived at Kennington in 1727, and that
Switzer's *Practical Kitchen Gardener* (1727) notices Dawley, along with Bathurst's nearby Riskins, as improved estates.[36] Jacques seems to suggest that
Dawley can be seen as an experiment in Tory noblesse oblige. In some
sense, Dawley exemplified the combination of wealth and moral responsibility for which Pope argued in the *Epistle to Burlington*. I doubt whether
even Pope, so ready to see in Bolingbroke an exemplar of the principles he
preached, was taken in by him as a farmer. Writing to Swift from Dawley
on 28 June 1728, Pope describes the haymaking and puts in a paragraph,
when Bolingbroke is no longer looking over his shoulder, which makes
clear that he regards his friend's farming as a posture:

> I now hold the pen for my Lord Bolingbroke, who is reading your letter
> between two Haycocks, but his attention is sometimes diverted by casting
> his eyes on the clouds, not in admiration of what you say, but for fear of a
> shower. He is pleas'd with your placing him in the Triumvirate between
> yourself and me; tho' he says that he doubts he shall fare like Lepidus,
> while one of us runs away with all the power like Augustus, and another
> with all the pleasures like Anthony. It is upon a foresight of this, that he
> has fitted up his farm, and you will agree, that this scheme of retreat at
> least is not founded upon weak appearances.
>   . . . Now his Lordship is run after his Cart, I have a moment left to my
> self to tell you, that I overheard him yesterday agree with a Painter for 200
> *l.* to paint his country-hall with Trophies of Rakes, spades, prongs, &c.
> and other ornaments merely to countenance his calling this place a
> Farm.[37]

Retirement, like religion, was an issue on which Pope probably did not
know Bolingbroke's true mind. But though Bolingbroke's practice failed to
square with his protestations in this matter, it is crucial to observe that the
political theory being evolved at Dawley in the late 1720s, which was
published in the *Craftsman* in the early 1730s, was such that it accommo-
dated many of the values implicit in the retirement ethos. Bolingbroke's
political ideals were so attractive to Pope because they were based on the
moral positives of friendship and homely virtue that also underpropped
the landscape gardener's idealism. It would not be distortive to describe

Bolingbroke's platform, in such works as *The Idea of a Patriot King*, as the politicization of private virtue. In many respects, his manifesto was as nonpolitical, even as utopian, as was conceivable; being so, it went some distance toward bridging the gap between private and public life that was apparent to Pope. On the terms proposed by Bolingbroke, Pope would find it possible to campaign in the public theatre for values that he embraced and tried to uphold in his private world.

1727–1730: A Servant of Two Masters

The correspondence for this period, during which Bolingbroke was so active in overseeing the *Craftsman*'s campaign, orchestrating the journalistic and the parliamentary opposition, conveys very little sense of Pope's being involved in political affairs. What evidence there is rather suggests that between 1727 and 1730, the poet became friendlier with Walpole and the court than at any other time in his career. Instrumental in promoting this entente were Mrs. Howard, the King's mistress and Pope's near neighbor, and William Fortescue, then Walpole's private secretary, who was to remain a lifelong friend of Pope's and a vital contact with the administration. On 5 August 1727, Pope lets Fortescue know that he has been bantering about him with Walpole.[38] Early in 1729, when Pope is collecting material for *The Dunciad Variorum*, he sets Fortescue to find out from Walpole the identity of the author of a libel entitled *Essay on the Taste and writings of this age;* Pope makes it clear that he is on visiting terms with the great man.[39] Shortly afterward, Walpole presented *The Dunciad* at court, where it was well received.[40] On another occasion, after the appearance of a pamphlet called *A Popp upon Pope* claiming that the poet was set upon and severely beaten as he took a constitutional near home, Pope complained bitterly to Walpole that Lady Mary Wortley Montagu was behind this libel.[41] But perhaps the best evidence that Pope was trying to put himself on terms with the government camp was his reaction to the publication in 1730 of Swift's "A Libel on Dr. Delany." Swift was by this time an implacably outspoken critic of the government. Had he been deliberately trying to embarrass his friend, he could scarcely have been more successful than in the verse compliment he chose to pay him:

> Hail! happy *Pope*, whose gen'rous Mind,
> Detesting all the Statesmen kind,
> Contemning *Courts*, at *Courts* unseen,
> Refus'd the Visits of a Queen;
> A Soul with ev'ry Virtue fraught
> By *Sages, Priests,* or *Poets* taught;
> Whose filial Piety excels

Whatever *Grecian* story tells:
A Genius for all Stations fit,
Whose *meanest Talent* is his *Wit:*
His Heart too Great, though Fortune little,
To lick a *Rascal Statesman's* Spittle. (71–82)

Such lines would be difficult to explain to Walpole when Pope dined at his table later in the year; to Fortescue, he wrote testily:

I've had another Vexation, from the sight of a paper of verses said to be Dr. Swift's, which has done more by praising me than all the Libels could by abusing me, Seriously troubled me: As indeed one indiscreet Friend can at any time hurt a man more than a hundred silly Enemies. I can hardly bring myself to think it His, or that it is possible his Head should be so giddy.[42]

But this is not the complete picture. It is difficult to see how Bolingbroke could have tolerated such liaisons, given that he regarded anyone who was not for him as being against him. Yet Pope and Bolingbroke were in regular contact during these years. 1728 was a typical year. Pope was at Dawley in February, June, and November of that year, when, as we have seen, he could not resist the temptation to poke wry fun at Bolingbroke's dilettante posing as a farmer; to Bathurst, he writes, "Lord Bolingbroke & I commemorated you in our Cups one day at Dawley—(Farm I should say & accordingly there are all the Insignia and Instruments of Husbandry painted now in the Hall, that one could wish to see in the fields of the most industrious Farmer in Christendome").[43] At times the conversation ran on antiquarian subjects, which Pope so loved to pursue with his learned friend. In one instance, James Stopford has sent Pope some "conjecture" on the ichnography of the Temple of Jupiter Olympius at Agrigentum, and Pope gives his conjectural description to Bolingbroke "to compare with Diodorus."[44] But at other times, the discussion must have been political. 1727 had been an election year, and the *Craftsman* had labored to find central issues of principle on which to fight it: week after week, the *Craftsman* stressed the dangers of exorbitant ministerial power in un-balancing the constitution; and in famous allegorical papers like the "First Vision of Camilick" and "The History of the Norfolk Steward," the *Craftsman* dramatized powerfully the venal, corrupting powers of ministerial gold.[45] Under cover of irony, allegory, dream, fable, Persian letter, and dialogue, the *Craftsman* conducted its campaign against placemen, pensioners, and all aspects of Walpole's political mismanagement: bribing juries, breaking into the sinking fund, mishandling of foreign affairs, inflating the land tax, and growing rich. At the same time, the historical numbers were beginning to offer the analysis of recent history that was to develop, in the 1730s, into a potent political ideology. *Craftsman* 40, for example, argues specifically against the two-party system on the grounds that the Protestant Succession and the monarch's popularity made it obsolete:

> If you ask a *Whig* for the Opinion of a *Tory*, he'll tell you, in general, that he is a *Jacobite* or a *Papist*; a Friend to *arbitrary Government*, and against the *Liberties* of the People both in *Church* and *State*.
>
> Take the Character of a *Whig*, in like Manner, from a *Tory*, and you will hear him describ'd to be a Man of *Republican Principles*; a *Presbyterian*; and a sworn Enemy to the Church of England, and the *regal Prerogative*; nay, it will be well for him, if he is not set forth as a downright *Atheist*, or Libertine, and an Enemy to *all Government* whatsoever.[46]

But the *Craftsman* was well aware that calls for a coalition government of national unity, like other issues in the debate at the center, did not significantly affect local elections. Caleb D'Anvers, the authorial persona, kept a weather eye open for sensitive issues in local constituencies. Above all, this campaign was coordinated with parliamentary activity. Particularly heated was Pulteney's motion on 21 February 1727 demanding a detailed account of the sum of £125,000 allegedly spent on secret service business, which, like other such debates, received back-up discussion in the *Craftsman*.[47] Pope expressed little overt reaction to this frenzied activity in his letters, though on 17 February 1727 he wrote to Swift, surely in connection with *Craftsman* exploits, "You see how much like a Poet I write, and yet if you were with us, you'd be deep in Politicks. People are very warm, and very angry, very little to the purpose, but therefore the more warm and the more angry."[48] But Pope's main opposition business was being done in the *Dunciad*.

In its major themes, the early version of the *Dunciad* is decidedly political. The progress of dullness from city to court cannot but be an arraignment of the government. Mercenary venality is the poem's major target. Certainly, the poet's personal animus is not yet fully controlled by the poem's ethical principles. Book 4 was added to the 1742–1743 version largely to combat the narrowness of the early *Dunciad*'s aim to give personal enemies their comeuppance. Not until 1743 can we speak of the poem's subject as, in Aubrey Williams's terms, "England on the verge of cultural breakdown."[49] Book 4 secured the culturally apocalyptic connection between bad politics and bad art, which is scarcely articulated in the early version beyond the level of suggestive analogy. But it cannot be any accident that virtually all the major Whig hack-writers are stigmatized in the early poem. Indeed, if we read the *Dunciad* in parallel with the *Craftsman* for 1727, we find a degree of similarity that puts Pope's objectives beyond doubt. The *Craftsman* was already making the connection between the decay of government and the decay of the arts and polite learning that is the *Dunciad*'s informing spirit:

. . . When no Regard is had, in the Dispositions of Offices and Favours, to the Fitness or Unfitness of Men; when Ability, Merit, and former Services are of no Weight in the Scale; when the Muses pine in Obscurity, and Learning is look'd on as a Disqualification, rather than a valuable Endowment; when, in short, the Favours of *great Men* are heaped only on Themselves, their own Relations and immediate Dependants; when all Places of Trust, Honour, and Profit center in *two* or *three Families* at most; when Pensions, Presents, Grants, Patents and Reversions are either *sold* or *engross'd;* and every thing runs in the same fowl Channel of *Corruption* and *Self-Interest;* then, I say, Men of Merit and Ability have just Reason to complain, remonstrate and protest; and it is ridiculous to expect that Arts, Wit or Learning should flourish, in any Degree, under such a rapacious, selfish and usurious Administration.[50]

One sign of cultural degeneration is the popular taste for debased art forms: Italian opera is the *Craftsman's* chief bête noire, and in, for example, *Craftsman* 29, historical examples of the enervating effects that bread and circuses have had on free nations are adumbrated to show that there is nothing harmless about the opera. On the contrary, such state-sponsored luxury is the instrument of arbitrary power.[51] This helps to explain why Gay's *Beggar's Opera,* first performed shortly before the appearance of the *Dunciad,* must be seen as a political play even in its objectives with respect to music. Etiolated Italian music had become, to *Craftsman* readers, an index to the nation's spiritual ill health. This *Craftsman* argument helps to elucidate the potency of such lines in the *Dunciad* as the following, which seem to refer innocuously enough to rather trivial entertainments:

> Thy dragons Magistrates and Peers shall taste,
> And from each show rise duller than the last:
> Till rais'd from Booths to Theatre, to Court,
> Her seat imperial, Dulness shall transport.
> Already, Opera prepares the way,
> The sure fore-runner of her gentle sway. (3.299–304)

Here, bad art has all the potential to run the nation that was claimed for it by the *Craftsman.* Shortly before this passage, Theobald has been invited by Settle to feast his eyes on a special effect, the kind used by John Rich in his immensely popular pantomime shows:

> He look'd, and saw a sable Sorc'rer rise,
> Swift to whose hand a winged volume flies:
> All sudden, Gorgons hiss, and Dragons glare,
> And ten-horn'd fiends and Giants rush to war.
> Hell rises, Heav'n descends, and dance on Earth,
> Gods, imps, and monsters, music, rage, and mirth,
> A fire, a jig, a battle, and a ball,
> Till one wide Conflagration swallows all. (3.229–36)

These breathtakingly fine lines are not only a satire on the crowd-pulling gimmicks of popular pantomimes, the more apropos because these actual effects were used in Theobald's own *The Rape of Proserpine*. Nor are they merely mimetic, in the verse movement and syntax, of the unleashing destructive energies that end in total ruin, the lines foreshadowing the final apocalypse of "And universal Darkness covers all." For *Craftsman* readers, there is another tissue of allusion. Harlequinades, Raree shows, and pantomimes in general occasioned the *Craftsman*'s withering scorn in 1727, and a particularly fine number recounts the history of harlequinades, leading on to a scenario entitled "The Mock Minister; or Harlequin a Statesman."[52] This purports to be a commedia dell'arte mime on the rise and fall of Harlequin/Walpole from his South Sea Company imbroglio to his eventual impeachment. The "sable Sorc'rer" of the *Dunciad* passage would be, in the political argot of the period, a reference to Walpole as the puppet-master working the nation's strings.

The *Dunciad*'s attack on party writers manifests a similar antigovernment bias. Pope's credentials as a neutral are seriously impugned by his exempting the *Craftsman* from attack. Some of the dunces, like Dennis and Gildon, are not political enemies, except in the general sense that Walpole's administration was seen to favor dunces over men of sense. Others, a very important group, were men like Roome, Duckett, and Burnet, who had made Pope's life a misery during the Atterbury trial by calling him a Jacobite. But a still larger group are those who, like Concanen, Pit ("Mother Osborne"), and dozens of others, wrote for the major government journals. In the 1735 edition of the poem, Pope characterizes Concanen as "a hired Scribler in the *Daily Courant*, where he pour'd forth much Billingsgate against the Lord Bolingbroke and others."[53] Again, Pope's poem can be seen to overlap with the *Craftsman*'s continuing campaign against government hacks in 1727 and 1728. At times, the parallels run very close indeed. Pope's deadly accurate attack on Orator Henley in 3.191–208 borrows even specific details of Henley's voice projection— "How sweet the periods, neither said nor sung!"—from a report on the orator's doings in the *Craftsman*.[54] Henley was absolutely certain that Pope was a *Craftsman* writer. As early as November 1731, his eccentric broadsheet, the *Hyp Doctor*, was claiming that Pope was responsible for the celebrated *Craftsman* paper "The History of The Norfolk Steward" and several others.[55] If this is true, it is of the utmost significance. This number launches the theme of false stewardship, which, in later attacks on such rapacious land stewards as Peter Walter, becomes so central to Pope's poetry.

The Scriblerians themselves certainly saw the *Dunciad* as part of the opposition campaign. In March 1728, Swift wrote to Gay excitedly, "The

Beggar's Opera hath knockt down Gulliver, I hope to see Popes Dulness knock down the Beggar's Opera."[56] This expresses the sense of reinvigorated Scriblerian activity in the period. Also, it reminds us of what should always be born in mind regarding this brand of satire, that it was as much written for its own peer group as for the war against corruption in government. Pope's attitude toward government patronage must have been hardened in 1727 by Gay's failure to gain a significant place at court. The offer of Gentleman Usher to the two-year-old Princess Louisa was regarded as derisory. There was, perhaps, nothing very logical about Gay's expectations; he was actually writing *The Beggar's Opera* while they were strongest. But his disappointment was considered proof positive of Walpole's contempt for men of independent spirit and true genius. Pope's letter to Gay on the occasion is worthy of a *Craftsman* essay:

> There is a thing, the only thing which Kings and Queens cannot give you (for they have it not to give) *Liberty*, which is worth all they have; and which, as yet, I hope *Englishmen* need not ask from their hands. You will enjoy That, and your own Integrity, and the satisfactory Consciousness of having *not* merited such Graces from them, as they bestow only on the mean, servile, flattering, interested, and undeserving. The only steps to their favour are such complacencies, such compliances, such distant decorums, as delude them in their Vanities, or engage them in their Passions. He is their Greatest favourite, who is their *Falsest*; and when a man, by such vile Gradations, arrives at the height of Grandeur and Power, he is then at best but in a circumstance to be *hated*, and in a condition to be *hanged*, for serving their Ends: So many a Minister has found it![57]

Job's comfort, doubtless, but it does suggest that, whatever the ostensible evidence, Pope was not an unqualified admirer of the King and his First Minister.

The *Craftsman* was not the only periodical that Pope was rumored to be contributing to at this point in his career. On Thursday, 8 January 1730, the first number of a new paper entitled the *Grub-street Journal* was offered to the London reading public. Insofar as the early numbers seemed to manifest a strong interest in Pope's literary quarrels and insofar as some contemporary sources (including the scarcely reliable unholy trinity of Orator Henley, Eustace Budgell, and Edmund Curll) identified Pope as the *éminence grise* behind this publication, Pope's name has always been closely associated with it. There is no hard evidence to suggest that Pope was more than an occasional contributor—certainly, he was not the mastermind behind it nor was he likely to have had any commercial interest in it—but nevertheless, it does seem that at least in the first few months of its operation, the *Grub-street Journal* extended Pope's *Dunciad* campaign against selected enemies and manifested certain political concerns in common with the *Craftsman* that suggest some directing influence from the Dawley circle. In a recent article on the subject, Bertrand Goldgar denies the connection between Pope and the *Journal*, but his argument actually supports the connection that he seeks to deny.[58] He argues that the *Journal*'s prime mover and principal editor Richard Russel was a non-Juror with strong Jacobite sympathies. This Jacobite leaning, Goldgar assumes, would distance Russel from Pope; as we have suggested, Jacobite sympathy was the crucible of Pope's friendship with Bolingbroke. Goldgar cites a mock-biblical genealogy of the *Journal* supplied by Henley in the *Hyp Doctor* 59 (25 January 1732) without pointing out that in this, Henley actually traces the pedigree of the publication back via sundry booksellers to Caleb D'Anvers, the sobriquet of the *Craftsman* editor:

> And this Suckling, the *Grub-street* Journal, being a weak Infant, was nurs'd up in the House of *Palmere*, which was the Son of *Quidnunc*, the Son of *Huggonsons*, the Son of *Batleys*, the Son of *Mottes*, the Son of *Bavius*, the Son of *Maevius*, the Son of *Brothertons*, the Son of *Conundrum*, the Son of *Willocks*, the Son of *Quibus*, the Son of *Caleb*, the Son of *Fog*, the Son of *D'Anvers*, which was—the Son of—BELIAL.[59]

And Goldgar's own examination of the early numbers of the *Grub-street Journal*, designed to show that it rarely reflects Pope's interest, does not show this. The opening number, in which the paper's ironic intention of defending the productions of Grub Street is announced, seems to me to be a precise reminder of Pope's project, conveyed in a letter to the *Spectator* of 14 August 1712, to found a magazine that would give *An Account of the Works of the Unlearned*, on which the Scriblerus project was based. As an example of the kind of interest that Pope would *not* share, Goldgar cites number 10 (12 March 1730) in which the *Journal* mounts an indirect attack on Walpole and Francis Charteris, the notorious rapist, whose trial had just ended. Quite unaccountably, Goldgar concludes that "all this is the stuff of the *Craftsman*, not of *Peri Bathous*" and is "fairly remote from the world in which Pope lived and wrote."[60] It is unlikely that this argument would recommend itself to any sympathetic reader of the present book. James T. Hillhouse, an earlier student of the *Grub-street Journal*, makes use of a compilation published in 1737 called *The Memoirs of Grub-street*.[61] This reprints some of the major contributions to the *Grub-street Journal*, with a preface by "Bavius" (Russel) which ascribes some of the articles (those marked with the signature letter *A*) to Pope. Goldgar does not dispute the ascription of the articles thus designated to Pope, who probably did have a hand in these. Their main function is to attack two of the poet's enemies, James Moore Smythe and Matthew Concanen, but they also concern themselves with the issue of the poet laureate. As Goldgar himself has shown, this issue became heavily political with the instigation of Cibber in

December 1730 and with the opposition press, the *Craftsman* and *Fog's Weekly Journal*, making all the capital possible out of this evidence for degeneracy in taste.[62] The question of Pope's hand in this, like so many questions in the biography of this most devious of men, remains shrouded in mystery, but there are tantalizing hints that the *Grub-street Journal* was in its early days an organ orchestrated by the opposition interest.

We have, then, two contradictory strains of inference regarding Pope's activity in the period 1727–1730. At the same time he was ingratiating himself with Walpole, frequently dining at his table, Pope's literary work was in important respects contiguous with the antigovernment campaign masterminded by Bolingbroke. To put it no more strongly, the *Dunciad* drew on a general receptiveness to political dimensions of apparently apolitical themes, a receptiveness engendered by the *Craftsman*. Could it be that Pope was a servant of two masters at this time? And if so, with what degree of premeditation? He was not, as is often claimed, aloof from politics altogether. It is tempting to suggest that Pope was actually encouraged by Bolingbroke to forge links with the government. Certainly, he was the only one of Bolingbroke's close associates who retained credibility enough with Walpole to penetrate his inner sanctum, and if the poet could have done so, he would have been a valuable source of intelligence. The role of opposition spy might not have been uncongenial to one who, in Lady Bolingbroke's words, "played the politician over cabbages and turnips." However, this must remain a matter of the merest speculation, since there is no evidence to support it. In the years that follow, however, Pope's commitment to the opposition cause becomes increasingly well defined.

Chapter 4

Bolingbroke and Pope, 1731–1735

Pope, Bolingbroke, and Political Verse Satire

Contact between the two friends probably increased after October 1730, when the poet's ailing mother fell into the fire, thus forcing him back into the role of nurse and giving him time for retirement and study. For some time, Pope had been putting together the fragments that were to be published as the *Essay on Man*, though of course Pope intended this to be part of a much larger work, and there are clear indications that the epistles to Burlington and Bathurst were also in progress. Already in January, Pope and Bolingbroke were together in the latter's library at Dawley: Boling-broke's letter to Swift at this time makes it clear that he sees Pope's work as part of the campaign against "national corruption" though he is uncertain about its power to stem the tide of vice:

> Pope is now in my library with me, and writes to the world, to the present and to future ages, whilst I begin this letter which he is to finish to you. What good he will do to mankind I know not, this comfort he may be sure of, he cannot do less than you have done before him. I have sometimes thought that if preachers, hangmen, and moral-writers keep vice at a stand, or so much as retard the progress of it, they do as much as human nature admits: A real reformation is not to be brought about by ordinary means, it requires these extraordinary means which become punishments as well as lessons: National corruption must be purged by national calamities.[1]

By the beginning of 1731, then, Pope was composing the *Essay on Man* in earnest. Later in the year, his worsening health necessitated his going on a regimen of asses' milk. In order to do this, Pope spent an extended period of time at Dawley. G. S. Rousseau and Marjorie Hope Nicolson have reconstructed the probable dates of this visit as being from 15 April to 2 June.[2] Pope slept at Dawley and made periodic visits to the pasture four miles away where he drank the freshly drawn asses' milk: to Oxford, he wrote, "I am daily drinking Asses Milk, which will confine me from rambling farther than betwixt this place & my Dam's Pasture, which is 4 miles off. I lye there & come hither daily, then go to Suck at night again."[3] Nicolson and Rousseau are almost certainly correct in concluding that it was at this time that, freed from the burden of nursing his mother, Pope finished epistles 1–3 of the *Essay*. As they put it:

There seems little reason to doubt that the major work of making into a
coherent, logical and poetical whole such "fragments" as he had shown
Spence and mentioned to Caryll was completed by Pope during the spring
of 1731, during comfortable and placid hours in Bolingbroke's home and
in his library.[4]

The much-discussed issue of Pope's debt to Bolingbroke in the composition and content of the *Essay on Man* I shall treat at greater length in the next
chapter. Clearly, however, Bolingbroke and Pope had repeated conversations on philosophical topics, and there is much evidence that Bolingbroke
was committing his thoughts to paper in a haphazard and unsystematic
way while Pope was composing. However, we know the drift of Bolingbroke's philosophical thinking, even without consulting his posthumously published works. On 2 August 1731, he writes to Swift regarding Swift's
friend Dr. Delany's treatise, *Revelation Examin'd with Candour*, on which
Bolingbroke's opinion has been sought.[5] Delany's central thesis was "that
the necessity of revelation, the truth of the Mosaic history . . . are . . . as
clearly proved in the following dissertations as any theorem in Euclid."[6]
This attempt to show that the Old Testament revelations are fully con-
sonant with reason was rather an embarrassment to Bolingbroke because it
relied on metaphysical hypotheses about final causes—the reasons for the
Creation and the nature of the Creator are not fit subjects for philosophical
discussion, in Bolingbroke's view, any more than is the putative existence
of a future life. Because his views of what is and is not the legitimate
province of philosophy prevailed over Pope, the *Essay on Man* was a less
recognizably Christian poem than it might have been. This caused Pope
much anxiety in later years.[7]

The *Essay on Man* brought Bolingbroke and Pope closer than they had
ever been. Apart from the philosophical cross-fertilization, I think it is
possible to read parts of the poem as a promulgation of Bolingbrokean
political principles. I shall develop this argument in the later chapter
devoted to the *Essay*. Indeed, it would be surprising if the *Essay* did not
have a political dimension, for 1731 was one of the stormiest years in the
Craftsman's history. The issue for 23 January exposed Walpole's negotiations with the Emperor over the Austro-Spanish disputes that resulted in
the Vienna agreement of March 1731.[8] For this breach of confidentiality,
the *Craftsman*'s printer Francklin was arrested. The pamphlet war between
the ministry's major writers Hervey, Yonge, and Arnall and the *Craftsman*'s team of Bolingbroke, Pulteney, and Amhurst reached its height in
1731. From September 1730 to May 1731, Bolingbroke contributed the
series of essays collectively named *Remarks on the History of England*, provoking the fury of ministerial writers. The *Craftsman* of 22 May, written in
defense of Bolingbroke and Pulteney, was particularly provocative. On the

day before its publication, Pope was still under Bolingbroke's roof, and the letter he wrote to the Earl of Oxford depicts Pope avidly drinking in a story he was told by Bolingbroke about a Whig attempt to assassinate Bolingbroke and Robert Harley, the then Earl of Oxford's father.[9] Later in the year, Pope was forced to break an engagement with Oxford to be with Fazackerly and Noel, who were the defense counsel in Francklin's trial.[10] Pope, then, was preserving an interest in the *Craftsman*'s fortunes at law. Perhaps Pope was acting for Bolingbroke in liaising with Francklin's lawyers, since Bolingbroke himself, being the alleged author of the offending issue, would not have wished to be directly associated with the *Craftsman*'s prosecution. In another area of activity too, Pope may have been acting in conjunction with Bolingbroke. Despite his later claim in the *Epistle to Dr. Arbuthnot* that "the Play'rs and I are, luckily, no friends," Pope was heavily involved in 1730 and 1731 with the promotion of plays by Aaron Hill and David Mallet. Mallet, who was later to become Bolingbroke's literary executor, had sent the manuscript of his *Eurydice* to Pope as early as autumn 1729, but it was not performed until 22 February 1731. The play was politically subversive, since the major characters—Eurydice, Periander, Procres, and Polydore—could be identified with, respectively, Queen Caroline, George II, Walpole, and Frederick, Prince of Wales, so that the play could be allegorized as being about the undue influence of Walpole over the Queen and the King's neglect of his constitutional duty.[11] Pope had reason to believe that Queen Caroline knew him to be the play's sponsor, which he had denied, as he tells Mallet in a letter of 29 December 1730.[12] But Pope had earmarked Mallet as a potential opposition writer. On Pope's recommendation, Bolingbroke invited Mallet to talk with him early in 1731, perhaps with the intention of grooming a new *Craftsman* journalist.[13]

All the evidence points to Pope's participation in opposition political activity in 1731, even if at a restrained level. Assuredly, Pope was not writing explicitly antigovernment satire as was Swift at this time. Swift's poem "To Mr. Gay," written, though not published, in 1731, contains a clear allusion to Bolingbroke's view of the need for a balance between King and Parliament undisturbed by the encroachment of a corrupt First Minister, as outlined in the *Remarks on the History of England*:

> The Law so strictly guards the Monarch's Health,
> That no Physician dares prescribe by Stealth:
> The Council sit; approve the Doctor's Skill;
> And give Advice before he gives the Pill.
> But, the *State-Emp'ric* acts a safer Part;
> And while he *poisons, wins* the Royal Heart. (77–82)

Here the medical allegory of Walpole the poisoning doctor draws us into the world of the *Craftsman*, where the image of Walpole as a quack doctor, purveyor of dangerous nostrums and fatal remedies, is frequently employed.[14] Nothing in Pope's writing had been as explicit as this, but the *Dunciad Variorum* and, I shall contend presently, parts of the *Essay of Man* are discreetly subversive. In 1731, while he continued to correspond with Fortescue, there are no longer any references to Walpole, and Pope seems to have given up the attempt to preserve his credit in government circles; his hopes of becoming intimate with the Prime Minister would seem to have come to nothing. And in December 1731, with the publication of Pope's *Epistle to Burlington* (originally published as *Of Taste*), Pope was drawn, possibly *malgré lui*, into the political arena. It is still very much a live issue in Pope studies as to whose house and estate was the object of satire in the "Timon's villa" passage.[15] A powerful case has been made by Kathleen Mahaffey for the view that Pope intended to satirize Walpole's Houghton and that the attribution of James Brydges, Duke of Chandos, was a red herring deliberately introduced by Leonard Welsted to deflect unwelcome attention from Walpole.[16] Pope's pamphlet *A Master Key to Popery* certainly takes this view and seems to redirect the satire toward Walpole by introducing Houghton as a possible target.[17] If this attribution is correct and if Welsted was attempting to draw Pope's political fire, it suggests that the government was sensitive to his poetry already by 1731 and that this year was the turning point in his career as a patent opponent of the administration. To my mind, 1731 was indeed the year when Pope ceased to work as a double agent—or otherwise to hedge his bets—and dedicated himself to Bolingbroke's cause.[18] But Bolingbroke was not yet satisfied that Pope was writing as usefully on politics as he might be. In the letter he wrote to Pope by way of a preface to his philosophical *Essays on Human Knowledge*, Bolingbroke commiserates indignantly with Pope's tribulations over the *Epistle to Burlington*—a campaign that Bolingbroke also thinks is politically inspired—and spurs the poet on to new heights with hints of martyrdom at government hands.

> You began to laugh at the ridiculous taste, or the no taste in gardening and building, of some men who are at great expense in both. What a clamor was raised instantly? The name of Timon was applied to a noble person with double malice, to make him ridiculous, and you who lived in friendship with him, odious. By the authority that employed itself to encourage this clamor, and by the industry used to spread and support it, one would have thought that you had directed your satire in that epistle to political subjects, and had inveighed against those who impoverish, dishonor, and sell their country, instead of making yourself inoffensively merry at the expense of men who ruin none but themselves, and render none but themselves ridiculous. What will the clamor be, and how will the same authority foment it, when you proceed to lash, in other instances,

our want of elegance even in luxury, and our wild profusion, the source of insatiable rapacity, and almost universal venality? My mind forebodes that the time will come, and who knows how near it may be, when other powers than those of Grub street, may be drawn forth against you, and when vice and folly may be avowedly sheltered behind a power instituted for better, and contrary purposes; for punishment of one, and for the reformation of both.[19]

Pope's poetry written between 1732 and May 1735, when the defeated Bolingbroke left England once again for France, would appear to be responding in no uncertain terms to the latter's suggestion that Pope "direct [his] satire . . . to political subjects"; and the reaction from the ministerial press was as St. John predicted also. The letters of 1732 show the poet collecting, or more probably verifying, information on the Man of Ross, whose charity and social concern becomes in the *Epistle to Bathurst* a monument of exemplary conduct.[20] At the same time, Pope was collecting evidence of the kind of corruption that the *Craftsman* claimed was rife in the land. The collapse through fraudulent management of the Charitable Corporation "for Relief of Industrious Poor," leading to the expulsion of Sir Robert Sutton and Sir Archibald Grant from the House, is the subject of an interesting letter from Peterborow to Pope.[21] Early in May, Peterborow wrote to Pope a letter that is very complex in tone.[22] The background to it is clearly the Parliamentary Committee's report on the Charitable Corporation brought on 20 April. It operates on a level of cynical seriousness: Peterborow has been cured of "some diseases . . . which tormented me very much in my youth. I was possest with violent and uneasy passions, such as a peevish concern for Truth, and a saucy love for my Country. When a Christian Priest preached against the Spirit of the Gospel, when an English Judge determined against Magna Charta, when the Minister acted against common-Sense, I used to fret." This ironic tone and the metaphor of the patriot as a man possessed, his "concern for Truth" a rabid hypochondria, is a *Craftsman*-like posture, suggesting the raised level of sensitivity to the stench of corruption created by that journal. Dennis Bond, the Charitable Corporation director, is also satirized in the *Epistle to Bathurst*. All in all, 1732 was to Pope a grossly corrupt year, and to Oxford, he laments in millenarian terms, "This whole year has seem'd the Expiration of the Reign of the Wicked."[23] Corruption also operated in literary spheres in 1732. Swift writes pessimistically to Gay on the probable fortunes of the second series *Fables*, adroitly inventing a fable appropriate to Gay's own situation:

> I approve of the scheme you have to grow somewhat richer, though I agree you will meet discouragements, & it is reasonable you should, considering what kind of pens are at this time onely employed & encour-

aged. For you must allow that the bad Painter was in the right, who
having painted a Cock, drove away all the Cocks & hens, & even the
chickens, for fear those who pass'd by his shop might make a comparison
with his work.[24]

To Swift, the advancement of hack authors was one of the darkest iniq-
uities of the times. The financially independent Pope could afford to take
a relaxed line on this, and he must have been somewhat chastened by
Gay's principled refusal of Pope's worldly advice to write a panegyric on
the new Royal Hermitage at Windsor.[25]

Pope and Bolingbroke were, as usual, seeing each other fairly regularly
in 1732. It was a quiet year for the poet, housebound by his mother's poor
health. Punctuating the overall deadness of life, his meetings with Bolingbroke were of a philosophical cast. In March, they wrote jointly to Swift a
letter in which Bolingbroke tells of his progress on a philosophical work
calculated to "render all your Metaphysical Theology both ridiculous and
abominable"; while Pope took the credit for having weaned Bolingbroke
away from active participation in politics toward "subjects moral, useful,
and more worthy his pen":

> I pass almost all my time at Dawley and at home; my Lord (of which I
> partly take the merit to my self) is as much estrang'd from politicks as I am.
> Let Philosophy be ever so vain, it is less vain now than Politicks, and not
> quite so vain at present as Divinity: I know nothing that moves strongly
> but Satire, and those who are asham'd of nothing else, are so of being
> ridiculous.[26]

It is true that Bolingbroke was politically quiescent in 1732, but this was
because he was involved in dangerous closet diplomacy at the time, as
Pope probably knew and as we shall shortly see. Later in the year, Pope
conveys to Bathurst Bolingbroke's whimsically extravagant compliment
on the improvements being made at Riskins:

> Lord Bolingbroke bids me to wish you all the joys of Nebuchadonozor, all
> the pensile Gardens, the proud Pyramids, the Ninevehs and Babels, to
> aggrandise and ornament your Territories; & that at length, you may be
> turn'd into a Happy Beast, loose among a thousand Females, to grass.[27]

On receiving a drawing or engraving of Bolingbroke commissioned from
Jonathan Richardson, Pope exults, "Posterity will thro' your means, see
the man whom it will for ages honour, vindicate, and applaud, when envy
is no more, and when (as I have already said in the Essay to which you are
so partial) 'The sons shall blush their fathers were his foes.' "[28]

The results of Pope's pensive and observant year were manifested in the
Epistle to Bathurst, published in January 1733, and in *To Fortescue (Imit. Hor.
Sat.* II.1), published shortly afterward in mid-February. Bolingbroke is

given the credit by Pope for having instigated the latter poem in one of Spence's anecdotes, perhaps too generously:

> When I had a fever one winter in town that confined me to my room for five or six days, Lord Bolingbroke came to see me, happened to take up a Horace that lay on the table, and in turning it over dipped on the First Satire of the Second Book. He observed how well that would hit my case, if I were to imitate it in English. After he was gone, I read it over, translated it in a morning or two, and sent it to the press in a week or fortnight after. And this was the occasion of my imitating some other of the Satires and Epistles afterwards.[29]

The *Epistle to Bathurst* is, broadly, an attack on the financial institutions of the City and on specific individuals who manipulated them—on usurers, stockjobbers, managers, directors of large corporations, in sum, on the moneyed interest, which target the *Craftsman* had been attacking since its inception. The poem is constructed round two central portraits; one, the Man of Ross, representing the ideally harmonious interaction between the substantial burgess and his dependent townsfolk, and the other, a composite portrait of Sir Balaam, whose niggardly uncharitableness is an early sign of cancerous moral nullity once he is exposed to the diabolically inspired temptations of the commercial City. The attack on the City is pursued on two flanks. Pursuit of money is seen to be dehumanizing, destructive of the charitable concern for the less fortunate that justifies the accumulation of wealth. On the other hand, "Blest paper-credit" facilitates the stockpiling of invisible wealth, allowing its owners to challenge the hegemony of the governing class. The money men, South Sea and other company directors like Blunt, Cutler, and Bond, or atttorneys-cum-stewards like Peter Walter, could quasi-magically circumvent the qualification for wielding influence—the possession of land. Only possession of land could make its owner sensitive to the wider community's needs.[30] Despite the unmistakably Tory implications of these views, the *Epistle to Bathurst* would not appear to have aroused a political furor.[31] This is probably because the relationship between the poem's moral argument about wealth—that it is a mixed blessing that needs to be handled properly if it is not to lead to the complementary vices of avarice and profusion—and the political argument outlined above is a subtle one and not easily available to hack writers. In addition, the portraits Pope paints either are general, as in Harpax, the Cottas, and Sir Balaam, or, when they are particular, tend to be of discredited men. *To Fortescue* is a good deal blunter. Fortescue plays Trebatius to Pope's Horace; and against the former's counsel to "write no more," or at least to write panegyric on the royal family, Pope runs through a gamut of increasingly serious counterobjections. He has aesthetic objections to the panegyricist's sound and fury; the royal family do not encourage poets anyway—with rich irony, Pope comments, "And justly CAESAR scorns the Poet's Lays, / It is to *History* he trusts for Praise" (35–36); it is his hobby to "pour out all myself, as plain / As downright *Shippen* or as old *Montagne*" (51–52); satire is his weapon in a world of "Thieves, Supercargoes, Sharpers and Directors"; and finally, while the world continues to be as it is, in despite of all opposition, even of violence, the poet will continue to assert his independence. By line 124, the poet has found in the din of protest occasioned by his satire a cure for the insomnia of lines 12–15 that caused him to write in the first place:

> Know, all the distant Din that World can keep
> Rolls o'er my *Grotto*, and but sooths my sleep.

By the end of the poem, Pope has redefined the nature of his art, rejecting the designation "Libels and satires" in favor of "grave *Epistles*, bringing Vice to light." The final irony of the poem is, of course, that however just Fortescue admits Pope's case to be, it requires the sesame of Walpole's name to succeed in a court of law, and the entire poem becomes mimetic of the corrupt institutional processes against which it is aimed. In its forward movement, the poem satirizes all the following: Walter and Charteris, continuing the "abuse of riches" theme from the *Epistle to Bathurst;* Lord Hervey and, viciously, Lady Mary Wortley Montagu ("From furious *Sappho* scarce a milder Fate, / P—x'd by her Love, or libell'd by her Hate," lines 83–84); Cibber the laureate, whose appointment was ipso facto evidence of degeneration in taste; Walpole himself in the explicit line "Bare the mean Heart that lurks beneath a Star"; and even the royal couple. There is even a passing hit at that Tory shibboleth, the standing army (73). What must have been more galling still to the government was that this antimasque of virtue's enemies was countered by the peaceful scene in Pope's garden and grotto where the friends of virtue, Peterborow and Bolingbroke, are to be found enjoying the poet's hospitality and helping him in arboriculture, quite unconcerned with the political world:

> There, my Retreat the best Companions grace,
> Chiefs, out of War, and Statesmen, out of Place.
> There *St. John* mingles with my friendly Bowl,
> The Feast of Reason and the Flow of Soul:
> And He, whose Lightning pierc'd th' *Iberian* Lines,
> Now, forms my Quincunx, and now ranks my Vines. (125–30)

To rub salt in the wound, Pope published the first three epistles of the *Essay on Man*, dedicated to Bolingbroke, between February and May 1733.

Not surprisingly, it was Lord Hervey and Lady Mary who first took up cudgels against Pope in the *Verses Address'd to the Imitator . . . of Horace.*

While this poem is largely a personal attack on the deformities of Pope's body and soul—"It was the Equity of righteous Heav'n, / That such a Soul to such a Form was giv'n" (50–51)—and on his inability to write proper satire, a later poem of Lady Mary's entitled *P[ope] to Bolingbroke* is a direct attack on this treasonable alliance. The poet is represented as a spiteful Puck, whose small acts of petty malice and chronic envy are pale imitations of his master Bolingbroke's treasonable acts:

> I own, these glorious schemes I view with pain,
> My little Mischiefs to myself seem mean,
> My ills are humble tho' my heart is great,
> All I can do is flatter, lie, and cheat.
> Yet I may say, 'tis plain that you preside
> O'er all my morals, and 'tis much my Pride
> To tread, with steps unequal, where you guide.[32] (44–50)

Pope is even envious of Bolingbroke's large-scale villainy! The poem ends, fittingly, in the couple's greatest vaunt—"You scape the Block, and I the Whipping-Post." And indeed, from 1734 onward, one of the recurrent charges made against Pope in government pamphlets and satires, often the most serious, is that he is Bolingbroke's friend. In *The False Patriot. An Epistle to Mr. Pope*, in *An Epistle to Alexander Pope, Esq.* (published in the *Daily Journal* for 4 February 1735), and in Thomas Bentley's *A Letter to Mr. Pope* of the same year, Bolingbroke is characterized as Pope's evil genius. Bentley, commenting on the line "To Virtue Only and Her Friends, a Friend" (*To Fortescue*, 121), exclaims irascibly:

> You make a great ado with your *Virtue only*, and your *Uni aequus virtuti atque ejus amicis*. VIRTUE ONLY in Capitals is one of the Marks to know you by. Is Bolingbroke one of your *Virtutis Amici*? Pray, let us know then what you mean by *Virtue*.[33]

The reason for this is not hard to find. By mid-1734, Bolingbroke was the most unpopular man in Britain. In the Commons debate on the Tory bill to repeal the Septennial Act, Walpole had replied to Sir William Wyndham with a blistering attack on Bolingbroke that stigmatized him as venomous, vainglorious, ambitious, self-interested, and a traitor.[34] At the time of saying this, Walpole had just survived the most serious crisis of his political life. The ill-fated scheme to extend the excise to cover spirits and tobacco, introduced early in 1733 for the perfectly respectable motives of cutting losses incurred through customs fraud and, with the revenue, reducing the land tax to one shilling in the pound, proved to be Sir Robert's gravest miscalculation. That such a seemingly sound and politically expedient scheme misfired was due, in some measure, to the *Craftsman*'s skill in persuading the House and the electors in the constituencies that it would lead to a proliferation of bureaucracy, which would be expensive, as well as tightening the government's stranglehold on the nation. When Boling-broke saw its potential as a political cause célèbre, he attempted to peg his court and country ideology to it, arguing that the excise was a court scheme that the country needed to unite against. Though the scheme was with-drawn, it remained the dominant issue of the 1734 election. Part of the Chief Minister's strategy for combating the excise threat was an assault on the court and country dichotomy, with a revival of the traditional party labels.[35] The election of 1734 would be fought between Whigs and Tories, claimed Walpole, and Tories were Jacobites. This was a familiar and time-tested tactic and the obvious line to take against an ideology that Walpole really feared: a genuine country opposition was a dangerous threat. But in 1734 there were very good grounds for the charge that leading Tories were Jacobite sympathizers, and once again, in this respect Bolingbroke was his party's Achilles' heel. Since 1732, he had been in close touch with the French ambassador Chavigny, with whom he discussed his hopes of fomenting a country opposition to Walpole. In addition, he and Wyndham discussed the Pretender's cause and the terms on which the English people might be persuaded to abandon the Hanoverian succes-sion. Worse still, in 1733 and 1734, he negotiated with the French the funding of the opposition's campaign, being promised both personal moneys and a grant of £10,000 or £11,000 toward party funds.[36] The loss of the election in 1734 was regarded by opposition Whigs, with some truth on their side, as owing to Bolingbroke's vulnerability. He was a liability to his own party, a fact that he himself recognized in his return to France the following year. Not everything emerged about his dealings with the French, but enough came out to make him persona non grata in England.

Favorable mention of Bolingbroke after 1733 was, therefore, an ipso facto political act. How could Lord Hervey have seen it otherwise? In January 1731, he had lampooned Bolingbroke and Pulteney in the pam-phlet *Sedition and Defamation Display'd*, to which Pulteney replied in the *Craftsman* for 20 January. Pulteney's well-chosen reply became the basis of Pope's "Sporus" portrait in the later *Epistle to Dr. Arbuthnot:*

> . . . It would be barbarous to handle such a *delicate Hermaphrodite,* such a pretty, little, *Master Miss,* in too rough a Manner.[37]

This pamphlet accused Hervey obliquely of homosexuality and resulted in a celebrated eighteenth-century duel. When the *Craftsman* resumed the subject, it was in the provocative paper of 22 May previously mentioned. To Hervey, sympathetic portrayal of Bolingbroke in verse would be tanta-mount to treason. Clearly then, even the relatively apolitical *Epistle to Dr. Arbuthnot,* published early in 1735, cannot be read as having no significance for affairs of state. Any poem that spoke of a longstanding friendship with St. John in the same lines while mounting a virulent attack on Hervey must be opposition inspired. The nature of Pope's attack on Hervey is of moment here:

> Whether in florid Impotence he speaks,
> And, as the Prompter breathes, the Puppet squeaks;
> Or at the Ear of *Eve*, familiar Toad,
> Half Froth, half Venom, spits himself abroad,
> In Puns, or Politicks, or Tales, or Lyes,
> Or Spite, or Smut, or Rymes, or Blasphemies.
> His Wit all see-saw between *that* and *this*,
> Now high, now low, now Master up, now Miss,
> And he himself one vile Antithesis.
> Amphibious Thing! that acting either Part,
> The trifling Head, or the corrupted Heart!
> Fop at the Toilet, Flatt'rer at the Board,
> Now trips a Lady, and now struts a Lord.
> *Eve*'s Tempter thus the Rabbins have exprest,
> A Cherub's face, a Reptile all the rest. (317–31)

Obviously, this description characterizes Hervey's relationship with Walpole, "the Prompter," and the Queen. He is presented as a tool-villain, part victim and part cause of the evil nexus in which all three are connected. About his capacity to cause real damage, Pope wishes to remain as noncommittal as he does about his gender. And of course, the sustained insect imagery secures the ambivalence on the figurative level. Insects have the power to repel and also, to the lepidopterist, to fascinate. But the description is raised to a mythical level by the allusion to *Paradise Lost* and to the Miltonic-Christian conception of evil. Hervey, like Satan, is endowed with the capacity for good or evil, but is inclined toward the latter by an implacable hatred of the social body that stems from "the corrupted Heart." Such a recasting of the Temptation and Fall is behind Dryden's portrait of Achitophel, and is indeed a pervasive structure in Tory satire.[38] Yet, on another level, we have seen that some of the passage's specific detail derives from particular numbers of the *Craftsman*, though much of it is the product of Pope's relentlessly keen observation. In general, too, the *Craftsman* lies behind the passage: Walpole as puppetmaster is a *Craftsman* characterization. And, more important, it was quite impossible by 1735 to use the term *corruption* without its being understood as part of a specifically political register. To the sensitized reader, it would suggest the erosion of constitutional liberty caused by ministerial encroachment on the rights and privileges of the Commons. Like the terms *virtue* and *liberty*, also made much of in the poem, *corruption* became almost a technical term, functioning in Bolingbroke's specialized vocabulary.

Pope's relationship with Bolingbroke seems to have been unaffected by the climate of detraction that existed by 1735. After his mother's death, he became freer to travel, and the summer of 1733 saw the formal instigation of his rambles round the south of England visiting friends that came to be his habitual practice.[39] In mid-September to early October 1734, he traveled in Bolingbroke's company to Bath, and at the close of the year he was with his friend a good deal at Dawley, while he was working on the *Epistle to Dr. Arbuthnot*.[40] In 1734, Pope made two very different mentions of Bolingbroke in verse. Epistle 4 of the *Essay on Man*, published in January, pays fulsome tribute to him as "my guide, philosopher, and friend" and, interestingly, attempts to give an impression of what conversation with him was actually like:

> Form'd by thy converse, happily to steer
> From grave to gay, from lively to severe;
> Correct with spirit, eloquent with ease,
> Intent to reason, or polite to please. (4.379–82)

Later, however, in December 1734, his imitation of Horace's *Sermones* 1.2 was published as *Sober Advice from Horace*, and in this risqué "sermon against adultery," it was fitting that he should include Bolingbroke, whose youthful reputation for indiscriminate sexual generosity is mocked:

> How much more safe, dear Countrymen! his State,
> Who trades in Frigates of the second Rate?
> And yet some Care of S—st should be had,
> Nothing so mean for which he can't run mad;
> His Wit confirms him but a Slave the more,
> And makes a Princess whom he found a Whore.
> The Youth might save much Trouble and Expence,
> Were he a Dupe of only common Sense.
> But here's his point; "A Wench (he cries) for me!
> I never touch a Dame of Quality." (61–70)

These lines are presumably a private joke, which Bolingbroke seemed to take in good part, commenting to Swift that "the Rogue has fixed a ridicule upon me, which some events of my life would seem perhaps to justify."[41] When Bolingbroke left for France in May 1735, it was for Pope the nadir of an already melancholy year. Arbuthnot had died in February, though he had mercifully lived to see the *Epistle* dedicated to him in print, while Peterborow sank into a decline that ended in his death in August, attended by Pope at his bedside. Yet Pope was already making new friends among the so-called "Boy Patriots," establishing relationships that would increase his sense of self-importance and, by an ironic reversal, make him a more significant political figure than Bolingbroke by 1740.

Chapter 5

Bolingbroke, Pope, and the "Essay on Man" Revisited

Influences and Chronology

We come now to consider one of the major issues arising from the relationship between the two men, the question of whether Bolingbroke's philosophy directly influenced the composition and substance of Pope's *Essay on Man*. Previous discussions of this problem have been insufficient in both their method of examination and in their use of all available evidence. John Barnard is correct in saying that "the true extent of Bolingbroke's influence has never been satisfactorily determined."[1] Virtually all biographers of both men have addressed themselves to the question of influence, and opinions lie along a spectrum ranging from the extreme claim that Pope simply versified a prose treatise written for him by Bolingbroke, to the extreme counterclaim that if there is internal evidence for influence, it must be attributable to Pope's influence on Bolingbroke rather than vice versa. There is very little agreement about the nature, extent, or direction of such a putative influence. Often, these questions have received an answer in terms of the biographer's own view of Bolingbroke's deistic beliefs regarding the doctrines of the soul's immortality, the existence of a future state of punishments and rewards, and the place of reason vis-à-vis revelation in arriving at a proper religious sense.

Owen Ruffhead, who produced the earliest biography of Pope "authorized" by Warburton and working from Warburton's papers, manifests in his biography a strong desire to protect the poems from adverse criticism. He is responsible for the view that Warburton was defending Pope not only from Crousaz, but also from Bolingbroke:

> The latter [Bolingbroke] *would have* given a bias to this admirable essay, which would have been disgraceful to our bard's understanding, dishonourable to his virtue, and injurious to society: the former [Warburton] . . . *did* give a bias to it, which will reflect mortal honour on the poet's sense, do everlasting credit to his virtue, and be for ever serviceable to mankind. Now let the world determine, which of the two deserves the incomparable praise of being—
> The Poet's *Guide, Philosopher* and FRIEND.[2]

Clearly, Ruffhead is retailing Warburton's own view here: this biography needs to be set in the context of the hostility that developed between Warburton and Bolingbroke in later years. But nineteenth-century editors of Pope follow Owen Ruffhead and Warton's edition in thinking Bolingbroke a pernicious influence who maneuvered the *Essay* in the direction of fatalism and deism. Says Warton, "Through the whole course of his life, Pope was firmly and unvariably convinced of the Being of a God, a Providence and the Immortality of the Soul. Though perhaps, when he was writing under the guidance of Bolingbroke, he entertained some unhappy and ill-founded doubts concerning the truth of the Christian Dispensation."[3] Adolphus William Ward, in his introduction to the Globe edition of Pope's *Poetical Works*, argues Bolingbroke's direct influence on the *Essay*, and the tenor of Ward's criticism reflects the purport of nineteenth-century discussion of the poem:

> In Pope's eyes an indescribable charm attached to the society and personality of this unrepentant Alcibiades. As Bolingbroke discoursed to him on his system of natural theology, clear and shallow as the streamlet in the grotto where they sat, and communicated to him those Essays which he never had the courage to publish, the mind of his friend became imbued with enough of the facile lesson to make him in his own belief the disciple of an exhaustive system, while he was in reality only the acolyte of a sophist and a man of the world. Thus Bolingbroke devised for Pope, or Pope devised with Bolingbroke's direct aid, the scheme of his *Essay on Man*.[4]

Elwin and Courthope similarly agree that the philosophical framework of the *Essay* was derived gratefully by Pope from Bolingbroke—and that its philosophy is both incompetent and ungodly; separating form and content, however, they argue that no one "thinks of the poverty of the argument as he listens to the melody of the verse."[5] This pharisaical tone continues into our own century in D. G. James's *The Life of Reason*.

That strain aside, two serious attempts have been made to discuss this question of influence, by Walter Sichel at the beginning of the century and by Maynard Mack more recently, though neither treatment is sufficiently rigorous in the extent of the evidence it examines. Sichel and Mack are at opposite poles of the spectrum in the question of influence: the former speaks of Pope as having "translated a part only of Bolingbroke's daring ideas into immortal verse" and is absolutely convinced that Pope was a versifier of the *Essays*, whereas Mack argues that it is chronologically impossible for any published work of Bolingbroke's to have influenced Pope and is only prepared to admit very weak claims for influence of a less specific nature.[6] Sichel's evidence for influence is based largely on verbal echoes—parallels in expression and simile—and he does assemble these in sufficient concentration to allow us to accept them as evidence. But evidence of what? Since he does not argue the chronological case for Bolingbroke's *Essays* to have existed *in some form* before Pope composed the relevant sections of the *Essay on Man*, his assumption that the direction of influence runs from Bolingbroke to Pope remains unproven. This is an inexcusable omission, since the nineteenth-century editor of Pope's works, William Roscoe, had already argued that a considerable part of the poem predated a "single word" of Bolingbroke's philosophical works and that the latter were "in many respects, rather a repetition of the same sentiments, than a model for that work."[7]

It is this argument that Mack reconstitutes in his influential and important preface to the Twickenham edition of the *Essay on Man*. Mack does discuss internal evidence for the attribution of influence provided by alleged similarities in the ideas—"the approach to the problems of man's life, the kinds of evidence drawn on, the texture of attitudes"—but he finds that the similarities are no more significant than the dissimilarities and that the similarities are often commonplaces that cannot be confidently designated "Bolingbrokean."[8] Though in my view Mack seriously underestimates the similarities in ideas between the poem and Bolingbroke's *Essays* and *Fragments,* I do not wish to make this the main point of my argument against him, because I share his distrust of this method of establishing influence. On purely internal grounds, I do not think it is possible to establish with sufficient precision or specificity the degree to which Pope was or was not indebted to Bolingbroke: we cannot say that the *Essay* is so remarkably like Bolingbroke's writing in certain respects that there is no other possible source or influence. Mack's own editorial work alone supports his claim that "everything Pope incorporated in the poem was available to him from other sources."[9] But he had not the benefit of an important book-length study of the poem by Douglas H. White, which demonstrates that not only did Pope use ideas that were in the common currency and depend on the traditions of classical and Renaissance ethical wisdom, but he also understood and held views on contemporary philosophical debates.[10] White's argument constitutes a major revaluation of the poem, which improves on Mack's hint that the view of Pope's mind as a tabula rasa and Bolingbroke's as a hard stylus is naive. Regarding such issues as the existence and origin of evil, God's status as immanent rather than external Creator, the degree of freedom in God's decision to create the world, the nature of his involvement in the created world (the functioning of providence), the sense in which this is the "best possible" world, the role of the passions vis-à-vis the reason in motivating and regulating human conduct, the extent to which the passions operate toward the establishment of social security, and the extent to which self-love is a "benevolent" passion, Pope takes up a position that can be placed

within the context of living controversy. This implies not only that Pope
is far from being the philosophical incompetent that nineteenth-century
and later critics have thought him, but also that the *Essay on Man* is not the
static encapsulation of received ideas (Bolingbroke's or anyone else's) that
many readers have thought it. Rather, it is a dynamic and motive poem
that really does steer "betwixt the extremes of doctrine seemingly opposite" in precise ways. It is therefore very hazardous to promote Bolingbroke into sole prominence as the poem's "onlie begetter."

But this is not Mack's strongest argument. He believes that for those
who think influence exists, the burden of proof lies on internal evidence
and on other more nebulous material, such as the content of oral conversations between the two and a philosophical "dissertation" or "letter" that
may have existed but no longer does, because on purely chronological
grounds, the published philosophical writings are too late to have influenced any but possibly the last of the poem's four epistles. He says of a
putative influence:

> The chronology is all against it. Bolingbroke's statements in his introduc-
> tory letter to his philosophical writings make it very plain that he is just at
> that moment beginning to *write* on the subjects they have previously
> discussed, and this introductory letter cannot be dated earlier than 14
> December 1731—about four months after the date when three epistles
> were completed and Pope was intent upon the fourth.[11]

If he is correct about this, the case for influence is considerably weakened.
Much of Sichel's evidence based on phrasal similarities, otherwise strong,
would be invalid. The chronological argument therefore needs to be ex-
amined at some length.

The history of composition of the *Essay on Man* is still obscure, but Mack
assumes on the basis of the relevant correspondence that the poem was
underway by November 1729, that by 2 August 1731 three epistles were
complete, and that the fourth was still undergoing revision in the summer
and autumn of 1733. We can add to this the literary detective work of G. M.
Rousseau and Marjorie Hope Nicolson, who have suggested that "the first
three epistles of *An Essay on Man* were brought into publishable form
under Bolingbroke's roof" during April and May 1731, when Pope was
recuperating from an illness at Dawley.[12] Furthermore, we can say that
during the summer of 1731, Pope was working on a version of the fourth
epistle, but that there was a hiatus in composition until August 1733.[13] The
work was certainly being published anonymously after January 1733,
though the fourth epistle did not appear in print until January 1734. We
have seen that Mack does not think Bolingbroke began his *Essays* before 14
December 1731. In a recent note, John Joerg argues an even later date for
the composition of the *Essays*; if he is correct, the *Fragments* would have

been written long after they could have influenced Pope, given the length of the *Essays*.[14] Joerg's argument runs that Bolingbroke refers four times to George Berkeley as bishop of Cloyne in the *Essays,* and once again in the *Fragments.*[15] But Berkeley was not consecrated bishop of Cloyne until 19 May 1734, thus proving that the *Essays* were not *begun* until after the publication of the *Essay on Man* in its entirety. However, Joerg does not cite the corpus of evidence that tells against his dating. Some of it is collected by James Osborn in his editions of Spence's *Anecdotes.*[16] In May 1730, Savage told Spence, "Lord Bolingbroke has sent Mr. Pope a long letter on these heads, and [Pope?] has by him what would make six or seven sheets in print towards a second, and does not know how far it may grow."[17] This, bolstered by a letter from Pope to Swift of 1 December 1731, in which he tells Swift, "You will see a word of Lord B–'s and one of mine; which, with a just neglect of the present age, consult only posterity; and with a noble scorn of politicks, aspire to philosophy," strongly suggests that Bolingbroke was putting a philosophical pen to paper in the very early thirties.[18] In March 1732, he writes to Swift:

> . . . You will be surprized to find that I have been partly drawn by [Pope] and partly by myself, to write a pretty large volume upon a very grave and very important subject; that I have ventur'd to pay no regard whatever to any authority except sacred authority, and that I have ventured to start a thought, which must, if it is push'd as successfully as I think it is, render all your Metaphysical Theology both ridiculous and abominable.[19]

Later, in a joint letter written by Pope and Bolingbroke to Swift on 15 September 1734, we are given a progress report on the "pretty large volume." Pope talks of "what my Lord B. is doing with Metaphysicks," and Bolingbroke admits to having "writ six letters and a half to him on subjects of that kind, and I propose a letter and a half more which would swell the whole up to a considerable volume."[20] By 1730, then, Bolingbroke had a philosophical treatise in progress, and by 1734 he was still writing; though whether he had finished the works that were eventually published as the four *Essays* and was now writing what were left as the eighty-one loosely connected sections of the *Fragments* is unclear. Doing some simple arithmetic on the data we have (and assuming that Bolingbroke's rate of output remained constant), we can say that Bolingbroke would have finished what he projected in April 1735.

What are we to say, then, about the anomaly pointed out by Joerg? It seems impossible that Bolingbroke could have begun as late as May 1734 in the face of this evidence. The answer is provided by the Advertisement to the *Fragments,* where Bolingbroke tells us that the *Essays* and the *Fragments or Minutes* were "all communicated to [Mr. Pope] in scraps, as they were occasionally written. But the latter not having been connected and put together under different heads, and in the same order as the former had been, before his death . . . I have contented myself to correct and extend them a little."[21] The clear import of this is that the *Essays* had been revised thoroughly before Pope's death in 1744, but that the *Fragments* had not yet; and so Bolingbroke intended merely to make small corrections and additions, presumably for publication. It follows therefore that the first printed edition is a later revision of the manuscript version that Pope would have seen. It cannot be used confidently for dating. Indeed, there is other "evidence" in the philosophical writings that "proves," in Joerg's method of dating, that the *Essays* were written after 1736! What it in fact shows is that certain sections were written later than the rest and were revisions. In the first *Essay*, Bolingbroke refers obliquely to Queen Caroline's fraternization with Joseph Butler:

> Our learned queen interests herself in nice and subtil disputations about space: from metaphysics she rises to theology. She attends frequently to the controversy, almost fourteen hundred years old, and still carried on with as much warmth, and as little success as ever, about that profound mystery the Trinity. She studies with much application the "analogy of revealed religion to the constitution and course of nature."—She understands the whole argument perfectly, and concludes, with the right reverend author, that it is not "so clear a case that there is nothing in revealed religion." Such royal, such lucrative encouragement must needs keep both metaphysics and the sublimest theology in credit; and in short, "Signs following signs, lead on the mighty year."[22]

The work referred to is Butler's *The Analogy of Religion, Natural and Revealed, to the Constitution and Course of Nature*, which was first published in 1736. Bolingbroke quotes from the Advertisement to the 1736 edition, perhaps from memory.[23] The "lucrative encouragement" is a sidelong response to the fact that Butler was appointed clerk of the court by the Queen in the same year; and her biographer tells us that the Queen used to spend the hours of 7 P.M. to 9 P.M. daily with Butler, discoursing on metaphysics.[24] This suggests that the passage was written after 1736 and before the Queen's death on 20 November 1737. But even this is inaccurate. E. C. Mossner has noticed that it is incorrect to refer to Butler as "right reverend" in the Queen's lifetime, since he was not then a bishop.[25] (He became dean of St. Paul's in 1740 and bishop of Durham in 1750). It seems that Bolingbroke wrote this snub of the Queen into the text at a much later date, goaded by the duncelike combination of bad politics and bad philosophy that Queen Caroline, the metaphysical supporter of Walpole, represented. He would have been accustomed by then to referring to Butler as a bishop and would have failed to notice that his insertion was anachronistic. Bolingbroke wrote the original text before 1736 and took the opportunity much later to satirize both Butler and the deceased Queen, writing in the historic present. If this is typical of the way Bolingbroke revised, it is clear that he could easily have updated Berkeley's title. Certainly, I think that Joerg's suggestion is simplistic and that the bulk of Bolingbroke's published philosophical writing was on paper by mid-1735. Quite possibly, Pope had all the papers in his possession immediately prior to Bolingbroke's departure for France in May of that year.

Let us return to Maynard Mack, who supplements what he says on the chronology of the works in question in his introduction to the *Essay on Man* by an appendix A, in which he gives the internal evidence for the earliest possible date of composition of the *Fragments* being late 1731 or 1732. His first point is that the *Fragments* contain references to works published after 1731, and he says those references show little sign of having been reworked, so that the allusions are not likely to have been later additions. In view of what has been said about such an allusion in one of the *Essays*, I would not endorse this remark with any confidence. The *Fragments*, Mack believes, are "pretty clearly . . . printed in order of composition, each discussion growing out of and referring to the one before."[26] This is, after all, at variance with what Bolingbroke himself says about them. The first *Fragment* not only refers to Cudworth's *Treatise on Eternal and Immutable Morality* (first published in December 1730) as having been sent to Bolingbroke by Pope "long ago," but it also refers to material already written by Bolingbroke to Pope. This is either a reference to his *Essays*—which "from internal evidence cannot be dated earlier than 1732"—or to a lost work. As I will show, the latter possibility cannot be ruled out. In conclusion, Mack argues that *Fragments* 42–57, which provide the majority of the parallels usually drawn with Pope's *Essay*, were probably written "at a blow" and therefore can be dated by 54, in which the allusion is made to Pope's characterization of the Man of Ross. Pope was first inquiring of Tonson about the Man of Ross as late as autumn 1731, so this again indicates the lateness of the *Fragments*. But the assumption that the section of the *Fragments* was written at one time is pure conjecture. I see nothing exceptionable in Mack's dating of the composition of Bolingbroke's philosophy except insofar as it is conjoined with an assumption of little mutual influence and is regarded as documentary evidence of that view. It is because I do not consider the date to have such a significance that I question Mack's view, to show that at least he has not said the final word on the subject. We cannot rule out a close ideational connection between the two on any a priori grounds; the question of influence is not put out of court by chronological evidence, but remains open.

A Lost Prose Work

Discussions of any influence that Bolingbroke's philosophy may have had on the *Essay* are dogged by persistent beliefs that he was writing some philosophical work parallel with parts of Pope's poem, an actual prose version of the poem itself. This work, if it ever existed, no longer survives so far as is known, and its relationship to anything that is now extant is unclear. But the possibility that such a work existed deserves to be treated more seriously than it is by Mack. An examination of the Pierpont Morgan manuscript of the *Essay* (one of two surviving *Essay* manuscripts) shows that there are prose marginalia interspersed with the draft of epistle 4 that are not similar in function to the other group of marginalia used by the poet to summarize the poem's thought and compile the Argument. In fact, these prose jottings are part of the poem and demonstrate quite clearly that this section of epistle 4 *was* versified prose. Mack himself has edited this manuscript for the Roxburghe Club and has said that the marginalia take us "about as close to the actual processes of composition as we are likely to get" and speaks of "verse sucking prose into its own vortex."[27] Rather illogically, he sees these prose fragments as a development from the verse. I think, as does Miriam Leranbaum, the most recent student of the manuscripts, that these prose notes and the verse itself grew out of the "large prose collections" that we know Pope kept by him.[28] There is no way of knowing what these "prose collections" comprised, but I would conjecture that Pope assembled not only anything Bolingbroke cared to commit to paper, but also the poet's records of spoken conversations with him. Again, the Morgan manuscript does not allow us to be sure that Pope composed the whole poem thus, because it shows the first three epistles in a more finished state, but it would be compatible with what George Sherburn believes to have been the poet's method of composition to think that throughout the entire work he assembled his prose notes, composed verse paragraphs on the basis of them, arranged the fragments and blocks in logical sequence, and later polished the lines.[29] In my view, the *Essay on Man* does indeed have a prose source—but is that source some lost work of Bolingbroke's? I should like to assemble the available evidence and allow the reader to draw his own conclusion.

Lord Bathurst told Hugh Blair on 22 April 1763:

> "The Essay on Man" was originally composed by Lord Bolingbroke in prose, and that Mr. Pope did no more than put it into verse: that he had read Lord Bolingbroke's manuscript in his own handwriting; and remembered well, that he was at loss whether most to admire the elegance of Lord Bolingbroke's prose, or the beauty of Mr. Pope's verse. When Lord Bathurst told this, Mr. Mallet bade me attend, and remember this remark-

able piece of information; as, by the course of Nature, I might survive his Lordship, and be a witness of his having said so.[30]

Another letter from Bathurst to the Rev. Joshua Parry, dated 3 April 1769, is quoted in a note by George Sherburn.[31] This also attests that Bolingbroke had shown Bathurst a "dissertation in prose" which Bolingbroke gave Pope permission to burn and which, Bathurst believes, he himself may be the only living man to have read. That Bathurst was fond of this story is witnessed by Joseph Warton, who claims in 1780 that "Lord Bathurst repeatedly assured me, that he had read the whole scheme of the Essay on Man, in the hand-writing of Bolingbroke, and drawn up in a series of propositions, which POPE was to versify and illustrate."[32] As Sherburn points out, this prose dissertation, if it ever existed, cannot be the actual *Fragments* or anything that is actually a published part of Bolingbroke's works, since Pope allegedly burnt it. But it seems very unlikely that Pope would have burnt anything by Bolingbroke. If there was such a manuscript, perhaps it was incorporated into the *Fragments* or even into the *Essays*. Perhaps Johnson's healthy skepticism might be the order of the day:

> Depend upon it, Sir, this is too strongly stated. Pope may have had from Bolingbroke the philosophick *stamina* of his Essay; and admitting this to be true, Lord Bathurst did not intentionally falsify. But the thing is not true in the latitude that Blair seems to imagine; we are sure that the poetical imagery, which makes a great part of the poem, was Pope's own. It is amazing, Sir, what deviations there are from precise truth, in the account which is given of almost every thing.[33]

Johnson would have the last word—if it were not for a confirmation of Bathurst's story that emanates from a very curious source. The famous Advertisement to the 1749 edition of the *Patriot King*, which accuses Pope of having pirated and printed 1,500 copies of a garbled text, drew vitriolic replies from various directions.[34] A reply presumably by Bishop Warburton was published in the *London Evening Post* for 23 May 1749, entitled "A Letter to the Editor"; and this drew, from Bolingbroke himself, *A Familiar Epistle to the Most Impudent Man Living*, and after it, the pamphlet in which we are interested, *To the Author of a Libel, entitled etc.* The pamphlet is anonymous, but the popular assumption has been that it was written by David Mallet, despite the latter's protestations to the contrary.[35] The author denies the recurring charge that Bolingbroke's reputation is due to his poetic immortalization by Pope, and he makes two claims of some interest in redressing this balance. When Bolingbroke went to France, he left to Pope "besides the Works written for Mr. P–'s own Instruction (which gave him ample Reason to call the Author his Guide, Philosopher

and Friend) several original Manuscripts on different Subjects, and among
the rest that of the Letters lately published."[36] It is clear from the context
that Mallet refers to Bolingbroke's departure for France in May 1735, and
though it is true that Bolingbroke did leave the manuscripts of his new
work on politics, the *Letters on the Study and Use of History*, this author is
clearly making the additional claim that certain philosophical works were
also in Pope's hands by this time. This ties in, except for a time lag of ten
months, with a letter dated 25 March 1736 from Pope to Swift in which he
says:

> I have lately seen some writings of Lord B's, since he went to France.
> Nothing can depress his Genius: Whatever befals him, he will still be the
> greatest man in the world, either in his own time, or with posterity.[37]

Again, it is ambiguous whether "have lately seen . . . since he went to
France" means "have lately been sent from France" or whether it means
that Pope has had possession of the papers since Bolingbroke went to
France and has just recently read them. And we do not know which papers
these are. The second claim made by Mallet to show that Bolingbroke's
debt was not to Pope but vice versa is the claim that an acquaintance of his,
"a certain Senior Fellow of one of our Universities," told him the following
story:

> [The Fellow] started some Objections one Day, at Mr. P–'s House, to the
> Doctrine contained in the Ethick Epistles: upon which Mr. P– told him,
> that he would soon convince him of the Truth of it, by laying the Argu-
> ment at large before him; for which Purpose he gave him a large prose
> Manuscript to peruse, telling him at the same time the Author's Name.
> From this Perusal, whatever other Conviction the Doctor might receive,
> he collected at least this, that Mr. P– had from his Friend not only the
> Doctrine, but even the finest and strongest Ornaments of his Ethicks.
> Now if this Fact be true (as I question not but you know it to be so) I believe
> no Man of Candour will attribute such Merit to Mr. P–, as you would
> insinuate, for acknowledging the Wisdom and the Friendship of the Man
> who was his Instructor in Philosophy; nor, consequently, that this Ac-
> knowledgement and the Dedication of his own System, put into a poetical
> Dress by Mr. P–, laid his Lordship under the Necessity of never resenting
> any Injury done to him by the Poet afterwards. In this Respect then let the
> World judge on whose Side the Obligation lay, and whether Mr. P– told
> more than the literal Truth, in calling L– B– his *Guide, Philosopher* and
> *Friend*.[38]

Giles Barber identifies the "Senior Fellow" as Dr. William King, the principal of St. Mary Hall, Oxford.[39] This "large prose Manuscript" could refer
to the same prose dissertation that Bathurst discusses, or it could refer to
the *Essays*, but Mallet's reference to the celebrated "guide, philosopher,
and friend" compliment in the *Essay on Man* (4.390) in the same breath as a

prose source lends weight to the view that Pope possessed papers that were influential on him. At any rate, Giles Barber is sufficiently impressed by the passage to comment, "Appearing while Bolingbroke was still alive and five years before the publication of the Essays, it must evidently support his claim to have provided Pope with at least, as he once put it, 'a hint or two.' "[40]

Classical Models

Insofar as any systematic attempt has been made to define the genre within which the *Essay on Man* is working, the frontrunners are the Horatian epistle and the Lucretian philosophical epic. The difficulty is one of tone. Regarding the poem as a series of epistles in the Horatian manner does justice to the wit and lightness of tone, but not to the attempt at logically structured argument; whereas if Lucretius is taken to be the model, the opposite is the case. Reuben Brower, the leading spokesman for the Horatian party, is himself uneasy about the shortcomings of his own view: "Pope had been tempted—perhaps by Bolingbroke—to write in Horace's manner a kind of systematic philosophic poem that is contrary to the genius of the style."[41] The conclusion to Brower's study of the poem will bear quotation at length because it makes considerable concessions to Bolingbroke as a major influence and supports the view propounded in my first chapter that he helped to shape Pope's mature poetic style:

> The Fourth Epistle also begins to show the suppleness in varying the tone and adapting the rhythm to changes of thought and feeling that marks the best of Pope's later work from the *Epistle to Burlington* to the Fourth *Dunciad*. In the satire on happiness there is clearer proof than in the other epistles that Pope has mastered the art described in the final address to Bolingbroke:
>
> > Form'd by thy converse, happily to steer
> > From grave to gay, from lively to severe;
> > Correct with spirit, eloquent with ease,
> > Intent to reason, or polite to please.
> > Oh! while along the stream of Time thy name
> > Expanded flies, and gathers all its fame,
> > Say, shall my little bark attendant sail,
> > Pursue the triumph, and partake the gale? (379—86)

The metaphor of poetic navigation (which Pope used also in describing "The Design" of the Essay) and the ideal of style in poetic "converse" are of course Horatian. Though the qualities mentioned are only in part those named by Horace, the aim of versatility in movement, feeling, and tone is basically the same for both poets. It has been the "little bark" of the poet (the figure is used by Horace too) that has carried the larger vessel of the

philosopher "along the stream of Time," and Pope's tribute indicates that
he learned more from Bolingbroke the master of conversation than from
Bolingbroke the philosopher. Perhaps the most important by-product of
their intimacy and the experiments with ethical poetry that it encouraged
was Pope's discovery of his role and style as a mature poet. It was
Bolingbroke who wrote, apropos of Pope's ease of "execution" in the
Essay on Man,

> . . . this is eminently and peculiarly his, above all the Writers I know
> living or dead; I do not Except Horace.

It was Bolingbroke also who suggested to Pope (in 1733) that there was an
analogy between "his case" and Horace's, a hint that encouraged Pope to
make his first *Imitation* of Horace. Viewed in relation to the poems that
Pope was working on during the same period and others that were to
follow immediately, the *Essay on Man* appears as a free and original
variation on the Horatian diatribe-epistle. The sources of its life and of its
limitations are alike Horatian. Pope had been tempted—perhaps by
Bolingbroke—to write in Horace's manner a kind of systematic philosophic poem that is contrary to the genius of the style, and hence the
sensation we have at times of hearing Sir Thomas Browne or Milton
speaking in the accents of the coffee-house; hence, too, the solemn exposi-
tions and the least convincing passages of "argument."[42]

More recently, however, the pendulum has swung toward Lucretius as
the source of Pope's inspiration. Miriam Leranbaum claims that "the
poem's structure and tone combine to suggest the predominant influence
of *De Rerum Natura*," though she later qualifies this by asserting that the
earlier poem exerts a *negative* influence on Pope, since he is opposed to
Lucretius's point of view in his handling of all the major themes.[43] We can
study the strength of the case for Lucretius in a recent essay by Bernard
Fabian—indeed, we must do so because an explicitly stated consequence
of his view is that Bolingbroke could not have been "the philosophical
designer of Pope's 'general map of man.' "[44] Fabian argues that the classical model for the *Essay on Man* is the *De Rerum Natura* and not the Horatian
epistle. In the course of the argument, this claim undergoes two important
sea changes: Pope's poem is not, Fabian allows, an epic since the epic had
become by then an outmoded, nonviable form; nor is the world view
presented by Pope in any way similar to the godless materialism propounded by the Roman poet. On the contrary, Pope is a Lucretius for his
times, using a modified form of the Lucretian poem to present the Newtonian universe in which science is the servant of Christianity. Implicitly,
in representing Pope as a Newtonian, Fabian must be identifying him with
the low-church Latitudinarians like Samuel Clarke who, under the aegis of
the Boyle lectures, popularized and Christianized the Newtonian system
of natural religion.[45] Since Clarke's *Evidences of Natural and Revealed Religion*

is Bolingbroke's main bête noire in his philosophical writings, Fabian is effectively signing Pope up for the opposition.

Let us consider first the form of the argument. Fabian begins with a somewhat scant historical argument to establish that at one time, both the matter and the manner of Lucretius were venerated and imitated in English poetry, but after the Restoration, the matter fell into disrepute, and therefore anyone still employing the manner would have to do so to refute the matter "unless he wanted to disqualify himself as an outmoded thinker."[46] This fearful threat is sufficient to persuade Fabian that Pope's poem, insofar as it is Lucretian, is anti-Lucretian. Later, he claims it to be a Newtonian counterblast to Lucretius.

But what is the evidence that the poem is Lucretian at all? Here Fabian puts together several of Pope's allusions to Lucretius, both internal to the poem and external to it, though even in sum they are hardly convincing evidence of any Lucretian intent. There is the very interesting observation recorded by Spence that Pope had intended to include in the *Essay* an invocation to Christ modeled on Lucretius's invocation to Epicurus, which Bishop Berkeley dissuaded him from doing—presumably because he did not consider Lucretius a fit source of allusion. The result, to Berkeley's mind, would have been virtual blasphemy. Then there is the fact that Pope spent much effort in characterizing the relationship between himself and Bolingbroke in the poem's opening, calling him Memmius (Lucretius's patron) at first, giving this up for Laelius (patron of Lucilius), but finally concluding that there was no substitute for the real thing and calling Bolingbroke by name. Both of these allusions seem to me to be evidence of the *rejection* of Lucretius rather than anything else. There follows the claim that the opening paragraph of the *Essay on Man* is an allusion to the famous "Suave, mari magno . . ." passage at the beginning of book 2 of *De Rerum Natura;* but since it has to be admitted that Lucretius's passage is not only serious but also starkly pessimistic and that Pope's tone is easy and informal, Fabian is forced to argue that the allusion is to Dryden's translation of Lucretius. But what is the evidence that Pope knew Dryden's translation? The only evidence given is that he certainly knew Dryden's translation of the *Aeneid*. To trade fact for fact, we might point out that Pope owned Lucretius in the original, published by Tonson and Watts in 1713.[47] Sticking to the facts, then, Pope's primary knowledge of Lucretius would seem to be of the original. But the point is that we are not in the realm of facts when dealing with Fabian's argument, which is at this and other points an example of what has been called "Fluellenism" after that egregious Shakespearean character who compared Alexander the Great to Henry V because both were born near rivers "and there is salmons in both."[48]

Fabian's next set of arguments are good examples of Fluellenism at work. Just as Pope is always urging the addressee (Bolingbroke, lest we forget) to "come along," "look" and "see," so in Lucretius this is also "the characteristic disposition of the dramatic speaker."[49] This example is taken not from the original, where his point is not borne out, but from Creech's translation of Lucretius.[50] What has happened, the reader wonders, to Dryden's translation? There follows Fabian's treatment of what is, he virtually admits, his most difficult problem—that the *Essay on Man* is far more satirical than *De Rerum Natura*. Fabian argues that *De Rerum Natura* is satirical, and to prove it he quotes a passage from 1.628–40, where the Epicurean doctrine of the indivisibility of basic matter is asserted and Heraclitus's view that fire is the raw material of all things is heavily criticized. Two points arise here. In the first place, Fabian is still quoting from a couplet verse-translation (Creech's, we are left to presume), which does have a satiric tendency inherent in the verse form that is not in the original. Secondly, Fabian's definition of satire is far too loose; that Lucretius sometimes dissents from the views of others in a full-blooded way, even coining the occasional epithet for their ideas, is no definition of satire. Fabian juxtaposes a passage of Pope with this of Lucretius (2.205–16), which is not really satirical either, but manifests the same method of putting forward a view (of the nature of virtue and vice) and briskly dismissing his opponents. Ironically, the quotation Fabian gives is directly paralleled in Bolingbroke's writing and owes its debt there—but more of this later.

Fabian then goes on to the final stage of his argument. The epistle is a misleading term for the *Essay on Man*, he argues, and it would be more useful to think of it as a satire, since, he claims, "epistle and satire were interchangeable" to Pope. He clearly does not know Howard Weinbrot's book *The Formal Strain*, in which the author convincingly argues that Pope did see a clear distinction between the epistle and the satire when imitating Horace. But qua satire, the *Essay on Man* again begins to look very unlike Lucretius, and here Fabian argues that literary taste turned Pope away from Lucretius, demanding a much briefer, essaylike treatment of philosophical material. Interestingly, the arbiter of taste here is Bolingbroke, whose introduction to the *Letters or Essays addressed to Alexander Pope* is cited, in which Bolingbroke specifically recommends Pope *not* to write a philosophical poem in the manner of Lucretius because "should the poet . . . pursue a long process of reasoning in the didactic style, he would be sure to tire his reader on the whole, like Lucretius."[51] Bolingbroke is very shabbily dealt with here and elsewhere. Earlier, Fabian cites this reference as proof that "the *Essay on Man* was seen by Pope and Pope's friends in close analogy to the *De Rerum Natura*," an absurdity in view of the fact that Bolingbroke is urging Pope not to bore the pants off his reader, as Lucretius does.[52] Later, when Fabian comes to the crux of his argument, the claim that Pope substituted Newton's world view for Lucretius's in the poem, he cites Warburton's statement to the effect that the argument does not propound Bolingbrokean naturalism but Newtonian natural religion. But Warburton is surely a discredited witness. He is well known to have Christianized the *Essay on Man* in his edition in an unwarrantable manner and to have hated Bolingbroke with inveterate malice.

What of Fabian's claim that the *Essay on Man* is a further propagation of Newtonian religio-scientific principles? There is evidence to suggest that by 1730, the tide was beginning to turn against Newton and that public infatuation was already giving place to the distrust of his certainties and the loathing of his mechanistic principles that are expressed by the Romantic poets. Surely the poem itself is evidence of this. In what seems to me to be a genuinely satirical passage of the *Essay,* written in the manner of *Gulliver's Travels* book 3, Pope inveighs against the scientific impulse and is, to put it mildly, ambivalent about Newton:

> Go, wond'rous creature! mount where Science guides,
> Go, measure earth, weigh air, and state the tides;
> Instruct the planets in what orbs to run,
> Correct old Time, and regulate the Sun;
> Go, soar with Plato to th' empyreal sphere,
> To the first good, first perfect, and first fair;
> Or tread the mazy round his follow'rs trod,
> And quitting sense call imitating God;
> As Eastern priests in giddy circles run,
> And turn their heads to imitate the Sun.
> Go, teach Eternal Wisdom how to rule—
> Then drop into thyself, and be a fool!
>   Superior beings, when of late they saw
> A mortal Man unfold all Nature's law,
> Admir'd such wisdom in an earthly shape,
> And shew'd NEWTON as we shew an Ape. (2.19–34)

This image of Newton in a cage, a clever monkey, an exhibit for the angels to marvel at as we marvel at the semihuman intelligence of an ape, is scarcely evidence of Pope's unqualified admiration for Newton. It is more accurate to say of the *Essay on Man* that Pope accepted the results of Newtonian science while remaining very distrustful of the methods used by scientists to achieve them. Latterly, this distrust of Newton turned into skepticism, as in the famous "high Priori road" passage of the *Dunciad* (4.453–82).

The Case for Bolingbroke

I have drawn attention in my first chapter to a passage (*Fragments* 42) in which Bolingbroke has occasion to allude to Lucretius, a passage that is particularly suggestive as the type that would have impressed Pope deeply. Bolingbroke there argues that poets are frequently either unduly optimistic or unduly pessimistic about the status of mankind in the creation. His example of the latter is Lucretius: he cites the "Tum porro puer, ut saevis projectus ab undis" passage (*De Rerum Natura* 5.222–28), where Lucretius describes the helpless child in a state of doleful abandon weeping bitterly as a concrete image of the human condition. Bolingbroke asserts, "There is a middle point between those extremes, where the truth lyes," and we cannot fail to detect an echo of this in Pope's Design for the *Essay on Man*, where he describes the poem's merit as "steering betwixt the extremes of doctrine seemingly opposite." Much of what Bolingbroke writes here is directly relevant to Pope's argument that threads through the whole of epistle 1 and the opening of epistle 2 of the *Essay* about man's place in the creation—"Plac'd on this isthmus of a middle state." Let us take as an example the passage Fabian cites as Pope at his most Lucretian and apply to it hypotheses no more speculative than Fabian's, but Bolingbrokean rather than Lucretian in sympathy:

> Extremes in Nature equal ends produce,
> In Man they join to some mysterious use;
> Tho' each by turns the other's bound invade,
> As, in some well-wrought picture, light and shade,
> And oft so mix, the diff'rence is too nice
> Where ends the Virtue, or begins the Vice.
>   Fools! who from hence into the notion fall,
> That Vice or Virtue there is none at all.
> If white and black blend, soften, and unite
> A thousand ways, is there no black or white?
> Ask your own heart, and nothing is so plain;
> 'Tis to mistake them, costs the time and pain. (2.205–16)

The immediate parallel to this aesthetic analogy is found in the later paragraph 59, in which Bolingbroke is making a similar observation to Pope's, that moral concepts seldom exist unalloyed:

> There is justice, and injustice, as certainly as there is white and black. But as the painter can, by diluting the two colors, not make them terminate in the midst insensibly, for these words are mere expletives and mean nothing; but as he can make them run into one another till no eye can distinguish them, so the casuist in law or divinity dilutes right and wrong, just and unjust, till no mind not even his own, can unblend and distinguish them again. (p. 409)

Additionally, perhaps, when Pope is making the point in lines 211–12 that people frequently take up extreme positions such as that neither virtue nor vice exist because they are difficult to distinguish, he has in mind Bolingbroke's examples of Lucretius and Ovid as such extremists.

Professor Fabian's article raises in an acute form the problem of the nature of Pope's allusions. When is an allusion a Fluellenism? In a crucial paragraph, he cites Pope's lines 1.17–34, which have usually been considered to contain an allusion to Lucretius both general and particular; Mack points out that the entire passage is a reply to Lucretius's celebration of Epicurus in *De Rerum Natura* 1.62–79 and that line 23 in particular—"He, who thro' vast immensity can pierce"—alludes to Lucretius's lines 73–74.[53] This is an "answer" to Lucretius because the context suggests that such a man as Epicurus could not exist. Fabian improves upon Mack by claiming that the allusion is really to Newton via Lucretius.[54] But Pope and his circle frequently employed planetary or cosmic imagery of this kind to pejorative effect. In paragraph 41 of the *Fragments*, Bolingbroke traces the history of the argument from evil for God's existence back to Epicurus and then comments, in imagery that calls Lucretius's complimentary address to mind, "Philosophers appear often, like comets, that rise out of our system, just cross it, disorder it, and go out of it again."[55] Piercing through vast immensity was not necessarily being recommended by Pope. As we have observed, Bolingbroke did not consider Lucretius any fit model for a philosophical poem because he is too prolix and in a sense too exhaustingly philosophical. Perhaps this was one reason why Pope, who spent much effort in characterizing the nature of his relationship with Bolingbroke and in securing for it an appropriate reference to similar liaisons of poet and philosopher in the past, rejects Memmius (Lucretius's patron) as a suitable way of apostrophizing Bolingbroke.

What sort of case can be made out, then, for Bolingbroke's thought and conversation as a direct source of inspiration for Pope? I wish now to examine the internal evidence for similarity between the *Essay* and Bolingbroke's *Essays* and *Fragments*. I intend to confine my discussion to epistle 3 of the poem, since, unlike epistle 4, very few claims have been made for Bolingbroke's presence here—indeed, Mack does not offer a single footnote reference to him in this epistle—and since, frankly, this kind of argument is liable to be tedious to the reader, so that brevity is a virtue. To the reader who wants to see possible parallels drawn outside this epistle, I would recommend Walter Sichel's *Bolingbroke and His Times*, with a caveat against the naive model of influence that Sichel accepts.[56]

Epistle 3 continues Pope's attempt to demonstrate that God disposes the entire created system for the providence and motivation of every creature. To this end, he submits three major positive theses: first, man and the animal kingdom are ecologically interconnected, and the multiplicity of created beings is bound together by a "chain of Love," whose mechanism is "plastic Nature." This is in part a Newtonian attraction between atoms and in part a symbiotic life cycle whereby decaying material enlivens a new species. Second, both animals and men are endowed with the directing power that suits them best, reason in the latter case, instinct in the former; and third, though self-love, the motivating principle of human action, can often drive men into excessive behavior beyond rational control, it ultimately works to secure the good of the society to which self-interested individuals belong—"Self-love and social [are] the same." Each of these positive theses generates a negative obverse that is used by Pope for the Swiftian purpose of mortifying human pride through abrasive satire, and to this end, the poet draws on established satirical strategies. From the first positive thesis, the poet develops the corollary that man is not lord of all creation. The prideful anthropocentrism that makes of the animal kingdom a banquet furnished for human delectation is ridiculed from the inverted perspective of the beast fable ("While Man exclaims, 'See all things for my use!' / 'See man for mine!' replies a pamper'd goose"). From the second, he draws the implication that instinct is superior to reason because it directly instantiates the power of God and therefore is not subject to error or abuse; standing conventional wisdom on its head and risking impiety, Pope again shifts the normal perspective disturbingly ("And Reason raise o'er Instinct as you can, / In this 'tis God directs, in that 'tis Man"). In order to establish the third thesis, Pope introduces the cultural and chronological primitivism of a regressive journey back to the state of nature, when, it is implied, instinct and reason were complementary and "Self-love and Social" indistinguishable. Early man is represented as responding to a personified voice of Nature that operates like the oracular prophecy of an epic. A patriarchal civil society was founded deriving its authority from love, not fear, owing its religious allegiance to the one true God and its political allegiance to the common good. In subsequent ages, tyrants perverted this ideal state, using superstition and self-created deities to terrify an enslaved, subjected people. At this point, the poem is an antiprogress poem, working up to the horrific, Gothic climax of reeking gore, smeared blood, and human sacrifice. This process of decline was arrested, however, by the uniting of men to curb the individual will-to-power with governmental and legal institutions. Self-love is responsible both for the individual's aspiration after absolute power and for society's counterattack on it. This counterinitiative is undertaken by "the studious head or gen'rous mind . . . Poet or Patriot" and consists of restoring, as nearly as possible, the prelapsarian state of moral and religious purity. In politics, it consists of creating "Th' according music of a well-mix'd State," that is, mixed government.

It will become apparent from the account given in the final chapters of this book that virtually the whole of the second half of the epistle from line 147 onward is an attempt to render into dramatically compelling verse Bolingbroke's view of the process by which the free and ancient constitution is corrupted by tyrannical encroachment. It needs to be cleansed by the patriotic uniting of the people, bringing it back to the balanced mixture of monarchical, aristocratic, and popular power that creates political stability. Pope's overt purpose is to demonstrate the ethical proposition that self-love is not incompatible with virtue, since the good of the individual is bound up with that of society: this is, in any case, found in Bolingbroke. Bolingbroke's view was that self-love, governed by reason, led men to benevolence and sociability. But he has also a covert purpose in the last hundred or so lines, the purpose of Bolingbroke's "patriot" literature, to rouse the people to a sense of their responsibilities under the constitution. As Bolingbroke says, "Good government cannot grow excessively bad, nor liberty be turned into slavery, unless the body of a people co-operate to their own ruin."[57] Pope's lines 303–4,

> For Forms of Government let fools contest;
> Whate'er is best administer'd is best,

are quite possibly a hit at the maladministration of the Walpole government.[58] It is precisely Bolingbroke's account of the origins of civil society in self-love and instinctive sociability and of the paternal nature of monarchical authority that Pope expresses in the *Essay on Man*. Pope, however, confuses what must have been to Bolingbroke a sound piece of political theorizing by conflating the state of nature with the poet's Golden Age:

> Nor think, in NATURE's STATE they blindly trod;
> The state of Nature was the reign of God:
> Self-love and Social at her birth began,
> Union the bond of all things, and of Man.
> Pride then was not; nor Arts, that Pride to aid;
> Man walked with beast, joint tenant of the shade;
> The same his table, and the same his bed;
> No murder cloath'd him, and no murder fed. (3.147–54)

This section of the *Essay* is a useful illustration of both the extent and the limitation of Bolingbroke's influence on Pope's ideas. Insofar as this passage assumes that primitive society was a perfect concord of man and the natural world, an ecological system in perfect balance, and a state of spiritual simplicity manifested in egalitarian worship and the "blameless priest" (lines 155–60), it is a refutation of Hobbes's premise that the state of nature was a state of warring confusion. Bolingbroke also attacks the Hobbesian world view in *Fragments* 3. Yet like the other serious political philosophers, he was irritated by the Golden Age myth as a rhapsodic "whitewash" and addresses the following remarks to Pope:

> You poets have given beautiful descriptions of a golden age, with which you suppose that the world began . . . Now, though I do not believe that men were as good, any more than I believe that other animals were as tame, by nature, as you represent them to have been in the primeval world; yet I do not believe neither, that such a state, as Hobbes assumed, ever did, or could exist, nor that men ever were in a state of absolute individuality at any time before the institution of civil society.[59]

This is possibly a dig at the facility of lines 152–53:

> Man walk'd with beast, joint tenant of the shade;
> The same his table, and the same his bed.

As poet, Pope was naturally steeped in the lore of the prelapsarian purity of the ancient world, and the Golden Age myth had been incorporated into his theory of the pastoral. In *A Discourse on Pastoral Poetry*, which prefaced the 1717 edition of his *Works* (but was written in 1704), Pope affirmed that "pastoral is an image of what they call the Golden age," so that "we are not to describe our shepherds as shepherds at this day really are, but as they may be conceiv'd then to have been."[60] This view is identified with the "ancient" or neoclassic view attacked by Fontenelle's "modern" view that pastoral is simply the representation of the quiet and leisured tranquillity of the shepherd's existence, which gave rise to the quarrel between the ancients and the moderns and such literary landmarks as Sir William Temple's *An Essay upon the Ancient and Modern Learning*, Swift's *Battle of the Books*, the *Pastorals* of Ambrose Philips, Tickell's defense of them in the *Guardian*, and Pope's brilliant and witty *Guardian* paper in which he gives Philips his quietus. (As we have seen, it was an extension of this quarrel carried across the Channel and conducted on the territory of Homer translation that was the main point of contact between Pope and Bolingbroke when the latter was in exile in France between 1715 and 1723.)

Conflations of this kind between the state of nature that had been the common property of political philosophers throughout the previous century and poetic versions of the myth of origin, the soft primitivism of the arcadian Golden Age, must have been the cause of Bolingbroke's complaint that Pope never understood his ideas. And indeed, there is a confusion here, because while the political philosopher attempts to show how civil society has developed out of natural society, the poet normally *contrasts* the state of nature with the present dispensation to illustrate the thesis of degeneration—"what a falling off was there." But the nature of Bolingbroke's political platform that he developed to fight the parliamentary and extraparliamentary battles against Walpole in the 1730s was such that it united both the philosophic and the poetic notions of a purer state of society. Crucial to Bolingbroke's ideology is the conception that there has existed in British political life a free and ancient constitution, functioning as an index of the health of that life and constituting the primary condition of political liberty. When the balance between the king, nobles, and commons that the proper functioning of the constitution requires is overturned, as Bolingbroke argued it had been by the Walpole clique, the result is a moral and political decline that can be described as a state of "corruption."

Pope follows very closely Bolingbroke's *Fragments* 11 in his account of the paternalistic origins of monarchical authority. Though Mack cites Aristotle's *Politics* and Locke's *Of Civil Government* as the likely sources, he fails to observe that Bolingbroke himself cites Aristotle as an authority for his view of monarchy as a development from paternal authority and that Pope follows Bolingbroke rather than Locke in considering familial bonds precedent to civil obligations. In paragraph 11 also, Bolingbroke praises the instinctual sociability of ants and bees (compare to Pope, lines 184–86), while at the same time pointing out both the shortcomings of reason—its fallibility and proneness to error—and its potential to move us beyond mere animal gregariousness. This is also discussed in paragraph 6, where the argument is very close to that given by Pope in lines 109–46. Pope's account of "Superstition" and of pagan religions whose vengeful, tyrannical deities are coined in the self-image of tyrants (241–68) is very close to the texture of Bolingbroke's writing on superstition and on "artificial theology," even in tone. In paragraph 22 of the *Fragments*, Bolingbroke is describing the purveyance of religion to "the vulgar":

> They who converted, with profane timidity, a reverential awe into a superstitious fear of God, and made the existence of a Supreme Being, which ought to be the comfort, the terror of mankind, ran into one of these extremes. They either screened him from human sight by the interposition of mediating, interceding atoning beings; or, fierce and cruel themselves, they represented him hating without reason, revenging without provocation, and punishing without measure.[61]

In addition, the central position accorded by Pope to the poet in "reluming the ancient light" and in teaching "Pow'r's due use to People and to Kings" is in accord with Bolingbroke's view of the satirist's role in political affairs; indeed, in the third epistle, Pope seems to take the advice given to him by Bolingbroke in the introductory *Letter to Alexander Pope*:

> Pursue your task undauntedly, and whilst so many others convert the noblest employments of human society into sordid trades, let the gener-

ous muse resume her ancient dignity, re-assert her ancient prerogative, and instruct and reform as well as amuse the world. Let her give a new turn to the thoughts of men, raise new affections in their minds, and determine in another and better manner the passions of their hearts. Poets, they say, were the first philosophers and divines, in every country; and in ours, perhaps, the first institutions of religion, and civil policy, were owing to our bards.[62]

In this epistle, Pope is again the arbiter of "religion, and civil policy," and it is Bolingbroke's policy he promotes.

The early part of the epistle is, in my view, not merely Bolingbrokean but Scriblerian. Bolingbroke held the view given by Pope in lines 1–78 that our failure to appreciate the teleological and uniform structure of nature as the instantiation of the divine will is owing to the hubristic premise that God made the world for man.[63] Pope's satiric point is made partly through the medium of beast fable. Beast fable as a genre is in some sense an attack on human self-importance, and the fourth book of *Gulliver's Travels* fulfills some of the generic demands, among them the challenge to man's belief that he is the final cause and capstone of the creation. John Gay has two relevant fables that between them provide both the positive and the negative sides of the issue: number 43, "The Council of Steeds," which makes the point that animals and men are reciprocally related by mutual wants; and number 49, "The Man and the Flea," wherein the man, wrought to a pitch of self-congratulation by surveying the created universe provided for his edification, exults, "Of what vast consequence am I!" A flea on his nose restores his sense of proportion by intimating that his place is to provide sustenance for the parasite. In the *Fragments,* Bolingbroke repeatedly pours scorn on the swagger and grimace of man's thinking himself lord of the creation (Pope does the same in *Essay* 1.131–64); at one point, Bolingbroke alludes specifically to Gay's satirical fable.[64] Finally, the Chain of Being notion that is employed by Pope in various guises throughout the *Essay on Man* is also employed by Bolingbroke.

Internal evidence like this is doubtless of limited use in supporting the case for Bolingbroke. Of itself it cannot determine either exclusively or precisely his influence on the poem, but when it is put in the context of the relationship that this book is arguing, it gains plausibility. Pope himself gladly acknowledged his debt to Bolingbroke, first to Joseph Spence:

> He [Pope] mentioned then, and at several other times, how much (or rather how wholly) he himself was obliged to him [Bolingbroke] for the thoughts and reasonings in his moral work, and once in particular said that beside their frequent talking over that subject together, he had received (I think) seven or eight sheets from Lord Bolingbroke in relation to it, as I apprehended, by way of letters, both to direct the plan in general, and to supply the matter for the particular epistles.[65]

and also in the fulsome and explicit tribute that he paid to Bolingbroke at the close of the *Essay:*

> Come, then, my Friend, my Genius, come along
> Oh master of the poet, and the song!
> And while the Muse now stoops, or now ascends,
> To Man's low passions, or their glorious ends,
> Teach me, like thee, in various nature wise,
> To fall with dignity, with temper rise;
> Form'd by thy converse, happily to steer
> From grave to gay, from lively to severe;
> Correct with spirit, eloquent with ease,
> Intent to reason, or polite to please.
> Oh! while along the stream of Time thy name
> Expanded flies, and gathers all its fame,
> Say, shall my little bark attendant sail,
> Pursue the triumph, and partake the gale?
> When statesmen, heroes, kings, in dust repose,
> Whose sons shall blush their fathers were thy foes,
> Shall then this verse to future age pretend
> Thou wert my guide, philosopher, and friend? (4.373–90)

I have little doubt that Bolingbroke deserved this credit.

Chapter 6

The Last Phase, 1736–1744

Pope and Jacobitism

When Bolingbroke left England in May 1735, his departure occasioned many expressions of regret from Pope. But there are signs that the poet had already made a new group of friends with political ambitions. One of the most interesting of these was Henry Hyde, Viscount Cornbury. Cornbury is first mentioned by Pope in August 1734, when Pope asks Bethel to pass on his regards.[1] But Hyde's behavior had come to Scriblerian notice earlier. The story of Cornbury's refusing a government pension of £400 per annum secured by Lord Essex is well known, in the version that Pope gave to Spence in December 1743:

> On Lord Cornbury's return from his travels, his brother-in-law, the Lord Essex, told him with a great deal of pleasure that he had got a pension for him. It was a very handsome one and quite equal to his rank. All Lord Cornbury's answer was, "How could you tell, my Lord, that I was to be sold? or at least how could you know my price so exactly?"[2]

This incident made its mark on Pope's imagination, leading to the honorable mention of Cornbury in the *Epistle to Murray (Imit. Hor. Ep.* I.6): "Disdain whatever CORNBURY disdains" (line 61). Back in 1732, Cornbury seems to have been residing with Gay and the Queensberrys after having been elected M.P. for Oxford University; to Swift, Gay wrote, "Lord Cornbury refus'd the Pension that was offer'd him. He is chosen to represent the University of Oxford . . . without opposition: I know him and I think he deserves it. He is a Young Nobleman of Learning & Morals which is so particular that I know you will respect & value him, & to my great comfort he lives with us in our family."[3] It is surprising that Cornbury should have been regarded as an ideal exemplar of upright incorruptibility, since from January to April 1731 he had been meeting the Pretender secretly in Rome, discussing plans to win over Tories and Opposition Whigs with promises of lucrative employments after the Restoration. Prominent in promoting these negotiations was the Duchess of Buckingham, James II's daughter, who was, at least until 1729, on good terms with Pope although she was later lampooned by him in the Atossa portrait of the *Epistle to a Lady.*[4] We have seen that during this period, Bolingbroke himself was at least discussing, if not plotting, a Stuart restoration, and Cornbury seems to have been even more committed than Bolingbroke to this cause until he renounced it in 1735. In 1733, he got the length of a trip to Paris to communicate to Louis XV the details of a plan for an English rebellion. It seems that one of the reasons for Cornbury's having given up Jacobite intrigue was the accusation made against him that he had discussed the plans with Bolingbroke—as he surely had.[5]

This was the man with whom Pope became increasingly friendly, probably through Bolingbroke, after 1734. Friendships such as this do suggest that Jacobitism was a significant factor in explaining Pope's lifelong closeness to Bolingbroke.

As we have seen earlier, the soil in which the first phase of Pope's friendship with Bolingbroke grew was the last days of Queen Anne's reign and the vital few months after her death. The succession problem had loomed on the horizon for several years, and for some time Bolingbroke had been considering the options, to put it no more strongly. When he failed to achieve office in 1714, his bitterness doubtless threw him into the Jacobite camp. While these decisions were being made, Pope was coming to know Bolingbroke well. Surely the conversations that took place while Pope was staying with him in January 1715 may have helped to cement the poet's own commitment to the cause and to create a lasting basis for the friendship.

The opprobrium that surrounded Bolingbroke's name again in the mid-thirties does not seem to have lowered him in Pope's estimation even though it certainly did in the eyes of his own party. Perhaps this is because, as we have suggested, Pope himself had a fund of sympathy with the Jacobite cause. Howard Erskine-Hill has considered this possibility with respect to Pope and his Catholic friend John Caryll, who was closely connected to prominent Jacobites by marriage. His view is that, despite having expressed disaffection toward the British government on two occasions—after the 1715 rebellion, when Pope and his family moved from Windsor Forest to Chiswick, and in various ways with respect to Atterbury's Jacobite conspiracy—Pope was probably no Jacobite.[6] But there is, it must be said, some evidence in Pope's life and in his writings that must give us pause. It is apparent that his association with Bolingbroke's campaign of opposition at least until 1735 brought him into contact with men like Wyndham and Cornbury to whom a Jacobite rising was an ever-present possibility, as it was to Bolingbroke. Shortly after this period, Pope expressed what appear to be pro-Catholic and possibly even pro-Jacobite sentiments in the *Imit. Hor. Ep.* II.2, where he gives this account of his father's doings in 1715:

> But knottier Points we knew not half so well,
> Depriv'd us soon of our Paternal Cell;
> And certain Laws, by Suff'rers thought unjust,

Deny'd all Posts of Profit or of Trust:
Hopes after Hopes of pious Papists fail'd,
While mighty WILLIAM's thundring Arm prevail'd.
For Right Hereditary tax'd and fin'd,
He stuck to Poverty with Peace of Mind. (58–65)

This implied criticism of William III's anti-Catholic legislation, along with an affirmation of Pope's father's, if not his own, belief in the principle of hereditary right, refers us back to Pope's early expression of loyalty to the Stuarts in *Windsor Forest*. Scholars now assume that the long passage on England in decline under William the Conqueror (lines 43–84) points beyond itself to the conduct of William III on the throne; his tyrannical behavior murdered "Liberty" and reduced the countryside to ruin, in contrast with the happy times in which "Rich Industry sits smiling on the Plains, / And Peace and Plenty tell, a STUART reigns."[7] This need imply no more than a Stuart commitment and does not entail that Pope would be ready to betray the Hanoverian succession, as did Bolingbroke comparatively soon after this poem's publication. But the Stuart cause certainly remained present in Pope's consciousness throughout his life.[8] In 1743, Pope was infuriated by the Duchess of Buckingham's perverse decision to appoint Walpole her trustee and Lord Hervey her executor in charge of her private papers, many of which might have been incriminating. To Bethel, Pope expressed a concern that some of his letters to her might be published piratically, though "I am sure they make no part of her Treasonable Correspondence."[9] The letters are not now extant, but I am certainly not so sure as Pope that they would not implicate him in the Jacobite cause. Pope probably decided to complete the vindictive Atossa portrait on the grounds of his suspicion regarding those papers.

To imply that Pope, with his insatiable appetite for intrigue, was party to Jacobite plotting through his intimacy with Cornbury and Bolingbroke and that his nostalgic loyalty to the House of Stuart was a significant element in his friendship with the latter is not to make a very strong claim after all. By the 1730s, Bolingbroke himself could not be spoken of as a Jacobite, if by that is meant the kind of extreme Tory who could not adjust to the Revolution Settlement, whose conscience was still ravaged by the breach of the principles of divine right and indefeasible hereditary succession that the Hanoverian line represented. It is more likely that his Jacobitism was simply the refusal to put all his eggs in one basket. Ideologically, he was far from Jacobite. From the early days of the *Craftsman*'s instigation until the appearance in that periodical of the series of essays collectively entitled a *Dissertation upon Parties*, Bolingbroke had labored to establish ideological consensus between the Whigs and Tories, based on acceptance of such essentially Whig notions as the existence of an ancient constitution that must be protected, the legislative sovereignty of the crown, Lords, and Commons, and the post-Revolution establishment. Political conflict was now focused through court and country oppositions, which were not about the nature of a desirable political establishment, but were about the forms of corruption that prevented agreed constitutional arrangements from working. Increasingly, with works like *A Letter on the Spirit of Patriotism*, dedicated to Lord Cornbury in 1736, and *The Idea of a Patriot King*, Bolingbroke turned his attention to exhorting all men of civic virtue to become watchdogs of the constitution, to find the court and government factions wanting in their adherence to it, and to unite behind a reforming figurehead, to wit, Frederick, Prince of Wales. Pope was very firmly caught up in this. His letters adopt the rhetoric of "Virtue"; he becomes friendly with the group of active politicians—led by Cobham, Lyttelton, Cornbury, West, Chesterfield, and later Marchmont—who pressed for the cleaning up of the administration as recommended by Bolingbroke; and indeed, his later poetry can be read as part of this campaign. As I will suggest in the closing chapters of this book, the objectives established by Bolingbroke in the late thirties are very close to those of the satirists; the enterprise of being a politician was conceived similarly to that of writing moral satire. And by 1742, when Walpole's resignation caused the "Patriot" program to lose its impetus, Pope was in many respects a more cherished and significant opponent of government than was Bolingbroke himself. To the frustration of this for Bolingbroke was added that of his being replaced in Pope's trust by the arriviste Warburton, who had in the period 1740 to 1744 a far better claim than Bolingbroke to be Pope's "guide, philosopher, and friend."

Pope the Patriot

Links were being forged with the Patriots as early as October 1733, when the poet had received a visit from the Prince of Wales himself at Twickenham.[10] But in March 1736, Pope first referred to his ties with them in a letter to Swift: "Here are a race sprung up of young Patriots, who would animate you." The same letter to Swift states that Pope had seen some recent writings of Bolingbroke's, on which he comments, "Nothing can depress his Genius: Whatever befals him, he will still be the greatest man in the world, either in his own time, or with posterity."[11] The reference here is probably to the *Letters on the Study and Use of History*, in which Bolingbroke elaborated a view of history that was of the greatest consequence to the satirist. "History," argued Bolingbroke, "is philosophy teaching by examples."[12] The study of history is that branch of the educational process that conduces most to the moderation of the passions, in which virtue consists. Learning properly the general lessons to be derived from historical example involves constructing a system of ethics that will improve both private and public virtue and will teach us how to act in the future. There is a clear link between Bolingbroke's view of the relationship between exemplary history and the improvement of virtue and Pope's view of exemplary or particular satire as a weapon in virtue's war against vice. Pope expresses this philosophy of history in a letter of 30 April 1736 to his comparatively new friend, Ralph Allen, whose friendship with Pope was one of the most significant in Allen's life. His home at Bath became Pope's habitual winter resort, and Pope found in him a living example of that unobtrusive Christian charity and patrician concern for dependent fellowmen that the Man of Ross had become in his imagination.[13] Pope gives Allen advice on the kind of historical engravings with which he should decorate his walls:

> A Man not only shews his Taste but his Virtue, in the Choice of such Ornaments: And whatever Example most strikes us, we may reasonably imagine may have an influence upon others, so that the History itself (if wellchosen) upon a Rich-mans Walls, is very often a better lesson than any he could teach by his Conversation.[14]

The *Letters on the Study and Use of History* were punctuated in composition by a short work that was the blueprint for Bolingbroke's political and ideological activity until the early forties, *A Letter on the Spirit of Patriotism*. In it, Bolingbroke points to the dangers of ministerial corruption and the strengthening of the executive's hold over Parliament, which threatened to destroy the constitution's delicately balanced mechanism. This is hardly novel, but also stressed is that the men of superior gifts, the aristocracy of talent whose duty it is to resist such depredations, were failing to halt them. Corruption is not only the proliferation of crown patronage or the ascendancy of the moneyed interest: it also means a lack of the "spirit of patriotism" or civic virtue in those who should be opposing these abuses. This is the *Idea of a Patriot King* without the patriot king. Clearly, the catalyst in forming Bolingbroke's later view that Frederick, Prince of Wales could be a figurehead for the aristocrats of talent was the quarrel between the prince and his father in the following year. But Bolingbroke was already founding the ideology that motivated the opposition during the period when, with the death of Queen Caroline, the tide was turning against Walpole.

In his personal life, however, it seems that Bolingbroke was not the virtuous, dedicated patriot that he was in his writing. Swift had for some time been exhorting him to draw in his horns and warning him that his extravagance would bring him low. It seems that some disparaging remarks made by Swift to someone outside their circle—"the prophane,"

Pope calls such people—had reached Pope. Pope denies that such a report is true and suggests that Swift feels slighted by Bolingbroke's failing to keep in touch: "He has fixed in a very agreeable retirement near Fontainbleau, and makes it his whole business *vacare literis.*"[15] We do not know quite what Swift said to whom, but my guess is that he mentioned to Pulteney wild rumors of Bolingbroke's bacchanalian orgies at his country house in France. In November 1735, Pulteney had written to Swift a bitter letter on the failure to win the election, for which he blamed Bolingbroke's taking a pension from France merely to subsidize his high living:

> You inquire after *Bolingbroke,* and when he will return from *France.* If he had listened to your admonitions and chidings about oeconomy, he need never have gone there . . . When I see lords of the greatest estates, meanly stooping to take a dirty pension, because they want a little ready money for their extravagancies, I cannot help wishing to see some papers writ by you, that may, if possible, shame them out of it. This is the only thing that can recover our constitution, and restore honesty. I have often thought, that if ten or a dozen patriots, who are known to be rich enough to have ten dishes every day for dinner, would invite their friends only to two or three, it might perhaps shame those who cannot afford two, from having constantly ten, and so it would be in every other circumstance of life: but luxury is our ruin.[16]

It is clear that, unlike Pope of *To Bethel (Imit. Hor. Sat. II.2)*, "Content with little, I can piddle here / On Broccoli and mutton, round the year" (137–38), Bolingbroke thought temperance no blessing. In an extraordinary digression in *A Letter on the Spirit of Patriotism,* he asserted that a patriot's life is far from all work and no play. The passage is clearly self-defense:

> The common, the sensual pleasures to which nature prompts us, and which reason therefore does not forbid, though she should always direct, are so far from being excluded out of a life of business, that they are sometimes necessary in it, and are always heightened by it: those of the table, for instance, may be ordered so as to promote that which the elder Cato calls *vitae conjunctionem.* In the midst of public duties, private studies, and an extreme old age, he found time to frequent the *sodalitates,* or clubs of friends, at Rome, and to sit up all night with his neighbors in the country of the Sabines. Cato's virtue often glowed with wine: and the love of women did not hinder Caesar from forming and executing the greatest projects that ambition ever suggested.[17]

Arguments ad hominem like this must have saddened Pope, the author of poems like *To Bethel* and the *Imit. Hor. Ep.* II.2 in which the moderation of sensual appetites is so firmly recommended. In this important respect, Bolingbroke must have been a disappointment to his friend, though Pope never acknowledged this. He could not really be put in the category of those friends, like Digby and Allen and Bathurst, who practiced the country-house ideal responsibly and with moderation. In *To Bethel*, lines 131–65, Pope expresses this ideal of plain but free-hearted hospitality, an ideal that is untarnished by anti-Catholic legislation and the cupidity of businessmen like Walter. But Bolingbroke's behavior hardly conformed to this vision of Penshurst-like graciousness, nor was he particularly noted for charitable acts, so revered by Pope.

Pope's attitude toward his friend's sensual indulgence is normally to turn a blind eye, as he does in the letter to Swift of 30 December 1736, where he speaks of a "change of life," of Bolingbroke becoming "a settled and principled Philosopher." In the same letter, he acknowledges his links with the Patriots, though in terms which are hardly very flattering to them:

> . . . As when the continual washing of a river takes away our flowers and plants, it throws weeds and sedges in their room; so the course of time brings us something, as it deprives us of a great deal; and instead of leaving us what we cultivated, and expected to flourish and adorn us, gives us only what is of some little use, by accident. Thus I have acquired, without my seeking, a few chance-acquaintance, of young men, who look rather to the past age than the present, and therefore the future may have some hopes of them. If I love them, it is because they honour some of those whom I, and the world, have lost, or are losing. Two or three of them have distinguish'd themselves in Parliament, and you will own in a very uncommon manner, when I tell you it is by their asserting of Independency, and contempt of Corruption. One or two are link'd to me by their love of the same studies and the same authors.[18]

In this last sentence, Pope refers to George Lyttelton. Lyttelton was, by 1737, secretary to Frederick, Prince of Wales, whose favorite he had been since 1734; on making his parliamentary debut in 1735, he had formed with the Pitt brothers and George Grenville the anti-Walpole grouping directed by Lord Cobham and known as "Cobham's Cubs." His friendship with Pope predated his political career: he addressed to Pope the first eclogue of his early poem *The Progress of Love,* and in 1730 wrote to Pope a verse epistle from Rome in which the ghost of Virgil appears to Lyttelton with a message for Pope, advising him to give up "meaner satire" and turn his attention to the epic![19] In October 1738, Lyttelton wrote to Pope regretting the latter's failure to attend a house party at Lord Bathurst's Cirencester Park where Prince Frederick was present, stressing the poet's importance as upholder of public virtue in terms familiar to any reader of Bolingbroke:

> Be therefore as much with him [the prince] as you can, Animate him to Virtue, to the Virtue least known to Princes, though most necessary for them, Love of the Publick; and think that the Morals, the Liberty, the whole Happiness of this Country depends on your Success. If that Sacred Fire, which by You and other Honest Men has been kindled in his Mind,

can be Preserv'd, we may yet be safe; But if it go out, it is a Presage of Ruin, and we must be Lost. For the Age is too far corrupted to Reform itself; it must be done by Those upon, or near the throne, or not at all: They must Restore what we ourselves have Given up. They must save us from our own Vices, and Follies, they must bring back the taste of Honesty, and the Sense of Honour, which the *Fashion of Knavery* has almost Destroy'd.[20]

Pope's reply to this letter is instinct with Bolingbrokean sentiment, with regard to both general political principles and particular issues. Pope alludes to a letter of political instruction that he would have written for the prince's benefit had he had time, and goes on to manifest his familiarity with the mechanics of diurnal politics by expressing his suspicion of "two Persons" (Carteret and Pulteney) whom he believed to be acting in their own interests to the detriment of a united opposition. He ends the letter with a Bolingbrokean address to Prince Frederick, the hoped-for Patriot King, which embraces the nonpartisan platform as an ideological commitment:

> Pray assure your Master of my Duty & Service: They tell me he has every body's Love already. I wish him Popular, but not Familiar, and the Glory of being beloved, not the Vanity of endeavouring it too much. I wish him at the Head of the Only Good Party in the Kingdome, that of Honest Men; I wish him Head of no other Party.[21]

Pope could rest secure in the knowledge that in writing to Lyttelton, he addressed a confirmed Bolingbrokean: Lyttelton's *Persian Letters* of 1735 had echoed Bolingbroke's major beliefs. By this stage, we can see that political nonpartisanship, which Pope had professed all his adult life, is now an explicitly ideological commitment to the country manifesto. Throughout Pope's correspondence, expressions of regret for the narrowness of "party spirit" occur, as do expressions of self-congratulation at being above it. But by the time he writes to Fortescue in March 1739 of himself as a man who "owed not a sixpence to any Party, nor any sort of advantage to any Mean or mercenary Methods; and who lamented not any part of his fortune here, but that of living to see an Age, when the Virtue of his Country seem'd to be at a period," he is clearly adopting the Patriot rhetoric.[22]

When Pope wrote this letter, Bolingbroke had been in England for several months. In the intervening months, Bolingbroke had been corresponding regularly with Wyndham and had seen the political potential of the quarrel between the King and his son over allowance money and of the late breach over the prince's decision to have his wife lie in at home rather than at court. To Wyndham, Bolingbroke was already expressing ideas of making the prince into the incorruptible Patriot who would return the constitution to its original purity, sacrificing his own interests to those of the nation.[23] But by July 1738, Bolingbroke's financial situation was so grim that he needed to sell Dawley, and ostensibly came to England for that reason. Between July 1738 and April 1739, Bolingbroke and Pope saw much of each other. Pope's pride at having the great man once again under his roof was boundless. Twickenham again became a meeting place for the disaffected: in November, he entertained Cornbury, the Duchess of Queensberry, Lyttelton, Bolingbroke, and Chesterfield.[24] It is likely that *The Idea of a Patriot King* was written during this period, and, at Pope's request, copies were made and circulated round the Patriot circle.

But Pope himself had not been idle about his own business. Together, Pope and Bolingbroke oversaw the literary campaign of opposition, particularly that waged in the theatre. Thomson, Glover, Mallet, and Brooke were all writing *pièces à clef*, which in varying degrees express the ideas of the Patriot opposition.[25] Pope had much to do with the promotion of these plays, not all of which passed the censorship of the Lord Chamberlain applying the new Licensing Act.[26] Aaron Hill was, as usual, particularly troublesome concerning his play *The Roman Revenge*. Both Pope and Bolingbroke regarded it as a potentially significant Patriot play, but seem to have doubted, in the end, whether it carried enough conviction as such, despite the lines in the prologue that insinuated the Patriot theme. I suspect that Bolingbroke regarded the play as sheer fustian.[27] At all events, it was never performed. In addition to this literary work, which, according to Malcolm Goldstein, was no more than "fun—an intellectual parlor game which England's most respected poet and most famous elder statesman, pencils in hand, could play in the pleasant summer air,"[28] Pope and Bolingbroke applied themselves to the sale of Dawley. Pope tried to persuade Orrery to become a customer. The behavior of one Joshua Vanneck, in trying to cheapen Bolingbroke's already rock-bottom price, roused Pope to fury—"some Child of Dirt, or Corruption; at best, some Money-headed & Mony-hearted Citizen"—and Pope was, typically, afraid that the new owner would not be worthy of the house he inhabited.[29] In 1737, he had published the *Epistle to Augustus (Imit. Hor. Ep. II.1)*, which framed an extended debate on taste in literature with two ironic panegyric passages extolling the virtues of King George II. Unlike those past kings whose living reputations were subverted by envy and who were only given their due posthumously,

> To Thee, the World its present homage pays,
> The Harvest early, but mature the Praise:
> Great Friend of LIBERTY! in *Kings* a Name
> Above all Greek, above all Roman Fame. (23–26)

Employment of such an emotive term as *liberty* in the context is the semaphore that would alert the reader to the presence of irony, though the entire venture of conducting a literary argument for the benefit of such a philistine king is a pervasive structural irony.

One recent critic has argued that the entire poem is ironic, not merely at one but at two removes from the literal. The accepted interpretation is that Horace's original is an entirely deserved panegyric on a benevolent prince, whereas in applying Horace's praise for Augustus to George II, Pope is praising him only mock-heroically: Augustan values serve as a norm from which present values have departed. But Howard Weinbrot has offered a revisionist view of both Horace and Augustus in the so-called Augustan period.[30] According to this view, Augustus Caesar had become the byword for the tyrannical king, the repressive monarch who conspicuously failed to reward men of literary talent, keeping only his tame publicist Horace to advertise his virtues. Thus, Pope's intention in the *Epistle to Augustus* was to divorce himself from Horace as well as Augustus, to assert his poetic independence, and in writing the epistle he was signposting his desire to ally himself with opposition political journals, where the identification of George with Augustus was a commonplace. If this reading is accepted, the poem represents the high-water mark of the involvement of literary issues with political ones in the Walpole era.

However, much of the poem is not obviously political, except in the general sense that kings like George II are responsible for the demise of taste in their reigns, so that the passage (lines 139–60) in which Charles II's luxurious court is blamed for an emasculation of literary standards—"The Soldier breath'd the Gallantries of France, / And ev'ry flow'ry Courtier writ Romance"—is an example to the present king. Pope's point is that popular taste will admit virtue only to the ancients and rejects those poets whose work lacks the patina of age, and that this also has been the situation with respect to kings, present company excepted of course. Two extended passages contrast a corrupt present with the idealized liberty of "Our rural Ancestors" (lines 161–80, 241–62), and such normative use of the remote past has a political dimension, due to the use being made of history in political ideology. But the poem's ending is unmistakable. It carries an ironically fulsome tribute to the nation's peace policy, which by the late 1730s had become extremely unpopular. Like the earlier *Epistle to Fortescue*, there is a deliberately contrived false ending, for the poem looks as though it will end in conventional panegyric until the persona suddenly becomes self-conscious:

> But Verse alas! your Majesty disdains;
> And I'm not us'd to Panegyric strains:
> The Zeal of Fools offends at any time,
> But most of all, the Zeal of Fools in ryme.

> Besides, a fate attends on all I write,
> That when I am at praise, they say I bite. (404–9)

Three reasons are given for Pope's refusal to flatter the King. One is that he is obtuse to the arts; this has been the complaint of the entire poem. Second, the poet's independence will not allow him to adopt a line taken by progovernment writers; this suggestion is amplified into the *MacFleck-noe*-like supplication at the end: "And when I flatter, let my dirty leaves . . . Cloath spice, line trunks, or flutt'ring in a row, / Befringe the rails of Bedlam and Sohoe." And finally, the persona adopts a naively quizzical tone about the misconstruction of his praise, which, somehow, is always translated into scandal. This *méchant* exploitation of irony's ambiguity is audacious. In fact, irony did gain for the poem an immunity from prosecution, but also, it would appear, an immunity from serious regard.[31] It is a mixed blessing, too, as far as the poem's success is concerned, since Pope's employment of the ironic mode, especially with respect to judgments on individual poets, is not always very deft, and often we are left at the mercy of the literary historian to resurrect the ingenuous statement.[32]

Pope's poetic output for 1738 was far less ambiguous, and the *Epilogue to the Satires*, published in two dialogues as *One Thousand Seven Hundred and Thirty-Eight* in May and July, transformed Pope into the leading exponent of antigovernment principles outside Parliament itself. No case need be made for the political import of a poem which celebrates by name Lyttelton, Chesterfield, Pulteney, Argyll, Wyndham, Cobham, Polwarth, and St. John: indeed, the epithet "All-accomplish'd" applied to Bolingbroke (*Dialogue II,*139) was, as usual, the single most exceptionable detail in the poem, provoking repeated attacks in the government-sponsored *Daily Gazeteer.*[33] Not only is the poem an attack on vice and corruption mounted in terms fairly close to those of the *Idea of a Patriot King*, but insofar as it continues from the *Epistle to Fortescue* and the *Epistle to Dr. Arbuthnot* the debate on the ethics of satire, it elaborates the view that satire itself is the ultimate form of political activity. We will discuss this aspect of the poem further in a later chapter. What is remarkable is the extent to which Pope was by now absolutely at the center of events. He now conceptualized his task in an exalted light:

> I have two great Tasks on my hands: I am trying to benefit myself, and to benefit Posterity; not by Works of my own God knows: I can but Skirmish, & maintain a flying Fight with Vice; its Forces augment, & will drive me off the Stage, before I shall see the Effects complete, either of Divine Providence or Vengeance: for sure we can be quite Saved only by the One, or punish'd by the other: The Condition of Morality is so desperate, as to be above all Human Hands.[34]

And there is a new confidence in his mien. His summer ramble of 1739 took him to Stowe, where he met Cobham and Grenville, to Hagley (Lyttelton), and to Adderbury (Argyll). To Swift, he wrote a letter that, for all its insouciance, glistens with pride at the elevation of his connections: the prince is furnishing his garden with urns and his library with busts of the famous poets, the *Gazeteer* rails at him, and the Duchess of Marlborough woos him:

> Yet I cultivate some Young people's friendship, because they may be honest men, whereas the Old ones, Experience too often proves not to be so. I have droppd ten, where I have taken up one, & hope to play the better with fewer in my hand: There is a Lord Cornbury, a Lord Polwarth, a Mr. Murray, & one or two more, with whom I would never fear to hold out against all the Corruption of the world.[35]

His role seems to have been to state the cause of the opposition as idealistically as possible to the self-interested sections of the opposition council, as well as to the outside world.[36] By the early 1740s, he and Bolingbroke were mounting a joint campaign to persuade the Earl of Marchmont out of retirement and back into muscular opposition.[37] By this time, Pope was certainly more significant to the cause of opposition than was his one-time mentor. In September 1740, after the tragic death of Sir William Wyndham dealt a cruel blow to opposition hopes, Pope wrote to Bolingbroke in reply to one of Bolingbroke's own letters (now lost) in which the latter had indicated his desire to return to England if needed by his country. This disinterestedness in one who has no hope of office is commended animatedly by Pope as "not so much Love to your Country as to God: It is not Patriotism, but downright Piety, & instead of celebrating You as a Poet should, I would (if I were Pope) Canonize You, whatever all the Advocates for the Devil could say to the contrary."[38] There is more than a hint of irony here, especially since the rest of the letter manifests such intimacy with the movements and states of mind of Marchmont, Lyttelton, and Chesterfield. Bolingbroke must have been painfully aware of being dependent on Pope for such information. In this letter too, Pope sent to Bolingbroke a version of the *Verses on a Grotto &c.*, a poem which must have taught him how far he had appropriated his master's teaching and made it his own:

> Thou who shalt stop, where *Thames'* translucent Wave
> Shines a broad Mirrour thro' the shadowy Cave;
> Where lingering Drops from Mineral Roofs distill,
> And pointed Crystals break the sparkling Rill,
> Unpolish'd Gemms no Ray on Pride bestow,
> And latent Metals innocently glow:
> Approach. Great NATURE studiously behold!
> And eye the Mine without a Wish for Gold.
> Approach: But aweful! Lo th' *Aegerian* Grott,

> Where, nobly-pensive, ST. JOHN sate and thought;
> Where *British* Sighs from dying WYNDHAM stole,
> And the bright Flame was shot thro' MARCHMONT's Soul.
> Let such, such only, tread this sacred Floor,
> Who dare to love their Country, and be poor.[39]

Here Pope's grotto at Twickenham is made an icon of the very qualities, of innocence, humility, and frugality, that the Patriot needs to possess. It is further represented as a shrine to the memory of such true Britons as Wyndham, who drew his last breaths there, Marchmont, who was inspired with patriotic zeal there, and Bolingbroke, whose Aegerian or prophetic thoughts, it is inferred, predicted the nation's fate that the worshiper at his shrine has come to know. For Pope himself, the grot is an emblem of his involvement in, and centrality to, the Patriot cause. A letter from Lyttelton to Pope on 7 November 1741 further underlines the extent to which Pope's and Bolingbroke's roles had reversed since the early and middle thirties. He wishes that Bolingbroke were in England, if for no other reason than to exhort Pope to write even more "in the Service of Virtue":

> I wish he was in England upon many accounts, but for nothing more than to Exhort and Animate You not to bury your excellent Talents in a Philosophical Indolence, but to Employ them, as you have so often done, in the Service of Virtue. The Corruption, and Hardness of the present Age is no Excuse; for your Writings will Last to Ages to come, and may do Good a thousand years hence, if they can't now; but I beleive they wou'd be of great Present Benefit; some sparks of Publick Virtue are yet Alive, which such a Spirit as Your's might blow into a flame, among the Young men especially; and even granting an impossibility of Reforming the Publick, your Writings may be of Use to private Society; The Moral Song may steal into our Hearts, and teach us to be as good Sons, as good Friends, as Beneficent, as Charitable as Mr Pope, and sure *That* will be Serving your Country, though you cant Raise her up such Ministers, or such Senators as you desire. In short; my dear Friend, though I am far from supposing that if you don't write, you *Live in Vain;* though the Influence of your Virtues is felt among all your Friends, and Acquaintance, and the whole circle of Society within which you Live, yet as your Writings will have a still more extensive and permanent Influence, as they will be an Honour to your Country at a time when it has hardly anything else to be proud of, and may do Good to Mankind in better Ages and Countries, if not in This, I wou'd have you Write till a Decay of your Parts, or at least Weakness of Health shall Oblige, and Authorise you to lay down your Pen.[40]

Unlike Bolingbroke, Pope was entirely an advantage to the cause of opposition, since he had no personal stake in gaining office. He seems to have responded to Lyttelton's exhortation, judging by the fragment *One*

Thousand Seven Hundred and Forty, which was never published in Pope's lifetime, perhaps because of potential or actual government pressure. Steeped in Patriot lore as it is, the fragment shows how much Pope was in command of the specifics of politics by the end of his life.

Pope, Bolingbroke, and Warburton

While Pope was becoming politicized in this way, deriving a thrilling pleasure from his growing commitment to opposition politics and from his own recognition in these circles, other aspects of his life were in less satisfactory order. There was an initial honeymoon period after the publication of the *Essay on Man* when it was very well received by the public, but as time went by, serious doubts arose, and the articulation of these doubts threw Pope into confusion. In 1737, J. P. de Crousaz, a Swiss philosopher, responded to the challenge of the *Essay on Man* by accusing it of deistic or atheistic tendencies deriving from Spinoza and Leibniz, though of course he had read the poem only in a totally distortive French prose translation by Silhouette and in a verse translation by Du Resnel that conflated it with the *Essay on Criticism.* Thereafter, Pope found himself at the mercy of outraged Catholic theologians over the poem, which had at first attracted unmitigated praise.[41] For all Catholics, but especially for Catholics of Pope's stamp, there was a very short cord connecting religious issues and political ones. To be a deist was not only to be a heretic in speculative theological matters, but it was also to dissent from the governmental arrangements, which were a microcosmic instantiation of the cosmic order. To the early-eighteenth-century mind, there was a strong connection between deism or freethinking and radical republican politics.[42] Neither in Pope nor in Bolingbroke did the rebellious spirit encouraged by freethinking take this form, but doubtless it did foster a critical attitude to the status quo that was expressed in outspoken criticism of the King and his ministers. I believe that through contact with Bolingbroke and through their philosophical discussions, Pope veered dangerously in the direction of deism in the 1730s. The manifestation of all this uncertainty in verse is the *Epistle to Bolingbroke.* Because this poem is, like the *Essay on Man,* so directly a product of the relationship between the two, I shall deal with it in a separate chapter.

Warburton rescued Pope from this invidious and confusing predicament by publishing a series of monthly letters in *The History of the Works of the Learned* from December 1738 to May 1739, which was finally published as *A Vindication of Mr. Pope's Essay on Man.* Pope's relief and gratitude to Warburton for his Christianizing of the poem is apparent from this ingratiating letter:

> . . . You have made my System as clear as I ought to have done & could not. It is indeed the Same System as mine, but illustrated with a Ray of your own, as they say our Natural Body is the same still, when it is Glorifyed. I am sure I like it better than I did before, & so will every man else. I know I meant just what you explain, but I did not explain my own meaning so well as you: You understand me as well as I do myself, but you express me better than I could express myself.[43]

Warburton's influence on Pope was exerted in the direction of bringing him back to the fold of Christian orthodoxy, where, no doubt, Pope was happiest. This influence affected Pope even before they first met in April 1740. Late in 1739, Henry Brooke, author of *Gustavus Vasa,* the Patriot play, wrote to Pope anxiously requesting assurance that Pope was a Christian: "I have often heard it insinuated, that you had too much wit to be a man of religion, and too refined a taste to be that trifling thing called a Christian."[44] Pope replied thus:

> I sincerely worship God, believe in his revelations, resign to his dispensations, love all his creatures, am in charity with all denominations of Christians, however violently they treat each other, and detest none so much as that profligate race who would loosen the bands of morality, either under the pretence of religion or free-thinking. I hate no man as a man, but I hate vice in any man; I hate no sect, but I hate uncharitableness in any sect.[45]

As this relationship with Warburton developed, it became exclusive of, and gradually supplanted, that with Bolingbroke. Just as Pope's friendships among the Patriots and the greater self-reliance he drew from them rendered him more critical of Bolingbroke's expertise, his friendship with Warburton introduced him to a system of philosophy that was far removed from Bolingbroke's. Warburton introduced Pope to his own remarkable work, *The Divine Legation of Moses Demonstrated,* in which he "demonstrated" the divine authority of Jewish revelation by arguing that since the doctrine of a future state is necessary to the well-being of society, and since it is not to be found in the Jewish religion, "therefore the law of Moses is of divine original." Lacking a central doctrine, the entire Jewish system must be supported by God's particular providence.[46] Small wonder that Pope was "struck with Veneration & Wonder" by this work, though he felt he needed the author's guiding hand to understand it![47] Clearly, such a work would be anathema to Bolingbroke, who was in England between early May and 14 June 1742 to settle his father's estate, and to whom Pope gave one of literature's most tactless going-away presents—Warburton's works.[48] Pope and Warburton's friendship grew apace after their first meeting, and by the end of 1742, they were collaborating on numerous projects: a formal edition of Warburton's *Vindication,* published in August 1742, and a revised edition of the *Essay on Man*, complete with Warburton's notes. By early 1743 Warburton was more or less performing the role of editor-in-chief of all Pope's poems, though only the *Essay on Man* and the *Ethic Epistles* appeared in Warburtonian form before Pope's death.[49] The role that Bolingbroke had once played in promoting Pope's poetic endeavor was by this time being filled by Warburton, to whom Pope gives the credit for the fourth book of the new *Dunciad*:

> The Encouragement you gave me to add the fourth book, first determind me to do so: & the Approbation you seemd to give it, was what singly determind me to print it. Since that, your Notes, & your Discourse in the Name of Aristarchus, have given its Last Finishings & Ornaments.[50]

In return for this editorial and annotatory work, Warburton received the social benefits of being Pope's intimate friend. Soon after they first met in 1740, Pope was carrying him to Bathurst, Oxford, Lyttelton, and Burlington, society that must have been edifying to so ambitious a man. But the most important introduction was to Ralph Allen, at whose residence in Bath the *Dunciad* was finished in 1742, with Pope closeted as closely together with Warburton as he had been with Bolingbroke over the *Essay on Man*. Warburton took very quick advantage of Allen's friendship. In summer 1743, there was a temporary lull in the intimacy with Pope owing to an incident that took place at Allen's. It seems that Allen's mischiefmaking niece Gertrude Tucker saw Pope's good friend Martha Blount going into his bedroom in the morning and spread an absurd scandal.[51] No doubt Warburton saw his advantage and sided with Gertrude Tucker and Mrs. Allen against Martha Blount, for which Pope said, "W. is a sneaking Parson, & I told him he flatterd."[52] Gertrude Tucker later married Warburton. But this quarrel was mended, and at various times, Pope attempted to secure preferment for his new friend.[53]

In the last few months of Pope's life, he saw a good deal of Bolingbroke, who was in England from March to May 1743 and again from October until Pope died in May 1744. Again, he lived conveniently close to Twickenham, at the family manor in Battersea, where he was within reach even when the act forbidding Catholics to live within ten miles of London was reinvoked in February 1744. Throughout this final period, Pope exerted every effort to bring Bolingbroke and Warburton face to face in the naive belief that two such men of genius could not let personal differences come between them. It is quite evident, however, that a clash was inevitable. Most of our information about Warburton's dealings with Bolingbroke around this time derive from Warburton himself and may not be reliable. To Spence, Warburton reported an incident that occurred at dinner with Murray in spring 1744:

> Pope [was] shocked at overhearing Warburton and Hooke talking of Lord
> Bolingbroke's not believing the moral attributes of God. "You must be
> mistaken," [said he]. (He [Warburton] mentioned it as a proof of Mr.
> Pope's excessive friendliness.) Pope afterwards talked with Lord Boling-
> broke about it; he denied all, and Pope told his friends of it with great joy,
> and said, "I told you you must be mistaken."[54]

Warburton himself, in *A View of Lord Bolingbroke's Philosophy*, gives two
reasons for Bolingbroke's animosity toward him. One was general—that
Bolingbroke was jealous of his pupil being "reasoned out of his hands."
The other was particular—that in Twickenham in 1742, Warburton told
Pope that the digression on Old Testament history in the *Letters on the
Study and Use of History* was derivative. Pope prevailed on him to write a
critique, which he did "with all the civility Mr. W. was likely to use to a
friend . . . but the word *prevarication* . . . chanced . . . to escape his pen."[55]
Whether the two men met during Pope's lifetime is not certain, though if
they did not, they missed one another by the merest whisker.[56] Warburton
claimed, in the life of Pope by Owen Ruffhead that he inspired, that they
did and that he bested Bolingbroke in debate.[57]

Pope and Bolingbroke certainly did not come to open rupture in the
poet's lifetime. Indeed, Bolingbroke's behavior during his friend's last
illness is an ennobling testament to the strength of this intricate bond.
" 'Oh great God! What is man?' (Looking on Mr. Pope, and repeating it
several times, interrupted with sobs.)," he ejaculated on one occasion; and
again, " 'I have known him this thirty years, and value myself more for
that man's love and friendship than—' (sinking his head and losing his
voice in tears)."[58] But in truth, Pope had been weaning himself away from
Bolingbroke's influence over a period of some years, at first through the
acclaim given by the Patriots to his poems and the subsequent status he
carved out for himself with that group—a status greater than Bolingbroke's
own. Whereas the latter's political ambition was an embarrassment to his
friends, Pope became their cultural mascot, his poems presenting the
acceptably idealistic face of their program. As far as religion and philosophy are concerned, Pope was by 1738 quite ready to have his beliefs
replaced on the shelf of orthodoxy. Warburton responded to genuine
needs that Pope felt deeply in his latter days. During his last illness, Pope's
thoughts ran on the immortality of the soul, and in the end, he received
consciously the last sacraments from a Roman Catholic priest. As Dean
Audra remarked, however much Pope refused to be limited to any one
sect, he preferred to pass for a Catholic rather than a deist.

The *Epistle to Bolingbroke* further indicates the respects in which Pope felt
confused and disappointed by Bolingbroke's counsel. The posthumous
episode that sullied the memory of this extraordinary relationship has its

roots, I believe, in resentments on Bolingbroke's part that took several years to mature and did not break the surface in the course of Pope's lifetime. Too often, the jealousy that developed between Bolingbroke and Warburton is the sole motivation offered for the sour aftertaste that the relationship with Pope left in the former's mouth. As we have seen, the roots lie much deeper.

Postscript

This part of the story can be quickly told, since it has been extensively and admirably chronicled elsewhere.[59] The bare facts are as follows. In May 1749, Bolingbroke published an authorized edition of the *Patriot King* in response to pressure created by a serialization in the *London Magazine* of extracts from Pope's text of that work (that is to say, the text given to Pope probably around April 1739, for very limited circulation only). Prefixed to this edition was an Advertisement written by Bolingbroke in which he told the whole story of Pope's having printed an illicit edition of 1,500 copies, callously edited and in despite of Bolingbroke's express prohibition. That Pope had in fact done so was ascertained by Bolingbroke shortly after the poet's death, and he ordered Marchmont to burn as many copies as could be retrieved. The Advertisement provoked a rash of pamphlet literature, in which accusations against Pope grew wilder; pamphlet attacks accused Pope of plagiarism, desire for financial gain, and a malicious wish to defame Bolingbroke, none of which charges are likely in the least.[60] It is probable that Pope did print a small authorized edition and a larger, modified one which he failed to destroy. There can be no question of any of the above motives operating; it is likely that Pope was prompted by respect for Bolingbroke's ideas and a sincere desire to propagate them. This incident was the second occasion on which Bolingbroke had spitefully sabotaged Pope's posthumous reputation. In 1746, he had published Pope's Atossa portrait accompanied by a note claiming that the Duchess of Marlborough had paid the poet one thousand pounds to suppress these lines. Presumably, Bolingbroke did this to prevent Warburton from publishing a biography of Pope that would be uncomplimentary to Bolingbroke. It was an unsavory end to such a friendship.

Chapter 7

The "Epistle to Bolingbroke"

The Poem in Context

It is to be hoped that, at this stage in the book, the privileged treatment I am about to extend to Pope's *Epistle to Bolingbroke* need not be justified. But even if special consideration was not warranted by the structure of argument I have been conducting, I should still think that the poem occupies a unique position in Pope's oeuvre. In several of Pope's poems, the addressee plays more than a conventional part, but only in the *Epistle to Bolingbroke* is his role of greater than structural or symbolic significance. In the *Moral Essays*, especially in the *Epistle to Burlington*, the addressee symbolizes the properly integrated life and enshrines the moral and social positives recommended by the poem. Fortescue and Arbuthnot in the epistles addressed to them function as the satirical *adversarius* against whom Pope argues: their function is mainly a structural one, though of course the *Epistle to Dr. Arbuthnot* is irradiated by personal glances that bring the implicit *adversarius* to life: "Friend to my Life, (which did not you prolong, / The World had wanted many an idle Song)" (lines 27–28). Murray's presence in the *Epistle to Murray (Imit. Hor. Ep. I.6)* is stilted, the well-nigh anonymous colonel of *Imit. Hor. Ep. II.2* scarcely lasts beyond the opening line, and Augustus is only ironically present in the epistle addressed to him. Only in the *Epistle to Bolingbroke* is the relationship between the poet and the addressee genuinely *interrogated* by the poem; this poem alone can be said to be *about* its dedicatee. There is a sense here, not present in the others, of the poem making its mind up about its subject, a sense of process rather than product, an ambiguity that results from Pope's inability to decide in advance how the dedicatee will serve the poem. I will suggest that the reason for this is Pope's uncertainty, at the time of writing, as to whether Bolingbroke was an influence for good or ill on his life. To see how this came about, we need to have the context of writing in sharp focus before us. Since this chapter is the last of the strictly biographical ones, let us take this opportunity of recapping the main lines of the relationship as we have charted them previously, even at the risk of some repetition.

*   *   *

Initially, Bolingbroke's place in Pope's life was that of sagacious elder brother. Throughout his life, Pope sought out the company of older, more distinguished men like Sir William Trumbull and Bishop Atterbury, who were able to tutor and instruct him but who held his precocious talents in proper esteem. Bolingbroke was a man of great charm and charisma. Conversation with him that was learned and extensive, while also being leavened by his ability to mock intellectual opponents, was to become Pope's great delight. During his exile in France from 1715 to 1723, Bolingbroke had embarked on a grueling reading program in history, political theory, and philosophy, returning to England as the most improved mind of his generation. His knowledge was encyclopedic and was matched by great rhetorical skill as well as by the elegant manners of a courtier and man of the world. Pope saw him in the romantic light of an omnitalented individual, combining the accomplishments of the active and the contemplative man. In contrast to the narrowly circumscribed life that Pope's delicate constitution and unfortunate physique forced him to lead, Bolingbroke was always at the center of events, and Pope benefited vicariously from his exploits. In Queen Anne's reign, St. John had been the most powerful politician in the land, and although on the fall of his Tory ministry he had fled to France, he later claimed his exile to be self-imposed, a noble reaction to the native land that had turned its back on him. In many respects, he seems a role model for his junior colleague. Ludicrously, in spite of Pope's actual physical incapacities, the poet liked to imagine himself something of a rake; in Bolingbroke he found the genuine article. Peter Wentworth wrote to his brother the Earl of Strafford on 29 October 1714 a letter that tells a picaresquely robust story of Bolingbroke's wedding day, when he got drunk, delivered a harangue to the astonished Queen, and "at night was put to bed to a beautyfull young lady [not his new wife], and was tuck't up by two of the prettiest young peers in England, Lord Jersey and Bathurst."[1] The reputation of whoremonger followed Bolingbroke to the grave, and in 1734 Pope published his salacious imitation of Horace's *Satire* I.2, under the title *Sober Advice from Horace,* which includes a satire on Bolingbroke's penchant for street girls, couched in terms of knowing intimacy (lines 61–70). In short, "all accomplish'd St. John" was everything that Pope aspired to be in his imagination.

Bolingbroke became Pope's near neighbor in 1725 when he bought Dawley Farm near Uxbridge, a very short ride from Pope's villa at Twickenham. In the years that followed, Dawley became an organized cell of political opposition to the Walpole regime, a gathering place for the disaffected, and the seedbed of the influential political journal called the *Craftsman,* begun in December 1726, which ceaselessly strove to oust Walpole from office. Pope was deeply involved in the Dawley circle's activities, and the result of his association was the politicization of his poems throughout the 1730s. The *Craftsman* was forced to develop an artillery of sophisticated literary techniques like allegory, fable, Theo-phrastian "character," "Persian" letter, dialogue, and dream vision, partly to escape prosecution and partly to widen its readership. It succeeded in developing an argot of intimate political allusion that gave the reader a strong and satisfying sense of being at the center of events: this was, to the contemporary reader of Pope's poems, equally a source of great pleasure.

Dawley became, then, the focus of English hopes for an alternative society in the 1730s. It was also an expression, in architecture and land-scape, of its owner's personality. Bolingbroke posed as a gentleman-farmer in Dawley and tried to camouflage it as a working farm. He ostenta-tiously engrossed himself in rustic pursuits, even going to the length of having the hall painted in monochrome with farm implements and dec-orating the rooms with paintings of mythological figures in georgic pur-suits, such as cupids guiding the plough. Pope contributed materially to the shaping of Bolingbroke's environment. As is only now being recog-nized, Pope was perhaps the foremost landscape gardener of his genera-tion and a considerable authority on architecture. Pope's architect, James Gibbs, remodeled the house, while Pope himself gave advice on improve-ments in the garden and the outlying fields. It was to very familiar sur-roundings that Pope went in 1731, therefore, when his worsening health forced him onto a diet of asses' milk and he spent some months in residence at Dawley. He used to sleep at Dawley and make periodic visits to the pasture four miles away where he drank freshly drawn asses' milk. These weeks were the most perfect in the intercourse between the two men. During this period, Pope put into their final form epistles 1–3 of the *Essay on Man,* working comfortably in Bolingbroke's library, a room that probably reflected Pope's own taste in statuary. To have had Bolingbroke looking over his shoulder while he was giving the lines their final polish must have been invaluable to Pope. Bolingbroke was intimately concerned in the making of this poem. He took the closest interest in Pope's career from the time he returned to England in 1723. It was Bolingbroke's idea that Pope should begin imitating Horace in English, and thereafter, as Pope's attacks on the Walpole regime became more and more outspoken, Bolingbroke was responsible for ensuring that the poet presented to the nation the acceptable face of the opposition platform. With the publication of the complete *Essay on Man* in early 1734, Pope paid his finest verse tribute to his mentor and friend (4.373–90).

But with Bolingbroke's return to France in 1735, the relationship's secure phase came to an end. When he left the country on this second occasion, he was again the most unpopular man in England. His party had failed to win the 1734 general election, despite the golden opportunity presented by the excise crisis, because he had again been caught plotting with French

Jacobites. He was branded a traitor by Walpole and regarded as an Achilles' heel by his own supporters. Friendship with him became increasingly hazardous for Pope, who was attacked in pamphlet after pamphlet by government hacks for his intimacy with the traitor Bolingbroke. This detraction would not have shaken Pope in itself, because he had, I believe, a strong romantic attachment to the Jacobite cause. But shortly afterward, there was more personal cause for concern. In 1737, the *Essay on Man* came under attack from the Swiss scholar J. P. de Crousaz, who claimed that the poem manifested deistic or atheistic tendencies deriving from Spinoza or Leibniz. For Pope, this was a case of the worst coming to the worst, because he had been uncertain from the outset about what sort of reception it would get, insofar as the poem does not mention particular Christian beliefs. In 1731–1738, Pope experienced something of a spiritual crisis. Religion was perhaps the most delicate area of Pope's entire personality. Against his interests, he was a lifelong Roman Catholic, perhaps not especially devout, but nevertheless he did attend Mass and had numerous friends who were strict adherents of the faith. On more than one occasion, notably in the Atterbury trial, Pope was forced to abjure his Catholic faith, and there must have accumulated a considerable weight of guilt about the whole question of belief. Partly as a defensive tactic, he adopted the rhetoric of Erasmian Catholicism, professing himself to be an ecumenical, nonpartisan Catholic who believed in a spiritual Christianity based on charity that was greater than any individual denomination.[2] This predisposition toward ecumenicalism and the sinking of differences was partly responsible for his susceptibility to Bolingbroke's influence in the late 1720s and early 1730s. While Pope was composing the *Essay on Man*, he was receiving from Bolingbroke prose letters that urged him toward natural religion or deism.

The question of Pope's deism, bedeviled as it is by the failure to agree on any definition of deism, has frequently blocked a sympathetic understanding of his friendship with Bolingbroke. The common ground of eighteenth-century definitions is the belief that all we know about God is discoverable by the light of reason, unassisted by revelation. This view is certainly not incompatible with Pope's ecumenical leanings. Bolingbroke regarded natural religion as the middle way between out-and-out atheism and those divines who, in Pope's words, "nobly take the high Priori Road / And reason downward, till they doubt of God." He presented his own view as an appropriately limited use of the rational faculty in discovering religious truth, fulminating against the presumptive arrogance of divines like Samuel Clarke and William Wollaston, who, in *The Religion of Nature Delineated* (1722), argued that only the doctrine of a future state can vindicate the ways of God to man, and that doctrine is received through revelation. I see no difficulty in believing that Bolingbroke convinced Pope that deism *was* a moderate system, which stripped religion of everything that was inessential to it, reducing it to the lowest common denominator of beliefs that all Christians could share. Deism would then become an aspect of Pope's moderate antisectarianism. Concentration on revealed religion opened the floodgates to doctrinal exegesis. This gave rise to dispute and faction, to which simple, commonsense piety fell victim. Arguments like this are the mainstay of Bolingbroke's attack on metaphysical theology, and I have no doubt that they would recommend themselves to Pope. Deism was a moderate system, avoiding the extremes of atheism and of metaphysical theism. It eschewed theological debate over doctrinal niceties and rejected most biblical exegesis. It was simple, commonsense piety, quite acceptable to a moderate antisectarian like Pope.

Douglas Atkins, in an essay designed to show that Pope was not a deist, concludes, "To argue still that Pope was a deist commits us to one of two possible positions, neither of which is defensible: either Pope was willfully deceptive all along or he became a deist, probably under Bolingbroke's influence in the early thirties, and then by 1737 either abandoned those views or falsified his true sentiments."[3] I do not see why the latter view is "indefensible." I think it is exactly what did happen. In the early thirties, Pope was convinced by Bolingbroke that deism was the solution to the problem of sectarianism and as such was complementary to his own Erasmian stance. This was all very well while Bolingbroke was actually present to sustain him in the belief, but when he was away and when Pope was exposed to the not-so-tender mercies of professional theologians in 1737, he found that his religious beliefs were now eclectic and unclear, nothing better than a muddle. When, after 1736, the *Essay on Man* began to be accused of unorthodoxy and irreligion, Pope started to experience serious doubts. He revised his earlier poem with deistic tendencies, the *Universal Prayer*, in view of these doubts, but the *Essay on Man* got into even hotter water in 1737, and Pope recognized himself to be in a predicament for which Bolingbroke was in some degree responsible.[4] In a spirit of perplexed injury, he wrote the *Epistle to Bolingbroke*, upbraiding him for causing the muddle that was now Pope's religious position. Then Warburton appeared as a deus ex machina in 1739 and, together with Pope, set about putting the poet's views to rights. After 1739, Pope several times expressed orthodox views of religion on request. We have already seen this in his answers to Henry Brooke's rather impertinent query in 1739. By the time Pope came to write book 4 of the new *Dunciad* under Warburton's wing, he was confident enough to include a passage (4.459–92) that not only eschewed deism, but also could be read as rejecting much of Bolingbroke's own theology.

The *Epistle to Bolingbroke*, in imitation of Horace's first epistle of the first book, was published on 7 March 1738 and probably begun around the turn of the year. Like the *Epistle to Dr. Arbuthnot*, it seems to be a verse letter written in reply to a specific letter of Bolingbroke's. Bolingbroke's letter does not survive, but something in it must have threatened to "break the Sabbath of [Pope's] days" (line 3). By early 1738, Bolingbroke firmly intended to return to England in the summer, partly because he was in serious financial difficulties and needed to sell Dawley, and partly because Frederick, Prince of Wales was now in open breach with his father George II and Bolingbroke believed he could exploit this tension in forming a reinvigorated opposition. Pope's *Epistle* is, I suspect, a reply both to Bolingbroke's announcement that he would be returning to England—as he did in July 1738, staying for ten months, mostly at Twickenham—and to his friend's request that he renew the poetic propaganda campaign at what might be a crucial political turning point. The poet sets himself two major tasks. One is to comply as far as possible with Bolingbroke's request to reopen hostilities in the propaganda war; the other is to investigate the present state of his feelings for Bolingbroke.

This, then, is the immediate context of writing. Bearing this in mind, we are unlikely to regard as purely arbitrary Pope's choice of Bolingbroke as addressee. Before arriving at our own reading, we can study the results of ignoring the personal relationship between dedicator and dedicatee in the influential chapter devoted to the poem by Thomas Maresca.[5] Maresca's view of the poem is that Pope is representing his society and its leaders as the perpetrators of a "coherently developed antireligion that perverts point by point the tenets of orthodox Christianity" (p.157). To show this, Maresca disinters with great diligence and profit a systematic use of allusions both to the Bible and to Renaissance commentaries on Horace that Christianized the Roman poet. (It is part of the book's overall purpose to show that the Horace Pope inherited was the Christianized, not the classical poet.) In harmonious opposition to this antimasque of "concentric rings of corruption spread outward from a vicious and devil-like king, through court and nobles, through rich and poor, to encompass the entire life of the nation" (p.172), the poet represents himself as exemplar of "the properly concordant man . . . a harmonic, properly ordered individual who is . . . fully discharging the Christian's duty to imitate Christ in leading the mixed life" (pp.179–80), a man who can reconcile the active life to the contemplative and the spiritual to the material. Again, the evidence presented for this view is a formidable array of allusions that, in Maresca's arrangement, turn Pope into a Jeremiah, prophet and preacher to an infernal society, then into an incarnation of Divine Wisdom, and finally into "a creator of God's own order, a 'Demi-god' who reproduces in himself and his works the pattern of God's own creation" (p.187). Maresca's reading is a traditional one, lending authority to the view of Pope as a poet with roots deep in the Christian Renaissance, but also bringing to this a strong belief in the classical ideal of *concordia discors* in its social application as a doctrine of moderation, balance, and eclecticism.[6] The poem is, once again, a public and traditional statement from the most self-assured and stable of poets.

Leaving aside the question of whether Maresca's allusions are admissible—and many are not—we must ask whether his reading really does justice to the poem's tone and the poet's voice. It is true that one of the poem's purposes is to continue the attack on the court and the ministry that Pope had been conducting under Bolingbroke's aegis in the 1730s. But is there really the apocalyptic fervor of a systematic attack on antireligion? I find it, by contrast even to the *Epistle to Dr. Arbuthnot*, not an especially outspoken piece, but rather a relatively restrained and half-hearted anti-government satire. There are only two direct hits. Line 62, "Slave to a Wife or Vassal to a Punk," certainly alludes to the unfortunate plight of King George II, subjected to his imperious wife Caroline as well as to the Junoesque tyranny of Madame de Walmoden; and lines 95–96, "Be this thy Screen, and this thy Wall of Brass; / Compar'd to this, a Minister's an Ass," are equally certainly a hit at Walpole, whose name is suggested in the Wall/Walpole pun and whose nickname gained after the South Sea Bubble debacle, "Screenmaster General," is also evoked.

Otherwise, the poem's central portion, which is devoted to an attack on the materialistic mores of Georgian England (lines 77–119), makes its impact by capitalizing on already sensitized areas of the reader's imagination. This section depends heavily on images and allusions that were already part of the stock-in-trade of Bolingbroke's mouthpiece, the *Craftsman*. Pope does his opposition business in an allusive political shorthand, utilizing tactics and a form of rhetoric made familiar to the reader by a decade of *Craftsman* campaigning. Lines 76–80, as well as engendering one of the poem's principal metaphors, the gap between spiritual and material wealth, attack the acquisitive citizens of London who provided the Whigs with their main voting strength. London was Walpole's true power base in the Commons. Following this, Pope makes the point in lines 85–90 that social status is frequently inversely proportional to true worth. While the bugs and dormants of this world step into a peerage by way of a government sinecure, Sir John Barnard, a truly worthy man, is despised by them as a mere "Cit" or tradesman. It is interesting to speculate as to why Pope should include Barnard by name in a poem that is otherwise very sparing of such particularities. I detect here the guiding hand of Bolingbroke's Tory opposition. Throughout his career, Barnard had been enthusiastically supported in his candidacy for Parliament by the *Craftsman*. Barnard was a Tory whose credibility as a nonpartisan moderate remained very high and whose personal morality was beyond reproach. The *Craftsman* had virtually won the 1727 election for Barnard by ruining the reputation of his adversary Sir John Eyles;[7] and he richly repaid the investment by becoming a powerful Tory spokesman on financial affairs. In early 1738, his stint as lord mayor of London was drawing to a close, and no doubt Pope wanted to draw attention to this sad loss, perhaps prompted by opposition leaders.

The lines that follow (91–119) are, to readers of the *Craftsman*, dense with political implications. The concept of virtue is insisted upon in this central section. Readers of Pope's poems and of Bolingbroke's political treatises would recognize it as partly the Christian conception of an innocent and pure soul and partly the Roman conception of public-spirited action. Bolingbroke sought to restore this concept as a central motive for political conduct. Another *Craftsman* tactic is adopted by Pope in lines 97–100:

> And say, to which shall our applause belong,
> This new Court jargon, or the good old song?
> The modern language of corrupted Peers,
> Or what was spoke at CRESSY AND POITIERS?

This exemplary use of history, the testing of the present against the constitutionally pure past, is one of Pope's most potent strategies.[8] Edward III, the monarch who won famous victories at Crécy and Poitiers, is implicitly contrasted with George II, whose "peace at all costs" policy was despised by the opposition. In the passage that follows, all England is turned into a giant opera house and pleasure garden; the government leaders become famous *castrati* and the King the principal spectator at the frivolous decline of his nation. Pope's imagery evokes the controversy surrounding opera that went far beyond musical and artistic issues. Bolingbroke took the view that the promotion of opera was part of the government's bread and circuses policy, a spectacular entertainment designed to keep the nation sweet while Walpole and his associates lined their pockets.[9] It also served to keep the subversive theatre in the background, such as Fielding's Grand Mogul's Company, operating under strict surveillance at the Little Theatre in the Haymarket. Thus an opera-going monarch is, as in this poem of Pope's, a Nero fiddling while Rome burns.

There is, then, a good deal of political propaganda in the poem for the practiced ear, but nothing in it justifies Maresca's view that Pope sees his society on the brink of cultural collapse. Equally distorted is Maresca's conception of the poet's presence in the poem as an incarnation of divine

wisdom and of the poem as itself an example of *concordia discors*, in its own
structure an example of the proper order of providence. Maresca neglects
to consider the poem as an epistle written to a particular man at a particular
time; but it is only this particularity that can make sense of the poem's
relationship with the Horatian original. If we study this poem in conjuc-
tion with Horace's, we see at once that Pope's poem is personal to a degree
that makes Horace look very dégagé indeed. Horace's poem treats of his
resolution to put away childish things, to turn to the serious business of
moral philosophy and to the active putting into practice of its lessons. But
Horace is only half-serious about this and is deeply skeptical of the rele-
vance of Stoic wisdom to ordinary predicaments. Most men are foolish,
vicious, tergiversatory, capricious, addicted to the way of the world. Thus,
the truly wise man is a rare bird, and even when we find him, he is still a
victim of his own physical condition. The poem ends in a bathos: "To sum
up: the wise man is less than Jove alone. He is rich, free, honoured,
beautiful, nay a king of kings; above all, sound—save when troubled by
the 'flu!' "[10] Pope, on the other hand, is in deadly earnest about the
importance of moral achievement, and what worries him is not only that
he sees other people falling short of moral perfection, but also that he is
aware of his own shortcomings and unfitness to be called wise. Compare
Pope's lines 35–46 to Horace's lines 20–26:

> As the night seems long for one whose mistress proves false, and the day
> long for those who work for hire; as the year lags for wards held in check
> by their mother's strict guardianship: so slow and thankless flow for me
> the hours which defer my hope and purpose of setting myself vigorously
> to that task which profits alike the poor, alike the rich, but, if neglected,
> will be harmful alike to young and to old. (Horace)

> Long, as to him who works for debt, the Day;
> Long as the Night to her whose love's away;
> Long as the Year's dull circle seems to run,
> When the brisk Minor pants for twenty-one;
> So slow th'unprofitable Moments roll,
> That lock up all the Functions of my soul;
> That keep me from Myself; and still delay
> Life's instant business to a future day:
> That task, which as we follow, or despise,
> The eldest is a fool, the youngest wise;
> Which done, the poorest can no wants endure,
> And which not done, the richest must be poor. (Pope)

The Johnsonian seriousness of Pope's lines, the gravitas of "So slow
th'unprofitable Moments roll, / That lock up all the Functions of my soul; /
That keep me from Myself," is out of keeping with Horace's mild finger-

wagging. Throughout the poem, Pope has asserted his own sensibility over Horace's; it is both more serious and more agonized.[11]

There are two main reasons for the vast difference in tone between Pope's poem and Horace's. One is the reason given by Maresca, that Pope's poem is a Christian one and his explicitly stated purpose is to prepare himself for the Day of Judgment:

> What right, what true, what fit, we justly call,
> Let this be all my care—for this is All:
> To lay this harvest up, and hoard with haste
> What ev'ry day will want, and most, the last. (19–23)

To a limited extent, the poem can be placed in the *ars moriendi* tradition. The poet is examining his own preparedness to die, the readiness of soul and conscience for death and judgment. The sense of impending judgment on the poet and his community imparts to the poem a seriousness that is absent from Horace's humanistic epistle. But the more important reason is that Bolingbroke is present in this poem in a way that Maecenas, Horace's patron, is not.[12] These two factors are closely connected. As I have argued earlier, Pope's religious position in early 1738 was extremely precarious: when he takes stock of it in this poem, he finds his standing with the Almighty far from assured. And this is partly due to Bolingbroke. Thus, while Horace begins his poem with an elegant and formal compliment to Maecenas—"you of whom my earliest Muse has told, of whom my last shall tell"—Pope gives Bolingbroke credit for being a lifelong formative influence on his work: "St John, whose love indulg'd my labours past / Matures my present, and shall bound my last!" It seems that all Bolingbroke has to offer Pope, the reward for breaking his sabbath, is to place him again in the firing line, and Pope protests that he is now too old to bleed for this privilege. As we shall see, the epistle's end, like its beginning, takes its character from Bolingbroke's presence in the poem and the peculiar intensity of Pope's feelings for him. In choosing to imitate some poems of Horace's rather than others, Pope was governed by the extent to which the poem concerned was applicable to his case. Addressing this poem to Bolingbroke was a very deliberate gesture. Horace's *Epistle* I.1 was one of Bolingbroke's favorite poems, and while in exile in France, he had made a couplet translation of its most Stoic passage. Bolingbroke responded to Horace's attack on Roman materialism and was greatly cheered in his exile by Horace's Stoic advice that we should wean ourselves away from worldly pelf.[13] But clearly, Pope was far more aware of the difficulties involved in "easing the heart of all that it admires," and his poem is a rebuke to Bolingbroke's facile philosophizing.

The poem's center of gravity is not to be located in its public, political, topical content. Propaganda for the "Patriot" cause is certainly included, but it lacks the piquancy that a few personal victims would normally supply. Furthermore, the normal tactical basis of opposition propaganda is to separate off the main body of the people from the corrupt cabal of King and ministers that is bleeding them white. Lines 120–33, in following Horace's Latin very closely and identifying the people with the "many-headed Beast" of Revelation 13:1–2, deliberately blunt the cutting edges of partisan weapons. In fact, the satire is at once more personal and more universal than this. Pope's main concern is the chronic inconsistency of human behavior, the average man's failure "to act consistent with himself an hour" (line 137). In this respect, the *Epistle* is a throwback to the *Moral Essays* and especially to the *Epistle to Burlington;* indeed, the Sir Job portrait in the *Epistle to Bolingbroke* (lines 138–47) is a dramatized development of the Villario sketch in the earlier work (lines 79–88). What imparts to the later poem its tolerant ethos and gentler pose is the poet's self-inclusion in its satiric sweep. It is framed by a direct evocation of Bolingbroke as an ambiguous presence, both frustrating and hopeful. It is made clear that Pope himself is in an inconsistent and confused state, by no means certain of his fate, and this mutes the satire, turning the whole into a satire manqué. Apart from the perfunctory political satire, which operates as a kind of mnemonic checklist of Bolingbrokean themes, Pope indulges in a fairly delicate comedy of manners. Lines 148–60 mock the absurd preten-sions to fashion among the poor, who, in a Billingsgate parody of their betters, "Prefer a new Japanner to their shoes" (156). However, the poet's main business is to put his spiritual house in order, and the movement is from a firm resolve in the opening lines to journey unassisted through the quagmires of philosophy, through a loss of confidence occasioned, perhaps, by a conviction that he is not immune to the common fate of mankind, to an insecure appeal to Bolingbroke for help at the close. Thus, the poem's structure reverses that of the *Epistle to Dr. Arbuthnot*, which dramatizes a process of the physician healing himself. The two crucial passages that distinguish this poem from all others are lines 23–34 and 161–88.

Pope has announced at the outset his intention to abandon the active public life he has pursued hitherto: "Public too long, ah let me hide my age!" He is now forty-nine, and on the theory of the climacteric years, the theory that persons were particularly subject to changes of fortune or health every seven years and especially so on odd multiples of seven, a falling away of poetic power can be expected. Even "modest Cibber," who for several years has been coming in and out of retirement in a prima donna manner, has decided to leave the stage. It is a time, says Pope, for spiritual stocktaking. Line 23 comes in response to an implied question from his absent friend Bolingbroke—who will Pope regard as his spiritual mentors? The lines that follow (24–34) have never been satisfactorily explained by critics, who frequently pass them over without comment. Yet it is here that Pope most apparently departs from Horace. There is no basis in the original for this assertion of the claims of rival philosophies, and therefore we need to account for it. Dustin Griffin regards the lines as "an engaging portrait of [Pope's inconstancy] . . . viewed as eclecticism and flexibility."[14] Thomas Maresca argues that Pope here presents himself as a living example of harmonious opposites, as the properly concordant man who can reconcile completely divergent viewpoints within himself—who can assimilate Montaigne and Locke and the active life of the politician Lyttelton with the spiritual life of both the pagan Aristippus and the Christian St. Paul.[15] Neither of these views does justice to the tone of Pope's lines. There is something in the diction that alerts us to the possibility that Pope is not happy with his eclecticism:

> Back to my native Moderation slide,
> And win my way by yielding to the tyde.

The religious pun on "backsliding" into moderation and the pusillanimous metaphor of yielding to the tide suggest some weakening of principle, some invertebracy about this state of mind. Clearly, Pope contrasts Montaigne with Locke as representatives of different philosophical ways of thinking, and similarly contrasts Aristippus with St. Paul, asserting a capricious freedom to choose between them as the wind blows. Pope's eclecticism here is a deliberate affront to the reader; most affronted of all would have been the reader to whom the poem is dedicated.

Montaigne and Locke were regarded as opposites in the eighteenth century, in that the former typified the loose, unmethodical, rambling essayist and the latter the tight, strictly logical thinker. Prior wrote in 1721 *A Dialogue between Mr John Lock and Seigneur de Montaigne,* which ends with Montaigne reducing Lockean principles to absurdity by showing in Shandean detail the thought processes of Locke's servant John when enjoined to go downstairs and sup. But Pope's allusion here is not of that public nature. It is a purely private reference to Bolingbroke's own estimation of Locke and Montaigne. Bolingbroke considered Locke too gullible a Christian in that he accepted many theological arguments about the nature of the Deity, whereas Montaigne on the contrary was too skeptical about the narrow limits within which we can have certain knowledge of God's law of nature.[16] Similarly, Aristippus, the founder of the Cyrenaic school, was a great favorite of Bolingbroke's because he believed that particular pleasures were desirable per se and that bodily pleasures were superior to mental pleasures. Among the Twickenham circle, Bolingbroke was given the nickname *Aristippus* because of his addiction to the pleasures of the flesh and his chronic overspending.[17] St. Paul, on the other hand, was Bolingbroke's bête noire because he had corrupted Christ's teaching by introducing pagan practices and his own personal theories of predestination and unlimited passive obedience.[18]

The passage is, then, an assertion of the poet's freedom from his erstwhile mentor. Pope picks his way skillfully through the minefield of Bolingbroke's philosophical allegiances, signposting his own independence. After all, it has to be admitted that his trust in his "Guide, Philosopher, and Friend" had proved misplaced, leading to insecurity and muddle, so much so that at this late stage of his life, he is in need of re-education, as he admits in lines 47–48. In the poem's closing passage (161–88), Pope makes a final plea to Bolingbroke to put the poet's house in order. Bolingbroke is accused of regarding only the trivial inconsistencies in Pope's dress and external appearance. But Pope protests that the grubby wig and collar, the incongruous coat and breeches are an objective correlative to the state of his soul. The lines "I plant, root up, I build, and then confound, / Turn round to square, and square again to round" express in domestic gardening and building imagery the chaos of Pope's life. In Jeremiah 1:10, God entrusts the prophet with a mission: "I have this day set thee over nations and over the kingdoms, to root out, and to pull down, and to destroy, and to throw down, to build and plant." Will Bolingbroke be to Pope the prophet that he once was and turn him into "That Man divine whom Wisdom calls her own"?

The closing lines exploit a fruitful syntactic ambiguity. Pope ends the poem with a portrait of the truly wise man that is a composite of various of his friends—John Gay "without Fortune bless'd," Jonathan Swift "Great without Title," Bishop Atterbury "free, tho' in the tower"—and though the lines are in apposition to "me" (line 179), most of the references are also applicable to Bolingbroke. "Rich ev'n when plunder'd" may refer to the attempt to withhold an inheritance from Lady Bolingbroke because her husband was attainted; "Great without Title" to his gaining a viscountcy rather than the earldom he expected; "follow'd without power" to his being leader of the opposition despite not being permitted to take his seat in the Lords. "Just less than Jove" is very typical of the hyperbolical way Pope was wont to refer to him: to Warburton on 12 January 1744, he calls him "a Being paullo minus ab angelis." And Bolingbroke's fits of depression and giddiness are frequently mentioned in his letters. Thus, with the punctured climax that stops the poet in mid-flight just as his head is about to disappear into the clouds, the poet is seeing through his own preposterousness and, simultaneously, demythologizing Bolingbroke. He completes the process of reappraisal, and "a Fit of Vapours clouds this Demigod" is, I think, Pope's last word in verse about his former hero.

The Critics and the *Imitations*

The reading that I have offered is, like my reading of the *Essay on Man*, an example of biographical criticism. Throughout this book I have argued strongly that some of Pope's thought patterns were formed in the crucible of his friendship with Bolingbroke and that therefore an understanding of that friendship is germane to the appreciation of the poems. The *Epistle to Bolingbroke* is a special case because it is not merely influenced by its author's absorption of Bolingbroke's concerns and characteristic attitude toward them, but is actually *about* this absorption. It is a good test case for the entire argument. At stake here is an issue much wider than the question of whether Bolingbroke is judged to have influenced Pope's poetry: it is a question of the terms in which we discuss the literature of the Augustan era. Some years ago, T. S. Eliot introduced the phase *dissociation of sensibility* into his essay on the metaphysical poets to describe a disintegration of unified experience into the modes of thought and modes of feeling, a disintegration that he considered to have actually occurred in the seventeenth century. Now unfashionable as a view of intellectual and poetic history, this concept seems to describe accurately enough the way *critics* respond to the poetry of the eighteenth and early nineteenth centuries. In general, critics attribute "thought" to the poetry of Pope's era and "feeling" to that of Wordsworth. They see classical learning and the use of allusion as inimical to the expression of feeling and are hostile to the notion that Augustan poetry can be emotive at base, speaking, through a very personal use of allusion, directly to the heart. Satire seems to me to be the most emotive, least rational of art forms, founded as it is on atavistic satisfaction. Yet no poet has suffered more than Alexander Pope from the prejudice against a purely rational poetry.

There can scarcely be another poet writing in English who tells us more about himself than does Pope in the *Imitations of Horace*. However widely this observation is acknowledged, it remains a commonplace in Pope criticism that he does not tell us about himself in any intimate sense. What is normally implied by describing Pope as an "Augustan" against the group of poets referred to as "Romantics" is that while the latter laid bare their own souls in their verse, Pope asserted the social function of the poet in a public voice. He worked in well-defined areas of poetic expression; his poems are genre pieces—imitation, essay, the mock-heroic—so that, in the words of a recent critic, "they are all 'public' poems belonging to established forms or patterns recognizable by Pope's contemporaries."[19] Recent criticism has affirmed that despite the extraordinarily fecund detailing of the poet in his everyday circumstances that goes on in the *Imitations*, there is a concealment of the "real self." Those critics who believe that Pope's poems cannot be understood apart from the Horatian originals on which they are modeled have supported the conception of Pope the public poet by emphasizing that Pope is governed in what he *can* say by what Horace has *already* said. Pope's poems are represented as open systems of allusion to a publicly available referent (Horace's poems) and can be accounted for in terms of the classical tradition to which he belongs.[20]

The other major critical parti pris is that Pope's manipulations of Horace so completely efface the original that they must stand as independent poems and be appreciated in their own right. The impetus behind this approach has been supplied by those who, like Elder Olson, had bigger critical fish to fry.[21] Olson objected to recent revaluations of Pope which assumed that "man and work are inseparable" and went on to read the poems as unique structures rather than as illustrations of "some quality of Pope . . . the man." Subsequently, the *Imitations* have been regarded as purely rhetorical triumphs, and at least since Maynard Mack's article "The Muse of Satire," critics have imported from the language of dramatic criticism the concept of *persona* or *mask* to connote that the voices heard are not those of the historic Pope, but are deliberate distortions of the actual, undertaken with hortatory intentions.[22] Much of the time, using such terms implies a commitment to the disregarding of all so-called extraliterary considerations. Pope comes to be regarded as an orator or public speaker whose history and character are presumed irrelevant to the poems. Curiously, the two competing ways of reading the *Imitations* converge on the same ground in the end. Laying stress on manipulation, either of mode or of rhetorical strategy, they diminish the poet's actual and intimate presence in the poems.

In denying that the poems are instinct with their creator's own personality and in claiming that the words on the page are only ostensibly, but not actually, about the historical Pope, the critics have not served their author well. They have deprived the reader of one main source of pleasure to be gained from reading poetry, the pleasure of discovering a man; and since it has been regarded as a defining feature of "Augustan" poetry that this kind of pleasure is not to be had, there has remained little incentive to read the poems at all. I regard it as an entirely healthy sign, therefore, that these views have been losing ground in recent years. Critics can now be found who are prepared to say that Pope tries to be, as far as possible, convincingly himself in the poems and that he does speak about the "real self" as honestly as he knew how.[23] But even yet, few critics will go so far as to say that Pope ever speaks about his own inner feelings, emotional states, and deep-rooted insecurities. Accepting him as a personal poet, we still draw the line at considering him a private one.[24]

In the preceding argument, I have tried to take the present revaluation of Pope a little further by showing that in the *Epistle to Bolingbroke*, the poet is anatomizing and reconsidering one of the most important and formative friendships of his life. The poem was written at a sensitive and crucial period in Pope's relationship with Bolingbroke, and it reflects the poet's uncertainty about the nature of his mentor's influence and about his own spiritual health. In parts, it is as close to being a confessional poem as even Coleridge comes. Insofar as Pope performs the function of the public poet, the social critic who speaks from the standpoint of the public conscience, he does so without his accustomed conviction. Whereas elsewhere in his poems, notably in book 4 of the revised *Dunciad* and in the *Epilogue to the Satires,* Pope was able to elaborate a coherent view of his enemies as depraved sinners who have created an anti-Christian society, in this poem his social criticism is generalized and diffident. As a poem of spiritual introspection, it reflects the poet's mood at the time of writing in early 1738, and this, as we have seen, was far from confident. He no longer put his full trust in Bolingbroke, who had stood guarantor for the deism that replaced the Catholic faith of Pope's forefathers. Laying his harvest up for the last day, it seemed to Pope that he was not on the side of the angels any more than the vacillating Flavios or Jobs of his observation. The poet's voice is disillusioned rather than confident, and his modification of Horace ends with a confession of personal failure. Allusions to the Bible, to literary works, and to eminent persons in public office are subordinate to private allusions that draw their meaning from the context of a particular friendship. Literary criticism confirms the expectations that are formed by the reader familiar with Pope's biography. The *Epistle to Bolingbroke* is, therefore, an entirely candid work.

Chapter 8

The Common Language

Bolingbroke versus Walpole

With the facts of their lives in front of us, it is now time to examine Bolingbroke's political thought more closely in order to reconstruct its appeal for a poet with Pope's satirical gifts. It is very much a case of reconstruction because as the introductory chapter makes clear, recent historians find little enough in Bolingbroke's oeuvre to attract the reader. Walpole's career has been rehabilitated by revisionist historians who have challenged the hackneyed image of him as a bluff, red-faced Norfolk squire whose main policy was to have no policy, a noninterventionist who preferred to leave things as they were. On the issue of financial corruption especially, Walpole's reputation has fared rather better in recent times. P. G. M. Dickson's authoritative study of the financial revolution in England during this period concludes that Bolingbroke's views on the "Robinocracy," the political stranglehold exerted by the financial elite in collaboration with court politicians, were little more than hysterical prejudices. Walpole understood that his policies needed to coordinate the interests of both the landed aristocratic and gentleman farmers and the international City financiers. Far from letting sleeping dogs lie, he was concerned with "creating a helpful political and social climate for individual economic initiatives, strengthening the relations of the government with the financial community in the City of London and repaying as much as possible of the nation's debts while at the same time taking care to conciliate the traditional landed and farming interests of the country, and to make it clear that the supremacy of the Established Church was not in danger."[1] According to Dickson, Walpole sought political unity through social and economic progress. Dickson wholly approves Walpole's handling of the government's short-term and long-term credit requirement: indeed, his ministry allowed for a period of respite from war, during which landed and trading interests could unite behind a strong dynasty and the Commons could become the central policymaking agency.

Increasingly, modern historians such as Dickson seem to justify the means by the end when assessing Walpole's achievement, considering that the stability created by the Walpolean system could only be achieved by skillful manipulation of patronage. Practices denounced by Bolingbroke as corrupt are held to have been inevitable and therefore, in some sense, not corrupt. Bolingbroke's objections are considered shrill and exaggerated. Equally heavily criticized has been Bolingbroke's attempt to change the structure of politics from the party system to a model of political conflict based on the older court and country nomenclature. He argued that the party distinctions that really existed in seventeenth-century politics were obviated by the settlement of 1688; the political nation was now divided into the court interest—the chief minister and the financial paladins whose invisible wealth maintained him in office—and the country interest, which is that of the nation at large. Such a view inhibited the necessary growth of institutionalized opposition because it was based on the premise that a perfectly functioning government would command universal approbation. Opposition, to Bolingbroke, was a desperate remedy that could only be justified in a state of national emergency, when the constitution and civil liberty were endangered. The opponent of government was either a "Patriot," selflessly acting in his country's interest, or he was a factionalist and a danger to the body politic. Under normally functioning government, the M.P. would be "independent," that is, inert.

Historians who follow Edmund Burke in arguing that Bolingbroke did not contribute to the evolution of modern political institutions are often unaware of the extent to which opposition of any kind was regarded as an enterprise of doubtful legality. Bolingbroke constantly faced charges of sedition and treason, in the teeth of which he continued a de facto opposition. Although he did not attempt to justify opposition for its own sake, his unremittingly trenchant conduct of the antigovernment campaign indubitably paved the way for those later politicians who did argue the respectability of opposition per se. A recent historian of the period, B. W. Hill, accuses Bolingbroke of being both wrong and insincere about the nonexistence of parties: "Bolingbroke's assertion that the true division was 'between constitutionalists and anti-constitutionalists, or of a court and a country party' . . . [has] often been quoted as a description of mid-eighteenth-century politics rather than as what [it was]: part of a campaign to deny the reality of party differences which were obstructing his own advancement."[2] This view can be identified with those of Namierite historians who regard all political ideology as more or less hogwash. It deserves further examination, since Namierite historians have made the most effective assault on Bolingbroke's reputation.

One of the major reasons for the continuing interest in Bolingbroke is that his career brings into sharp focus the problematic nature of the relationship between political ideology and political action. Sir Lewis Namier's view that political ideas are irrelevant to the determination of action and that the only eighteenth-century reality was the struggle for power has had considerable influence. According to Namier, Bolingbroke's ideology is merely a function of his need to say *something*, to drape respectably the piano legs of ambition. This conception of politics as merely a frenzied hunt for office and place leads to biography that stresses the opportunistic and the instrumental in political action. As may be imagined, Bolingbroke does not fare well at the hands of such biographers, who regard his political indiscretions as good grounds for dismissing his ideas wholesale. Quite clearly, the pattern of this reasoning is circular. Quentin Skinner has pointed out, in a very shrewd article, that if Bolingbroke's ideas are in Namier's term *flapdoodle*, they are a peculiarly consistent brand, developed over a period of years, focusing on specific issues and with a specific content.[3] Namierites cannot explain why an ideology should be of one character rather than another. In the end, they cannot really account for the ideological element of political thought at all, since it is not convincing to regard it as merely another tactic. Recent work on Bolingbroke has partly resurrected his reputation in response to the Namierite challenge. In the last few years, historians sympathetic to Bolingbroke have argued that his ideology was a sincere expression of his fears for English political liberties.[4] Theories about the most desirable political dispensation, about the aims of government, and about the best way to exercise power were significant and did involve the conflict of sincerely held principles. Those historians who have best evaluated this period have been those who, like J. P. Kenyon, have not assumed that what happens in history is what is bound to happen and who, unlike Dickson, Hill, and often Plumb, have tried to represent the political choices of the period as they appeared to the men responsible for making them. Kenyon's conclusion about the Walpole era is as follows:

> . . . The Whigs became oligarchic and mercenary, with no thought for reform, toleration or popular participation in government. Having consolidated their power by the Septennial Act, they viewed with complacency an increasing electoral corruption which worked in the interests of the governing class . . . Modern cynicism applauds the skilful techniques employed, and justifies the means by reference to the end, which was constitutional parliamentary government unruffled by popular revolutions. But this begs the question; had another choice been made, a better, or at least a different kind of government could have emerged much earlier. Had the Septennial Act not been passed, had a firm line been taken with electoral corruption, had the abuse of patronage been curbed, had a proper system of government accounting been instituted and all placemen barred from the House of Commons, the face of eighteenth-century England could not have been worse, and might well have been better.[5]

The England that Kenyon is describing here is the England that Bolingbroke earnestly desired to see. He was convinced that a new England would rise out of the ashes of the old if two major changes of direction could be effected in national policy: the subsumption of the two-party system into a single party government of national unity, and the ascendancy to power of a Patriot King whose leadership would be by moral example rather than by political manipulation. To Pope, as I shall argue, the attraction of Bolingbroke's analysis of the nation in decay and of his proposed remedy was that it presented exactly the social vision that satire was best fitted to express. Bolingbroke's views were moderate, patriotic, and strongly ethical—suggestible to Pope because his own personality responded very ardently to these values and because, as I shall contend in the next chapter, Pope inherited the satirist's art at a juncture when the satirist still had to argue the legitimacy of his enterprise. Pope made a major contribution not only to the practice of satire but also to its apologetics, and he did this by stressing its ethical utility. It became, in Pope's hands, the art of the embattled moderate, determined to arrest the symptoms of national decline by effecting a wholesale improvement in morals. His satire and Bolingbroke's essays published in the *Craftsman* are twin weapons of a single campaign.

Bolingbroke's Political Program

It is hardly an exaggeration to say that the creation of political stability out of the unpromising materials of eighteenth-century political life was miraculous. Walpole performed the miracle by fostering what Isaac Kramnick calls "a rigorously articulated system of corruption."[6] Perhaps more subtly, J. H. Plumb describes Walpole's methods of creating dependable parliamentary majorities as a strengthening of the executive.[7] To Plumb, the potential for political stability was inherently present in post-Revolutionary society, but its realization required the managerial acumen of a Walpole. England's virtually unremitting state of war between 1689 and 1713 was more significant even than the constitutional settlement of 1689 in shaping the future of British political life. The wars required government spending far in excess of revenue acquired from taxation and necessitated the development of a complex system of public borrowing, ushering in the banks and the stock exchange, stimulating the growth of the insurance industry and the trading companies, and injecting into commercial life all the aspects of management of the national debt and paper credit. Effective naval, military, and diplomatic finance and the growth of the system designed to provide it called for efficient administration. Between 1680 and 1720, all the major state departments grew enormously, particularly the Treasury, which became a very large employer indeed, and government service became a magnet for place-hunters in search of lucrative advancement. Manipulation of such patronage as accrued from this strengthening of the executive would become the linchpin of ministerial power.

Coeval with these developments in public finance was the establishment of Parliament itself as the focus of British political life. It grew at the expense of the court, as the Revolution Settlement ensured that it would, and in 1695 the Triennial Act established its permanence and regularity.[8] Political power, office, and place would derive from membership; as membership became more desirable, the cost of election became higher, with prospective members being forced into extravagant spending in their constituencies. The high cost of electioneering, and the tendency to regard such spending as an investment to be repaid by the returns of office, helped to undermine the independence of the average M.P. and to ensure that there were always votes for sale. Again, adroit manipulation of such mercenary hunger by the ministry could impose on the conduct of parliamentary business a coherence that would certainly have been absent without it. Walpole's monopoly over all the important sources of patronage was assured by the 1730s, and this, as the Tory opposition plaintively cried, was one condition of the success and longevity of his ministry. *Corruption* to members of the opposition was a generic term for the methods through which Walpole sought to impose single-party government; it is perhaps slightly naive on Kramnick's part to accept the opposition's evaluation of the facts. In the absence of party discipline, or indeed any real basis for political unity, the exploitation of industrious, often talented placemen was the only means of ensuring that administrative work was carried on. If any of the various attempts to exclude placemen from Parliament by legislation had succeeded, the result would have been administrative anarchy. Under Walpole's management, parliamentary institutions stabilized but did not develop.

Changes in the structure of politics like these indicated above, which fashioned the Whigs into the party of government, were not the only conditions of stability. Both parties had to adapt themselves to post-Revolutionary circumstances in their ideological accounts of how and to what ends power was to be wielded. For the Tories, this involved relinquishing many of their central tenets—passive obedience, nonresistance, divine right, and indefeasable hereditary succession—whereas Whig ideology modified in a conservative direction, as the party elite strove to confine power to property owners. Thus, as the Tories became less authoritarian and the Whigs less radical, the conditions of ideological stability were gradually evolved. Partisan distinctions became less significant as both sides came to accept the notion of an ancient constitution and recognized the sovereignty of crown, Lords, and Commons. Conflict arose in the period we are studying out of dispute over the moral quality of those in power. There was no doubt that the English constitution and mixed-government system was as strong a dispensation as possible. But was it being worked properly? The danger arose from corruption, the inevitable result of the new financial system. This threatened to upset the delicate equilibrium between crown and Parliament that had been achieved in 1688. Opposition to the ruling clique at court based on the fear of corruption can properly be termed a country rather than Tory position. In the 1730s, Bolingbroke articulated the principles of country opposition in a forceful and coherent way. Because his faith in existing institutions was so strong, his critique was largely directed toward the moral fiber of those in office, and this made it a suggestive politics of satire.[9]

Bolingbroke's task as absentee leader of the opposition—absentee because the terms of his pardon did not allow him to take his seat in the Lords—was to formulate the principles on which all potential enemies of the Walpole administration could unite, to focus both on perennial and specific issues that could be raised in Parliament, and to orchestrate the coalition of M.P.s cemented by his ideological principles in the defeat of Walpole's parliamentary majority. Even the increased patronage wielded by Georgian administrations was insufficient to satisfy completely the appetite for power and lucre of their parliamentarians, and therefore there were Whig malcontents who could be useful allies. William Pulteney was such an ally, though his chief allegiance was always to himself rather than to Bolingbroke. And of course, there were independent members of both parties who were not being retained on pensions or in places by the chief minister. Such men as the principled Sir William Wyndham, leader of the independent Tories, were open to arguments about the need for coalition against the ruinously corrupt ministerial clique and did see themselves in the role that Bolingbroke cast them in, as watchdogs of the constitution and preservers of parliamentary purity. In a sense it was this group, especially the Whig sector, that provided the dynamic for the politics of the period, because Walpole also needed to solicit their support to supplement the assured votes of his dependents; and they were the target of the ideological and propagandist warfare.

Another major parliamentary grouping was the Jacobite Tories, but their support was increasingly an embarrassment to Bolingbroke. It was his Achilles' heel and his gravest political mistake that he had flirted with Jacobitism in France just after the 1715 Rebellion. That fact crippled his resistance to Walpole's tactic of, in Speaker Onslow's words, "having everybody to be deemed a Jacobite who was not a professed and known Whig." There was little-enough reason for Bolingbroke to be optimistic about his chances of gaining power. No one wanted to ally with the

Jacobites, anyone cooperating with the Pulteneyites could not be sure of his bargain, and the independent Whigs, particularly those who formed the nucleus of the so-called Patriot opposition in the mid and late 1730s, loathed the thought that to gain power themselves, they might have to open the gates to Tories. What is surprising is not that Bolingbroke failed to achieve his aim in over a decade of sustained political activity, but that on one or two occasions he came very close to doing so, notably in 1733 over the excise crisis. That he achieved so much is due in large measure to the quality of his journalism and to the sheer imaginative power and vivacity of the ideology, almost the mythology, that he created. Like the majority of contemporary historians, Plumb is uncharitable to Bolingbroke's ideas:

> His hope was a renewed, reinvigorated country-party—by 1734 a hope as utterly futile, as ridiculously unrealistic, as the rest of Bolingbroke's political philosophy.[10]

Plumb speaks here with the clear vision of hindsight. Let us inspect the ideas that captured not power, but rather the imaginations of the foremost literary men in England.

In his principal theoretical works, the *Remarks on the History of England* and *A Dissertation upon Parties*, and in the later treatise *The Idea of a Patriot King*, Bolingbroke elaborated a number of arguments.[11] England's ancient constitution is seen as preserving the traditional political liberties of the English nation as long as it is respected by the government whose duty it is to put it into practice. At times, Bolingbroke speaks as though this constitution is as old as the original contract that took men out of a state of nature and into civil society. He is unsure whether it is prehistorical in origin, but the pedigree of English constitutional liberty became verifiable historical fact in Saxon times; their Wittena Gemote was a prototype of a modern parliament.[12] The form of the constitution is described in terms deriving, most modern scholars agree, from Aristotle, Polybius, and Machiavelli, though Bolingbroke receives them in a version filtered through the tradition of seventeenth-century Whig political theory, and in particular from Harrington's *Oceana*.

In Bolingbroke's view, the constitution prescribes a mixed government in which the three estates—monarchy, aristocracy, and democracy—govern in harmony under the presidency of the king as chief executive. Such a constitutional government will function perfectly provided one of the estates does not attempt to encroach on the independent functioning of another and arrogate to itself more power than is its right. The crown rather than the peers or the people poses the threat in this respect. Kings, being so to speak a one-man institution, find it most difficult to separate their personal from their public interests, and are liable to pursue the power that gratifies personal ambition even if it is unhealthy for the constitution. Bolingbroke spends some time in his political writings refuting theories of absolute monarchy proposed by Hobbes and Filmer, though arguably Locke had left little to be done in this province.[13]

The term *corrupt*, in the first of the three important senses in which Bolingbroke uses it and its cognates, defines the state of the constitution when this usually royal encroachment takes place. Human nature and the nature of political institutions are such that corruption of this kind is endemic in a nation's history; it will break out periodically, and when it does the only remedy is a return to the original principles of constitutional government, to be achieved by a cleansing process more fully described in *The Idea of a Patriot King*. In recent history, the Stuart monarchs Charles II and James II provide an example of royal abuse of the constitution when they attempted to rule by arbitrary sway, imposing an illegal religion on the people and neglecting the opposition of the Commons as well as the attempted mediation of the Lords. This tyrannical behavior had a disastrous effect on the nation, driving men into opposing parties according to whether they upheld the divine right of the hereditary monarch and the principles of nonresistance and passive obedience (Tories), or alternatively recognized an immediate need to exclude a Catholic monarch from the throne (Whigs). This partisan struggle was resolved by the Revolution Settlement and the accession of William III, a triumph for moderation and reason, since the Settlement, in finding a constitutional solution to the succession problem, discovered a middle way between reactionary, slavish Toryism and anarchistic, republican Whiggery. The Revolution of 1688 in fact represented just such a check on corruption and a return to the balanced, purified form of the original constitution as Bolingbroke believed to be periodically essential. What 1688 also accomplished—and here is one of Bolingbroke's major convictions—was the dissolution of genuine party distinctions. Parties, Bolingbroke urged, were rendered obsolete in English political life, because since the Whigs had stopped short of republicanism and the Tories—all except the lunatic fringe of Jacobites—had abandoned the obtuseness of divine right, nonresistance, and passive obedience, there are now no genuine issues, religious or political, on which bona fide members of the body politic could possibly be divided. *Whig* and *Tory* are therefore now empty and meaningless labels, appertaining no longer to parties but to factions. It is characteristic of factions that they substitute private for public good. They are promoted and manipulated by unscrupulous men for their own ends, and their existence is an index of the corrupt state of society.[14] Dishonest ministries will promote factions in order to destroy the concerted criticism which alone can bring them down—and which Bolingbroke was trying to arouse.

In 1688, then, the constitution was compromised by the inordinate ambition of the crown. But, argued Bolingbroke, there are ways other than encroachment and arbitrary rule of the monarch by which a constitution can be traduced and a state of corruption begun. If the independence of Parliament is undermined by bribery—if money replaces royal prerogative as the stifler of liberty—an even more dangerous threat is posed. This, says Bolingbroke, is the state of the nation at the present time. In this respect the 1688 settlement was not a foolproof return to original constitutional principles: it blocked the patent, but not the latent attacks on the constitution, insofar as it limited the power of the monarch but failed to establish by law parliamentary independence of royal patronage. (Specifically, Bolingbroke is referring here to the failure to enact a bill for the exclusion of placemen and pensioners from Parliament.) Bolingbroke argues that at present there is a national state of emergency, even more serious than that of 1688, caused by the breach of the various constitutional safeguards.

Corruption, in the second sense of the term (besides the constitutional sense noted previously), is a specific word for the gamut of illicit practices being used by the Walpole ministry to do this damage. They include electoral bribery, the retention of placemen and the feeing of pensioners, the maintenance of a standing army, the refusal to hold frequent elections, the failure to account for government spending, and the artificial and malicious propagation of party distinctions. All these techniques were being pressed into the service of a governmental *divide et impera* policy. In Letter 13 of the *Dissertation upon Parties,* Bolingbroke integrates his political platform with its theoretical infrastructure by arguing that the constitution demands the independence of Parliament and the frequent convention and dissolution of it.[15] Triennial as opposed to septennial parliaments, for which the opposition strove as a means of breaking Walpole's continuity in office, are argued to be constitutional rights. Governments of the day are therefore not entitled to tamper with this right.

Bolingbroke's attack on financial corruption is conducted on a very wide front. His argument is not merely confined to the specific grievances designated above, which were always good for raising a heated debate in the House; it amounts to an attack on what he conceived to be the social and economic consequences of the financial revolution. Large financial institutions and corporations had become powerful pressure groups on government. Indeed, the relationship between the leaders of government and finance is best described as a cabal or a conspiracy to deny the landed gentry their stake in governing the country. The establishment of public borrowing was accompanied by taxation increases that bore most heavily on landowners and that created armies of civil servants, all working in the ministry's interest. Stock-jobbing was the apogee of self-interest and graft.

As Harry Dickinson has it: "Bolingbroke and the Tories could never accept that the system of public credit and the rise of the moneyed interest had been natural consequences of the Revolution."[16] The moneyed interest represented to him a dislocation of the social order, and its influence on government was wholly pernicious. To Bolingbroke, Parliament is as dependent upon the court in his day as ever it was prior to 1688, but the interests served by the present form of unconstitutional government are not those of the King himself. Rather, they are those of the chief minister and the financial elite who support him. In campaigns conducted in the *Craftsman* and in all his writings before the death of his hopes, Bolingbroke is careful to present the King as the too trusting, too good-natured dupe of unscrupulous, self-serving politicians.[17] He was well aware that no ministry could hope to prosper without the royal blessing, despite the limitations now placed on regal power. Isaac Kramnick's *Bolingbroke and His Circle* discusses at length Bolingbroke's conception of the effect that the new economic order and the social mobility that resulted from it was having on the traditional model of government; political control was being wrested away from its proper location, the landed gentry, whose stake in their country's prosperity was as tangible as the acres they improved. Little needs to be added to Kramnick's analysis.

The term *corruption* is given yet a third significance in Bolingbroke's political writings. It describes the national "spirit," the morale of the nation, when the people are degenerate enough to allow such violations of the constitution to occur. It is important to remember that Bolingbroke considered the constitution indestructible even by wicked ministers, as long as the people themselves do not collude. At present, Bolingbroke says, the people of Britain are infected by "party spirit," the toxic counterpart to "the spirit of liberty and patriotism," a collective ethical sickness, for which the emetic effect of satire is one possible cure:

> Nothing can destroy the constitution of Britain, but the people of Britain; and whenever the people of Britain become so degenerate and base, as to be induced by corruption . . . then may the enemies of our constitution boast that they have got the better of it, and that it is no longer able to preserve itself, nor to defend liberty. Then will that trite, proverbial speech be verified in our case, "that the corruptions of the best things are the worst"; for then will that very change in the state of property and power, which improved our constitution so much, contribute to the destruction if it; and we may even wish for those little tyrants, the great lords and the great prelates again, to oppose the encroachments of the crown. How preferable will [appear] subjection to those powerful landlords . . . when they shall see the whole nation oppressed by a few upstarts in power; often by the meanest, always by the worst of their fellow-subjects; by men, who owe their elevation and riches neither to

merit or birth, but to the favour of weak princes, and to the spoils of their country, beggared by their rapine. Then will the fate of Rome be renewed, in some sort, in Britain.[18]

This densely packed rhetorical passage contains many of Bolingbroke's characteristic attitudes and ideas. Caste attitudes, the notion of noblesse oblige and the patrician privilege to govern earned by talent and pedigree, are prominent at the end of the passage, alongside the intense contempt for the new men. The reference to that "very change in the state of property and power, which improved our constitution so much" is one of the many glances at the work of the seventeenth-century political philosopher James Harrington, whose *Oceana* was a utopian work greatly influential on Bolingbroke. Put simply, Harrington's view was that the constitutional balance of the three estates depended on the allocation between them of land. Greatest power would be wielded by the class who owned most land. Harrington's analysis of his own society revealed a shift in the distribution of land and therefore of power from the nobility to the gentry, occasioning a movement away from aristocracy toward popular government in the form of the constitution. At once consoling and disturbing, this theory presented Bolingbroke with an ideal exemplar of constitutional equilibrium at a specific juncture in history, but it also reminded him that the balance of power could shift again, this time in the direction of financial oligarchy. Kramnick accurately describes him as "a frightened Harringtonian."[19] That phrase is testimony to the use made throughout Bolingbroke's work of the exemplary significance of history. According to him, history has shown that if corruption is allowed to spread, the total emasculation of the nation will result. Elizabeth's reign was the zenith of good government according to the constitution; the Stuart monarchs, beginning with the perverse James I, caused the decline. Nations have been destroyed both because they lacked the mixed form of government and were riven by clashes between groups with opposing interests (ancient Rome and modern France), and because they had a mixed government but allowed one constituent to grow disproportionately powerful or failed to notice it happening (Spain and contemporary Britain). We are to learn from these precedents.

The last important link in the elaborate chain of Bolingbroke's reasoning is the inference from the view that the distinction between Whig and Tory is now spurious because it does not relate to any distinction in principle. This notion is stressed by Bolingbroke because he had to forge an opposition out of Tories as well as Whigs and needed to create a sense of common identity and purpose. Accordingly, Bolingbroke encouraged independent and honest parliamentarians to identify themselves as friends of the constitution: a genuine distinction in principle *does* now exist, between the friends and enemies of the constitution, to whom it is appropriate to apply the seventeenth-century nomenclature—the court and country parties. The country party of the 1730s, Bolingbroke pointed out, would carry on the older Whig tradition of guardianship of political liberty. For it was the Whigs, he admitted, who were zealous in their country's cause against the corruption of excessive royal prerogative during the reign of Charles II and his brother. Thus he was able to turn the tables on the Whigs by claiming that he was merely reviving the principles and values of their forebears, which the power of money had obliterated from their memories. He was, in Dickinson's phrase, "out-Whigging the Whigs."

Bolingbroke's Political Panacea

Recent scholars have shown that the ideas advanced by Bolingbroke have little originality. His concern with political liberty originates in Harrington and was propagated by Whig "neo-Harringtonians" at the time of the exclusion crisis. J. G. A. Pocock shows that many of Bolingbroke's concerns in the *Craftsman* campaigns and parliamentary debates after 1726 were developed in the writings of court critics in the reign of Charles II—standing armies, ministerial corruption, placemen, pensioners, the national debt, excise, and high taxation became shibboleths at that time. By the close of the seventeenth century and particularly from 1697 to 1700, we can find in writers like Henry Neville, Andrew Fletcher of Saltoun, Walter Moyle, John Toland, John Trenchard, and Robert Gordon attitudes that have the coherence of a country party manifesto.[20] From Pocock's summary of this manifesto we can see that its aims are to a large extent resurrected by Bolingbroke: in particular Bolingbroke agreed that it is the duty of most parliamentarians not to support or to work for the administration, but to supervise the operation of the executive, because the executive has various subversive means, collectively known as "corruption," of destroying the equilibrium prescribed by the constitution. Liberty and independence, the chief political virtues, are to be preserved by the catalogue of remedies familiar to readers of Bolingbroke: expulsion of placemen, frequent elections, disbanding the standing army, and so forth.[21]

Of course, the notion of the mixed government and the balanced constitution is not Bolingbroke's property or even that of the Whig commonwealthmen. Polybius in book 6 of his *History of Rome* argues that in addition to the simple constitutional forms of government, kingship, aristocracy, and democracy, there exists the mixed form of government that Lycurgus instituted in Sparta to protect against the vicious circle through which simple forms of government give way to their characteristic corruptions, tyranny, oligarchy, and mob rule.[22] The study of political degeneracy and declining liberty in the state was also undertaken by Machiavelli. From Machiavelli, Bolingbroke developed the quasi-scientific approach to the evils of corruption, the sense that by careful observation the process of decay could be arrested and the course of history changed. Returning to first constitutional principles is also Machiavelli's solution.[23] Neither is Bolingbroke's version of the contract theory original. In fact, it is closer to Aristotle than it is to Locke: the understanding that exists between ruler and ruled is in the nature of a bargain, to be maintained as long as the monarch holds the qualifications in virtue for which he is respected by the people. Aristotle's emphasis in the *Politics* on the virtue of the prince, the rule of law, and the willingness of subjects to be ruled is more influential on Bolingbroke than Locke's consent of free and equal individuals.

But lack of originality in Bolingbroke's work is not a serious defect since he himself presented his ideas as a record of "what oft was thought" but has now, grievously, been forgotten. There is still a virtuosity, even a brilliance in the rigorous application of his eclectic system to the specific instance of Walpole's corrupt ministry. Nevertheless, it must have been clear to him that after the defeat in the 1734 election and the failure to make due capital out of the excise, his ideology needed to point the way forward more clearly and positively. When the quarrels between Frederick, Prince of Wales and George II came into the open in 1737, Bolingbroke saw his opportunity of priming the prince with his ideas for a national and moral resurgence. His ideas on this were expressed in the form of an educative manual, *The Idea of a Patriot King*, that largely abandons the language of politics for that of morality. *The Idea of a Patriot King* was born out of battle fatigue, for it was written after the parliamentary campaign had failed, at a time when the younger members of the second-wave opposition known as Cobham's Cubs—men like Grenville, Pitt, and Lyttelton—were finding Bolingbroke a liability, a time also when he was conspicuously failing to persuade Carteret and Pulteney to unite in Chesterfield's "broad bottomed" opposition. But even allowing for the fact that the failure of Bolingbroke's practical campaigns manifests itself in this work in the form of future planning, the reader senses that Bolingbroke has entirely lost his grasp of politics as "the art of the possible." What sophistication the work has derives from its use of various *de regimine pricipum* conventions; particularly at the close of the work, Bolingbroke gives an almost Shakespearean account of the necessity of austere standards of personal behavior:

> Let not princes flatter themselves. They will be examined closely, in private as well as in public life: and those, who cannot pierce further, will judge of them by the appearances they give in both. To obtain true popularity, that which is founded in esteem and affection, they must,

therefore, maintain their characters in both; and to that end neglect appearances in neither, but observe the decorum necessary to preserve the esteem, whilst they win the affections of mankind. Kings, they must never forget that they are men: men, they must never forget that they are kings.[24]

This advice is not unlike that given by his illustrious namesake, Henry IV, to his son, and the criticism Henry IV makes of the "skipping King," Richard II, is in similar terms:

> The skipping King, he ambled up and down
> With shallow jesters and rash bavin wits,
> Soon kindled and soon burnt; carded his state;
> Mingled his royalty with cap'ring fools;
> Had his great name profaned with their scorns
> And gave his countenance, against his name,
> To laugh at jibing boys and stand the push
> Of every beardless vain comparative. (*Henry IV, Part 1*, 3.2.60–67)

In other respects than its often impressive stylistic elegance, the work is astonishingly naive. The argument can be briefly summarized. A return to the original and pure form of the constitution can now be effected only under the leadership of a Patriot King, who is prepared to put the nation's best interests before his own, ridding the administration of self-seeking ministers and their acolytes, subduing faction and promoting national unity, eliminating corruption in all its forms, and promoting trade and commerce. The quality of his rule is paternal:

> The true image of a free people, governed by a Patriot King, is that of a patriarchal family, where the head and all the members are united by one common interest, and animated by one common spirit: and where, if any are perverse enough to have another, they will be soon borne down by the superiority of those who have the same; and, far from making a division, they will but confirm the union of the little state.[25]

For the modern reader who grows up with a sense of tension between trades unions and government as the first postulate of political understanding, Bolingbroke's emphasis on national unity can seem very remote indeed. His ideal of government is not the arbitration between and conciliation of legitimately expressed, but opposing, interests; rather, he believed that a truly virtuous government would have no opposing interests to satisfy. They would drop away like so many rotten boughs of dead trees. This doctrine is indeed utopian—in three precise senses. It prescribes a uniform society in which there is universal consensus on prevailing values and institutional arrangements; it excludes structurally generated conflict—revolutions, or even a Parliament in which organized groups (parties) advance conflicting claims for power; and everything that happens in the reign of the Patriot King strengthens the status quo.[26] These objections are not mere anachronisms; nor is this the facile superiority of the modern mind. In his own time, Bolingbroke's opponents conceived the conflict between government and opposition in terms of the head-on collision of practical administration and utopian imagining.[27] Interesting in this connection is the pamphlet published by Edmund Burke shortly after Bolingbroke's death, *A Vindication of Natural Society*.[28] This clever parody is presented as a translation out of French of a work by Bolingbroke himself, and its stimulus is clearly the publication, two years previously, of the *Philosophical Works* in Mallet's edition. Many readers were outraged by the moral enormity of Bolingbroke's ideas on natural religion and considered them a thin cloak for atheism. Burke in his pamphlet adopts the persona of Bolingbroke himself. He first paints an appealing portrait of "natural society" as founded in "natural Appetites and Instincts" and argues that its replacement by political society, in which laws replace instincts, is a result of "the great Error of our Nature . . . not to know where to Stop." From there, he goes on to analyze the characteristic forms of government, including mixed government, support for which he acknowledges has been "a darling Mistake of my own," and shows that each breeds corruption, concluding that all forms of government are inferior to natural society, in which "life is simple, and therefore it is happy." Under the guise of Bolingbroke himself, Burke criticizes the utopian tendency of the former's writings: he makes his puppet Bolingbroke say, "I have defended Natural Religion against a Confederacy of Atheists and Divines. I now plead for Natural Society against Politicians, and for Natural Reason against all three."[29]

This spurious pamphlet is presented as a kind of *éclaircissement* similar to the philosophical writings. According to Burke, Bolingbroke was really driving at the destruction of all government, just as in the philosophical works he was really arguing for the end of all religion. He was in truth, suggests Burke, a rhapsodical, primitivist-anarchist. And it has to be conceded that *The Idea of a Patriot King* does not even allot to government the minimal policing function or even the very function for which other political philosophers think government instituted: the adjudication between competitive attempts by various individuals and groups to secure their own advantage. Logically, the virtues possessed by a Patriot King would work such a revolution in men's attitudes that governing them would be unnecessary. The realm presided over by the Patriot King would be the ultimate utopia, because it would combine an absence of authoritarian compulsion with maximal liberty of the individual and yet, at the same time, there would never be any conflict of interest. The demands of freedom and order would never create tension, as they do under most dispensations.

Nothing less than a revolution in human nature itself is being attempted by Bolingbroke in this treatise. His aim, it becomes clear, is not political change, but the moral transformation of the English nation. Quite simply, Bolingbroke's view is that unless men can somehow become morally superior, unless they can rise out of the sink of depravity and degradation that is present-day England, there is no hope for the future. Despite his own disclaimer—"I am not wild enough to suppose that a Patriot King can change human nature"—his thesis really belongs to the canon of moral literature. In his introduction, Bolingbroke belabors Walpole in evocative terms that E. M. Forster borrows in his essay "Two Cheers for Democracy," speaking of the "constant endeavour he has employed to corrupt the morals of men. I say thus generally, the morals; because he, who abandons or betrays his country, will abandon or betray his friend." Shortly after this he describes the task in hand thus: "to reinfuse the spirit of liberty, to reform the morals, and to raise the sentiments of the people." Such objectives as these are very close indeed to the satirical manifestos of Alexander Pope, insofar as both are concerned with the return to a state of primitive virtue, to be achieved through wholesale moral reform. One passage in particular in *The Idea of a Patriot King* stresses the magical powers the Patriot King possesses to effect a miraculous moral metamorphosis:

> As soon as corruption ceases to be an expedient of government, and it will cease to be such as soon as a Patriot King is raised to the throne, *the panacea is applied;* the spirit of the constitution revives of course; and, as fast as it revives, the orders and forms of the constitution are restored to their primitive integrity, and become what they were intended to be, real barriers against arbitrary power, not blinds nor masks under which tyranny may lie concealed. Depravation of manners exposed the constitution to ruin: reformation will secure it. *Men decline easily from virtue; for there is a devil too in the political system, a constant tempter at hand: a Patriot King will want neither power nor inclination to cast out this devil, to make the temptation cease, and to deliver his subjects, if not from the guilt, yet from the consequences of their fall.* Under him they will not only cease to do evil, but learn to do well; for by rendering public virtue and real capacity the sole means of acquiring any degree of power or profit in the state, he will set the passions of their hearts on the side of liberty and good government. A Patriot King is the most powerful of all reformers; for he is himself a sort of standing miracle, so rarely seen and so little understood, that the sure effects of his appearance will be admiration and love in every honest breast, confusion and terror to every guilty conscience, but submission and resignation in all. A new people will seem to arise with a new king. *Innumerable metamorphoses, like those which poets feign, will happen in very deed:* and while men

are conscious that they are the same individuals, the difference of their
sentiments will almost persuade them that they are changed into different
beings. [my italics][30]

In force, this passage could hardly be further away from the grave factual-
ity of political writing. Of particular interest to me are the sentences I have
italicized, which render political corruption in terms of the Christian
conception of evil and the degenerate British public as fallen men. Ronald
Paulson, in *The Fictions of Satire*, has argued that there is a "myth" or
"fiction" developed by Dryden and succeeding Tory satirists, especially
Swift and Pope, that is forged out of certain characteristic elements: in
Absalom and Achitophel, a civil war is established on analogy with the
rebellion of angels in heaven, a tempter who is the biblical and Miltonic
Satan, a dupe for the tempter to act upon, a fickle and apathetic mob, a plot
to sway them, and a countergroup of the loyal few representing God and
the angels.[31] Pope further develops the satanic image of evil and manipulated aspects of the Creation, the Temptation, and the Fall in the *Dunciad*,
the *Epistle to Dr. Arbuthnot*, and the *Epistle to Bathurst*. These elements
Paulson considers to be the identifying marks of "Tory" satire, though he
does not really say what is especially "Tory" about them. Reference to
Bolingbroke might well be thought to secure his argument, for in his
writings, Bolingbroke does present Walpole as a satanic tempter, whose
money and patronage seduce an apathetic public and dupe the unsuspect-
ing monarch. Bolingbroke and his friends are, of course, on the side of the
angels.[32]

Bolingbroke's writings are propped by what we might call a moral
ameliorism, a belief in the improvement of public morality and the cultivation of civic virtue as a route to political reform. This was exactly the
defense of their art that eighteenth-century satirists provided, Pope
among them—that it was an agency of social and political reform, perhaps
the only one now efficacious. Concern for national and individual virtues
is manifested in Pope's *Imitations of Horace*, in terms which owe a debt both
to classical and Renaissance moralists and to seventeenth-century country-house poetry. Bolingbroke also has a vision of an ideal society, a golden
age of the constitution, when the fair maiden Liberty was not besieged by
the dragon Moneyed Interest. Latterly, I have suggested, as the locus of
his concern became the nation's morals rather than its government,
Bolingbroke's writing increasingly shares the assumptions and stances of
the utopian satirist, constructing an image of an ideal society based on an
analysis of contemporary society's departures from that ideal. That his
political ideas were not intellectually strenuous, resting as they did on an
appeal to the nostalgic imagination of the "independent member," would
be no shortcoming in Pope's eyes. Indeed, Bolingbroke may have stressed

for Pope's benefit the purely fictional, utopian aspects of his thought. There is reason to believe that in matters of religion, Pope never really knew how far his friend's deistic beliefs stretched, and in Burke's pamphlet to which we have referred, *A Vindication of Natural Society*, we meet with a very interesting suggestion that the relationship between the two was never completely frank, that Bolingbroke was always forced to pull his punches and to deceive Pope in his political views. After Burke/Bolingbroke makes the admission that he was mistaken about the benefits of mixed government, he says:

> When I confess that I think this Notion a Mistake, I know to whom I am speaking, for I am satisfied that Reasons are like Liquors, and there are some of such a Nature as none but strong Heads can bear. There are few with whom I can communicate so freely as with *Pope*. But *Pope* cannot bear every truth. He has a timidity which hinders the full exertion of his Faculties, almost as effectively as bigotry cramps those of the general Herd of Mankind.[33]

Burke is suggesting, how seriously it is difficult to say, that Bolingbroke offered Pope placebos rather than opinions, and there is some truth in this. But certainly, the Patriot King was a political cure—and one of great appeal to the poetic imagination.

"A Talent to Abuse": The Mutual Language

What was it, then, that this political ideology had to offer Alexander Pope? Critics hostile to the view that Bolingbroke was a shaping influence on the poet are fond of remarking that Pope's mind was not a tabula rasa when they first met and that he had already formed very strong predilections deriving from his early reading. This is perfectly true. Perhaps the most conspicuous attribute of Pope's mental set was his commitment to the moderation ideal and the "middle way." His expressed intention in the *Essay on Man* of "steering betwixt the extremes of doctrine seemingly opposite" was not merely a means of organizing his material, but was a strongly held principle. The *Moral Essays* and *To Bethel* recommend avoiding extremes in conduct, establishing moderation as characteristic of the fully integrated personality. The habit of searching for the mean was ingrained in Pope by his situation as a Roman Catholic in a country where it was still very precarious, if not actually dangerous, to be one. In his early career, Pope's temperamental preference for the middle way was being shaped by the need to camouflage his Catholicism. His great discovery here was Erasmus. Pope claimed that, like Erasmus, he eschewed sectarianism and was a tolerant ecumenical Catholic. He made vocal protests against the narrow partisan spirit that split the European Catholic

church into Jansenist and Jesuit factions, led in France by Fénelon and
Bossuet:

> . . . Besides the small number of the truly faithful in our Church, we must
> again subdivide, and the Jansenist is damned by the Jesuit, the Jesuit by
> the Jansenist, the strict Scotist by the Thomist &c. There may be errors, I
> grant, but I can't think 'em of such consequence as to destroy utterly the
> charity of mankind, the very greatest bond in which we are engaged to
> one another [as Christians].[34]

Later, replying to a letter of Atterbury's of 8 November 1717 in which the
bishop pointed out that as Pope's father was now dead, there remained no
objection to Pope's converting from Catholicism and furthering the possibility of civil employments by taking the Test, Pope argued that there is a
spiritual Christianity far greater than any individual religious denomination, to which fraternity all true Christians belong, and he drew the parallel
between his nonpartisan politics and his ecumenical religion:

> In my politicks, I think no further than how to preserve the peace of my
> life, in any government under which I live; nor in my religion, than to
> preserve the peace of my conscience in any Church with which I com-
> municate . . . In a word, the things I have always wished to see are not a
> Roman Catholick, or a French Catholick, or a Spanish Catholick, but a true
> Catholick: and not a King of Whigs, or a King of Tories, but a King of
> England.[35]

Recent commentators have related such professions as this to Pope's larger
concern, manifested in his later poetry, with finding the middle way in
moral conduct and have accepted at face value Pope's stated ambition to be
catholic in the most general sense, with or without the orthodoxy. Powerful attempts have been made to answer the question "What kind of
Catholic was Alexander Pope?" in terms of the ecumenical spirit of De-
siderius Erasmus.[36] Pope had written to Swift on 28 November 1729, "Yet
am I of the Religion of Erasmus, a Catholick"; and at an early stage of his
career, he had to run the gauntlet of his Roman Catholic neighbors for his
attack on the abuses of the Roman Catholic Church, launched under the
banner of Erasmus:

> Thus long succeeding Criticks justly reign'd,
> *Licence* repress'd, and *useful Laws* ordain'd;
> *Learning* and *Rome* alike in Empire grew,
> And *Arts* still *follow'd* where her *Eagles flew;*
> From the same Foes, at last, both felt their Doom,
> And the same Age saw *Learning* fall, and *Rome.*
> With *Tyranny,* then *Superstition* join'd,
> As that the *Body* this enslav'd the *Mind;*
> Much was *Believ'd,* but little *understood,*

And to be *dull* was constru'd to be *good;*
A *second* Deluge Learning thus o'er-run,
And the *Monks* finish'd what the *Goths* begun.
   At length, *Erasmus,* that *great, injur'd* Name,
(The *Glory* of the Priesthood, and the *Shame!*)
Stemm'd the *wild Torrent* of a *barb'rous Age,*
And drove those *Holy Vandals* off the Stage.

(An Essay on Criticism, 681–96)

Subsequent letters to John Caryll in defense of Pope's Erasmian stance stress the need to end the in-fighting that has obscured the real bond uniting Christians, "the charity of mankind"—a characteristically Erasmian concern. Throughout his lifetime, Pope continued to venerate Erasmus: in his last testament, he bequeathed to Bolingbroke an eleven-volume set of the Dutch scholar's works.

It is doubtless too harsh to discuss Pope's Erasmianism as disingenuous; and yet, it is clear that, protected by this rhetoric, he would be able to operate in private devotions exactly as he wished. Erasmian ecumenicalism was both a usefully noncommittal position and a very attractive, almost glorious one. Pope certainly did not abandon his Catholic faith in private, but the evidence suggests that he was moderate in his religious practice.[37] A continuity exists between his professions of religious moderation and similar kinds of statements made about politics. At various crucial junctures of his life, such as when pressure was being put on him by the Addison circle to declare his hand, he adopted a similar middle-way rhetoric with respect to party interest. A clear analogy exists between his remarks about political neutrality, about his indifference to those both in power and out of it, about his abhorrence of faction and narrow partisan interest, about his being one who "owed not a sixpence to any Party," and his claim in religious matters that he was an antisectarian and that he exalted whatever united Christians and deplored whatever divided them. In both spheres, Pope claimed to rise above divisive self-interest. Virtue is not the sole property of either party, but is the attribute of enlightened individuals, argued Pope in letters to friends; and in religious doctrine, Pope also professed a preoccupation with the ideals of moderation, proportion, and eclectic balance.

Bolingbroke's theory of party obsolescence was a moderate, antiextremist view that provided a political and historical justification of the position Pope had always adopted. Pope was an instinctive moderate—his low profile was essential to the survival of a man in such a socially precarious position—but his moderation was rendered rational and vertebrate by Bolingbroke. Here was the most noted political philosopher of the generation arguing for virtue and public spirit, for moderation and compromise, for Whig and Tory alike to come together under the flag of the country opposition—a manifesto perfectly suited to Pope's own temperament and to his self-image as magnanimous, public spirited, and open hearted. Under Bolingbroke's tutelage, the via media myth became a political manifesto. And because the basis of the manifesto was an attack on vice and national corruption, involving invidious comparison to earlier, purer government and implying a degeneration in human nature, it was supremely fitted for satirical expression. Thus, in the following passage from the *Epistle to Fortescue*, one of the clearest expressions in verse of Pope's "moderation myths," the middle-way stance is both the expression of an ideal norm and an attack on party distinctions:

> My Head and Heart thus flowing thro' my Quill,
> Verse-man or Prose-man, term me which you will,
> Papist or Protestant, or both between,
> Like good *Erasmus* in an honest Mean,
> In Moderation placing all my Glory,
> While Tories call me Whig, and Whigs a Tory. (63–68)

When in the *Epilogue to the Satires* Pope professes himself one of those "Who know how like Whig-Ministers to Tory" (1.106), he is not professing himself apolitical, but rather identifying himself as a supporter of the country party.

Pope and the *Craftsman*

Bolingbroke also made more tangible contributions to the development of Pope's political satire. His political thought was a virtual invitation to the satiric poet because it held morality in such high esteem. But there was also a suggestibility about the opposition platform that was capable of capturing Pope's imagination, a suggestibility that amounted at times to an almost mythic power. This is most evident in the *Craftsman*, the periodical under Bolingbroke's editorship that was planned from Dawley Farm. It is not too impressionistic to suggest that very often when Pope came to call on Bolingbroke, he was engaged in writing or reading *Craftsman* copy; and there is at least some evidence to suggest that Pope was sucked into this enterprise. Bolingbroke's central ideas were expressed in the *Craftsman* until he left for France in 1735. The importance of this journal's contribution to the shaping of eighteenth-century satire has not been fully explored. There is only one full-length study of the *Craftsman* known to me, an unpublished University of Cambridge Ph.D. thesis by Simon Varey, which goes some way toward filling this important gap but does not explicitly investigate the relationship between the journal and the literary expression of its ideas in opposition writing.[38]

This journal was in great measure responsible for creating the mythology that conflated Walpole with Satan and with Mammon. It lost no opportunity to record with great sensationalism the appallingly corrosive power of *aurum potabile*. Very often, its satirical papers made their mark by delicate allusion to biblical or classical sources in the same way that Pope's mature satires do. The "Tree of Corruption" paper of 25 March 1732 is a minor satirical masterpiece.[39] The dream vision begins with a description of a utopian island in which "A Spirit of Liberty discover'd itself in the Faces of the Inhabitants"; but in the *"North-East Part of it"* (Norfolk) is located a tree hung with golden apples, which turns out to be "the TREE of CORRUPTION, which bears a very near Resemblance to the *Tree of Knowledge*, in the Garden of *Eden*; for whoever tasted the Fruit of it, lost his Integrity and fell, like *Adam*, from the *State of Innocence.*" In the middle of this tree, Walpole is to be found tossing apples to all who will partake, lifting them up beside him into the branches. Soon, a forest of such trees has grown, with the apples bearing legends like *"charitable Corporation."* The fruit and leaves soon destroy both the principles of the country's inhabitants and the natural beauty of its landscape, provoking the furious countrymen to cut it down, but they are prevented by "a numerous Body of *arm'd* Men."[40] The power of such a paper and the suggestibility of its allusions to biblical and Miltonic portrayals of evil is obvious; its influence on Pope's Sporus portrait in the *Epistle to Dr. Arbuthnot* is evident. Howard Erskine-Hill has analyzed in detail the theme of corruption in Pope's poems, though he has not seen how precisely the inspiration derives from Bolingbroke. But he very properly gives the *Craftsman* credit for having initiated the comparison between Peter Walter and Sir Robert Walpole as dishonest stewards of the country's wealth, accounting for the virulence and frequency of Pope's attacks on Walter.[41] Colonel Francis Charteris was also a powerful symbol of the degradation of moral and social standards for Pope. His imprisonment for rape in 1730 and his subsequent pardon were widely regarded as a perversion of justice effected by bribery. Pope's attacks on Charteris in numerous places, like Fielding's play *Rape upon Rape* and like the *Craftsman* of 8 August 1730, recognize the patron/client relationship that existed between Walpole and Charteris.[42]

It is outside my scope to investigate fully the symbiotic relationship between the *Craftsman* and Pope's poems, though I have already suggested that Pope's awareness of it was a fecund inspiration as early as the year 1727, when he was working toward the early *Dunciad*. It is impossible to say with any certainty who was responsible for which numbers of the *Craftsman*, so Bolingbroke's adroitness as a satirist cannot be judged from this. But clearly, Pope's intimate acquaintance with the contents of this journal edited in part by his closest friend was a formative influence on his own technique and helped to create the communal language that we are investigating.

To see what Pope was able to do with Patriot themes in verse, let us consider this passage from the *Epilogue to the Satires:*

> *Vice* is undone, if she forgets her Birth,
> And stoops from Angels to the Dregs of Earth:
> But 'tis the *Fall* degrades her to a Whore;
> Let *Greatness* own her, and she's mean no more;
> Her Birth, her Beauty, Crowds and Courts confess,
> Chaste Matrons praise her, and grave Bishops bless:
> In golden Chains the willing World she draws,
> And hers the Gospel is, and hers the Laws:
> Mounts the Tribunal, lifts her scarlet head,
> And sees pale Virtue carted in her stead!
> Lo! at the Wheels of her Triumphal Car,
> Old *England's* Genius, rough with many a Scar,
> Dragg'd in the Dust! his Arms hang idly round,
> His Flag inverted trails along the ground!
> Our Youth, all liv'ry'd o'er with foreign Gold,
> Before her dance; behind her crawl the Old!
> See thronging Millions to the Pagod run,
> And offer Country, Parent, Wife, or Son!
> Hear her black Trumpet thro' the Land proclaim,
> That "Not to be corrupted is the Shame." (1.141–60)

Before J. M. Osborn's important article was published, in which he traces a double allusion in the passage by way of Justinian and Theodora to Walpole and his mistress-turned-wife Molly Skerrett, Vice here was regarded as an abstract personification.[43] And it is true that Vice does function somewhat like the Vice in a morality play, the sinister yet comic tempter who jeopardizes the soul ("Old *England's* Genius") of the nation. Here again is a version of the Fall and the erection of a new temple to the pagan idol Gold that we have seen to be a pervasive mythos in Pope's satire. Yet there is also an intermediate level of allusion, difficult to characterize, in the use of terms like *Vice, Virtue, corruption,* and *Greatness.* They are abstract, but have a very specific range of application. *Corruption,* as we have seen, is a term used in three precise senses by Bolingbroke: it refers to the constitution unbalanced by ministerial encroachment, to the employment of illicit techniques, especially bribery, in unbalancing it, and to the national morale or "spirit" when the process is complete. "Old *England's* Genius," whose shame is so pictorially represented in this passage, is the "spirit of patriotism" that needs to be resurrected if the Gospel and laws of the land are to do their work. Insofar as it carries a specific allusion to Walpole's disgraceful marriage to his whore, the passage is doing opposition business. But it also carries the reader into the realms of political ideology, where words like *Vice* and *Virtue* and *Greatness* (as distinguished from *goodness* in the way that Fielding does in *Jonathan Wild*) have particular work to do. Within the passage itself, the terms *Court* and *Country* are both specified. With increasing frequency, Pope's poems had been employing such terms in the 1730s as well as making reference to specific issues, like the excise scheme or the standing army.[44] It is this quality in Pope's verse, of engaging directly in the diurnal strife of politics while simultaneously continuing a debate about ultimate sociopolitical values, that is the major legacy of Bolingbroke and the *Craftsman*.

Chapter 9

Satire and Political Theory in the Age of Bolingbroke and Pope

The Architectonic Impulse

In the preceding chapters I have supplied the biographical context for the friendship between Bolingbroke and Pope, analyzing its results in the *Essay on Man* collaboration and in the *Epistle to Bolingbroke*. What I have not yet attempted to do, except in general terms, is to show why Bolingbroke's particular brand of political ideology presented itself to Pope so suggestibly as the raw material of his satire. The question can be answered on many different levels. Frequently in this book I have stressed the areas of overlap between political issues and issues that we might now be disposed to regard as purely literary; and one recent writer has argued convincingly that there are good sociohistorical reasons for the proximity of satire and politics in this period, reasons that no longer exist. Bertrand Goldgar has argued that the Walpole era was the last historical epoch in which satire was capable of influencing state policy directly and that Walpole saw the danger in this situation. His deliberate refusal to patronize literary talent was no mere philistinism but was a calculated attempt to disarm the satirists with the weapons of economics.[1]

In my view, however, there are even more fundamental factors underlying the phenomenology of eighteenth-century practice. By the late seventeenth century, political discourse had reached a stage of evolution that brought it close to the discourse of satire in various respects, so that it became possible to regard satire as actually a form of political thought. In the *Tractatus Politicus* of 1677, Spinoza asserted the close connection between political philosophy and satire. Satire occurs when political philosophers present views of possible societies that are predicated on unrealistic assumptions about human nature—for example, that men are wholly rational creatures:

> [They] conceive men, not as they are, but as they would like them to be. The result is that they have generally written satire instead of ethics, and have never conceived a political system which can be applied in practice; but have produced either obvious fantasies, or schemes that could only have been put into effect in Utopia, or in the poets' golden age, where, of course, there was no need of them at all.[2]

Spinoza's remarks imply that when a political system is unworkably idealistic, it must stand in a satirical relationship to the actual society of its author, since it manifests the author's conception of what is wrong with his own society. Despite Spinoza's censure, the connection between political theory and utopian fiction is to some extent a necessary one. The "great tradition" in political philosophy has comprised works that contain not only factual or descriptive accounts of political institutions and activities, but also recommendations about the ideal ends of political activity— the dimension of ideology.[3] To the ideological dimension of political thought, Sheldon S. Wolin gives the name "the architectonic vision," by means of which the theorist gives imaginative expression to his fundamental values.[4] If a work of political theory is to be more significant than a mere pamphlet, a tract for the times, it must be conceived in terms of an overall vision of political and social progress transcending particular and ephemeral phenomena. A vision of the good outside the political order must shape the theorist's description of desirable institutions; and this degree of imaginative mediation of the actual is not peculiar to seventeenth-century theorizing. Nevertheless, the writings of the leading seventeenth-century theorists, Hobbes and Locke—and Bolingbroke even more obviously—expose the ideological dimension very starkly. Their theories are grounded on assumptions about human nature in prepolitical society, assumptions which dictate the nature of the social "contract" on which modern political society is based. To make these assumptions, they journey back to the prehistoric or remote past, intent on discovering man in his natural state. Once we know the nature of naked, unaccommodated man, we are able to determine the kinds of freedom that the contract must create and guarantee. In order to explain why men were prepared to mortgage the absolute freedom they possessed in prepolitical society and to invest some quantity of it in a sovereign, seventeenth-century theorists investigated more thoroughly than they need have done the state of prepolitical society. Arguing from first principles about human psychology, they posited a "state of nature" in which human behavior would be unadulterated by the constraints of legal and political institutions, in the establishment of which they would have alienated some of their rights and freedoms. Hobbes's description of this state is familiar, but will always bear repetition:

> . . . It is manifest, that during the time men live without a common Power to keep them all in awe, they are in that condition which is called WARRE; and such a warre, as is of every man, against every man. For Warre, consisteth not in Battell onely, or the act of fighting; but in a tract of time, wherein the Will to contend by Battell is sufficiently known: and therefore the notion of *Time*, is to be considered in the nature of Warre; as it is in the nature of Weather. For as the nature of Foule weather, lyeth not in a showre or two of rain; but in an inclination thereto of many dayes

together: So the nature of War, consisteth not in actuall fighting; but in the known disposition thereto, during all the time there is no assurance to the contrary. All other time is PEACE.

Whatsoever therefore is consequent to a time of Warre, where every man is Enemy to every man; the same is consequent to the time, wherein men shall live without other security, than what their own strength, and their own invention shall furnish them withall. In such condition, there is no place for Industry; because the fruit thereof is uncertain: and consequently no Culture of the Earth: no Navigation, nor use of the commodities that may be imported by Sea; no commodious Building; no Instruments of moving, and removing such things as require much force; no Knowledge of the face of the Earth; no account of Time; no Arts; no Letters; no Society; and which is worst of all, continuall feare, and danger of violent death; And the life of man, solitary, poore, nasty, brutish, and short.[5]

From the psychological description of human nature and the sociological account of human behavior that Hobbes derives from it, he accounts for the contracting into a form of civil society guaranteeing that self-interested behavior is also reasonable behavior—behavior likely to preserve the state of peace. Contract theory of this kind is utopian, and not only because it introduces a dimension of fictional history. Indeed, modern scholars point out that contract theorists like Hobbes and Locke need not be read as implying that such a state of nature ever existed, any more than the Golden Age of the poets ever existed. C. B. Macpherson argues that it is "a logical not an historical hypothesis" in that the political behavior Hobbes recommends should be *as if* men had contracted out of the state of nature he has described to receive the benefits he has described.[6] Sheldon Wolin considers the state of nature to have been a timeless model to illustrate the causes and consequences of political breakdown, a logical and moral absurdity because in such a state of maximization of rights and absolute freedom, the right of everyone to everything contradicts the right of anyone to anything, and because man the freedom lover, in such a state, becomes *homini lupus*.[7] But whether or not Hobbes believed there was ever such a state, the attempt to describe and explain the origins of society can only be expressed in terms of myth. Genesis is substituted for analysis in the account given by contract theorists of the origins of society, and the resultant theory is heavily ideological. A form of state authority is justified on the grounds that the qualities which necessitate it really are present in human nature when that nature is deprived of authority: in Hobbes's view, fear is the key to human behavior and motivates the destructive rapine of natural society.

Northrop Frye, in an article called "Varieties of Literary Utopias," indicates the relationship between the social contract myth and the utopia: the former begins in an analysis of the present society that confronts the mythmaker and projects it into the past, normally as an explanation of the present state of things, whereas the inventor of the utopia also begins in the present but projects into the future. He is accounting, not for the origin of society, but for the "*telos* or end at which social life aims."[8] Utopias are untrammelled expressions of what Wolin calls the "architectonic impulse," clearly recognizable statements of ideals—recognizable because they are fictional and the problems of arriving at the utopia from the fallen world of the present are ignored by their creators. But the theorists of contract are equally moving from unverifiable hypotheses about human psychology to the recommendation of a political settlement based on them. In this respect, they are "mythical" even if the states of nature that political philosophers have actually conceived have sometimes been the reverse of the perfect worlds created by the utopists. Hobbes's state of nature, for example, is, as described above, a counterutopia, but his idea in the precise form that it took was not influential except as a bogey. Locke's state of nature, described in the second of the *Two Treatises of Government*, obliterates the unacceptable face of Hobbes, as we would expect, given that it was a tract for very different times. Locke's *Treatises* legitimized the limitations on monarchy established by the Bill of Rights of 1689, whereas the actual form of political authority to which Hobbes's contractors had assented was absolute monarchy.[9] Locke's state of nature has nothing of the Gothic horror of Hobbes's: it is not a fearful environment, but an insecure one. It is governed by the natural law, which is quite manifest to all, but there are those who are degenerate enough to ignore its dictates, or are self-interested enough to reject its application to their own cases. This is inconvenient, and therefore the common law of the political society is superior.

Also inconvenient is the situation in which, in the state of nature, it is the duty of each man to be his own judge and executioner when his rights are infringed. It is to eliminate this inconvenience that men agree by the terms of Locke's contract, not to completely yield power as Hobbes had it, but to *delegate* power into the hands of a limited monarch (chapters 5 and 9). We can see that even in Locke's account, the state of nature falls very far short of the ideal society: indeed, Locke distinguishes the golden-age phase of the state of nature from the later phases when princes begin to abuse their power and become corrupted by their ambition to rule regardless of the interests of their subjects (chapter 8, paragraph 111). But Locke, like Hobbes, had to make the inference from a psychological and sociological theory of human nature uncontaminated by the influences of sophisticated society to the government theory most suitable for them; and the vital presuppositions are that man is a naturally gregarious and sociable creature and that his birthright is a state of "*Equality*, wherein all the Power and Jurisdiction is reciprocal, no one having more than another: there being nothing more evident, than that Creatures of the same species and rank promiscuously born to all the same advantages of Nature, and the use of the same faculties, should also be equal one amongst another without Subordination or Subjection" (chapter 2, paragraph 4).

Recent scholarship has shown the inadequacy of regarding post-Revolutionary political thought as beginning and ending with Locke.[10] H. T. Dickinson has argued that the full-blown contract theory proved less acceptable to Whig thinkers than did the appeal to the existence of a historically verifiable ancient constitution in accounting for the nature of political obligation. Locke's view appeared dangerously radical in that it conferred universal and inalienable rights on all men, since all men were parties to the original contract. Postulation of an ancient constitution that could be traced back to the Anglo-Saxon era and before served to adjust the balance of power between king and Parliament while excluding popular participation in the political process. Men of property retained control over the institutions of government, and inflammatory ideas of popular sovereignty were held at bay.[11] But even the historical version of constitutional origins depends on an appeal to the distant past for its justification, involving a regressive journey into the nation's childhood. And often, childhood is associated with purity, virtue, and other moral notions. Even if Locke's theory was not widely accepted, it was widely reckoned with.

Bolingbroke himself was not a follower of Locke, at least in respect of his version of contract theory. But he did inherit the idiom of Lockean political theory. In Fragment 13 of the *Fragments or Minutes of Essays,* he specifically attacks Locke's theory of the foundations of civil society on the basis of consent between free and equal individuals. The state of nature could not have been as Locke describes it, because noble savages roaming in splendid isolation could not propagate the species; neither could they come together on any common ground to accept the contract. The hypothesis is therefore unhistorical. More serious, a state governed by natural law, in which each man was his own judge and executioner, would not have been a state of perfect freedom but "a state of war and violence, of mutual and alternate oppression, as really as that which Hobbes imagined to have been the state of nature."[12] Anticipating Hume, Bolingbroke argued that conquest rather than consent was often the basis for the formation of political society. But even when consent was the catalyst, it was not the consent of individuals but of families. Before men were governed by civil authority, they lived in family groups regulated by paternal authority, and it was from among the various heads of families that the early monarchs were chosen.

This modification of Locke's theory is not a trivial quibble. Governing the selection of details for Bolingbroke's version of the myth of origin is his concern for the characteristic quality of the authority wielded in natural society, and therefore the quality of authority that present political arrangements must preserve. This is, in Bolingbroke's view, paternal benevolence. Isaac Kramnick's masterly analysis, in *Bolingbroke and His Circle* and elsewhere, spells out what he takes to have been the consequences of Bolingbroke's rejection of Locke's contract to protect rights and property. Locke laid the theoretical foundations of a bourgeois, liberal individualism that stressed personal freedom, self-interest, and competition. This was a philosophical sponsorship of the rising class of stockbrokers, financiers, and city bankers, the new commercial order bent on the destruction of the traditional order of society, an aim which, in Bolingbroke's view, was nearly realized in the debacle of the South Sea Bubble. By contrast, Bolingbroke's ideology was that of a family-centered aristocracy and gentry: "Fathers, paternal authority, subordination, rank, cooperation, and public service are the dimensions of this ideology's superstructure."[13] (Kramnick perhaps exaggerates the extent of Bolingbroke's disagreement with Locke; even if the content is entirely at odds with Locke's, the form and methodology is the same.)[14] Bolingbroke also derived his theory of the nature of original political authority from the presumed operation of natural law. The law of nature renders it necessary that a father care for and wield authority over his children, at least in their minority. What can be more likely therefore than that civil government should be modeled on this form of aboriginal authority, which is the most benevolent and concerned? Also like Locke, Bolingbroke deduced his account of the foundations of civil society from first principles about the psychological nature of humankind. Fragment 6 is Bolingbroke's clearest statement of belief about these principles: ". . . The all-wise creator . . . implanted in us another principle [besides natural reason], that of self-love, which is the original spring of human actions."[15] Self-love is at first an instinct and drives men instinctively toward the sociability essential to self-preservation. At a later stage of development, self-love is guided by reason into accepting the moral virtues of justice and benevolence, virtues which alone can preserve the body politic. Thus the various family units are driven into civil society and unity under a monarch who is *primus inter pares*, wielding a patriarchal authority for which his own virtue qualifies him.

Pope's Satire and Political Theory

We might consider Bolingbroke to be a "reconstructed" contract theorist insofar as he does not journey back to prehistory to locate the foundations of political obligation, but rather to Saxon times, when political freedoms were guaranteed by the Wittena Gemote, the assembly of king, lords, and freemen that was a prototype of the modern Parliament. As is apparent from the above account, the freedoms that Bolingbroke's version of the constitution was designed to protect were grounded on the domestic, home-and-hearth moral values, to which he gave a revitalized political currency. The development of Bolingbroke's political philosophy through the 1730s shows a movement toward allowing this ideological element to dominate the purely programmatic parts of his doctrine. This is partly why Pope found his ideas so congenial as a basis for satire. It was as if the qualities that Pope conjures up in his evocation of himself as a dinner-party host at Twickenham in *To Bethel*—of generosity tempered by moderation, humanity, Englishness, poetry, and godliness—could be directly trans-lated into those required to govern the country:

> But ancient friends, (tho' poor, or out of play)
> That touch my Bell, I cannot turn away.
> 'Tis true, no Turbots dignify my boards,
> But gudgeons, flounders, what my Thames affords.
> To Hounslow-heath I point, and Bansted-down,
> Thence comes your mutton, and these chicks my own:
> From yon old wallnut-tree a show'r shall fall;
> And grapes, long-lingring on my only wall,
> And figs, from standard and Espalier join:
> The dev'l is in you if you cannot dine.
> Then chearful healths (your Mistress shall have place)
> And, what's more rare, a Poet shall say *Grace*. (139–50)

As we have seen in the last chapter, Bolingbroke's political platform rested on the translation of private virtues into the sphere of public life. The values of friendship and benevolence, the cornerstone of the retire-ment idyll, became the basis for an alternative model of government. But at a more fundamental level, developments in the history of satire also combined toward an absorption of Bolingbroke's views into the marrow of Pope's work. As P. K. Elkin has shown, the status of satire as a mode of discourse in the Augustan era was very far from assured.[16] It operated within an area that included terms like *libel*, *lampoon*, and *slander*, from which the practitioners of the emergent art wished to dissociate them-selves. Thus, in the celebrated "Jack Ketch" passage of Dryden's *A Dis-course concerning . . . Satire*, he claims the superiority of "general" satire over personal and of "fine raillery" over malice (though the author of *MacFlecknoe* surely did not always practice what he preached).[17]

When, in the late 1720s, Pope "stoop'd to satire and moralis'd" his song, he found his new art in an equally unstable condition, and the systematic defense of satire became an objective as important as the practice of it. The nub of the defense was of course that satire was a moral teacher, a social therapeutic, and the duty of every reasonable man. It preserves law and order, maintains moral and literary standards, and exposes to correction those enemies of the state who are impervious to the law. In the same way as political theories based on contract made assumptions about human nature in the raw, satirists also held the vision of an ideal society founded on permanent principles of order, which was often thought to have been instantiated in the remote past. Thus, the historical comparison between the ideal past and the fallen present became for Pope a tactic of satire just as it was for Bolingbroke a tactic of politics. Pope journeyed into the past to locate his first principles of human nature, which in his satire act as standards and as evidence of present corruption. Here is his view of the past in the *Epistle to Augustus* as a progressive wasting disease:

> In Days of Ease, when now the weary Sword
> Was sheath'd, and *Luxury* with *Charles* restor'd;
> In every Taste of foreign Courts improv'd,
> "All by the King's Example, liv'd and lov'd."
> Then Peers grew proud in Horsemanship t'excell,
> New-market's Glory rose, as Britain's fell;
> The Soldier breath'd the Gallantries of France,
> And ev'ry flow'ry Courtier writ Romance.
> Then Marble soften'd into life grew warm,
> And yielding Metal flow'd to human form:
> Lely on animated Canvas stole
> The sleepy Eye, that spoke the melting soul.
> No wonder then, when all was Love and Sport,
> The willing Muses were debauch'd at Court;
> On each enervate string they taught the Note
> To pant, or tremble thro' an Eunuch's throat.
> But Britain, changeful as a Child at play,
> Now calls in Princes, and now turns away.
> Now Whig, now Tory, what we lov'd we hate;
> Now all for Pleasure, now for Church and State;
> Now for Prerogative, and now for Laws;
> Effects unhappy! from a Noble Cause.
>   Time was, a sober Englishman wou'd knock
> His servants up, and rise by five a clock,
> Instruct his Family in ev'ry rule,
> And send his Wife to Church, his Son to school.
> To worship like his Fathers was his care;
> To teach their frugal Virtues to his Heir;
> To prove, that Luxury could never hold;
> And place, on good Security, his Gold.
> Now Times are chang'd, and one Poetick Itch
> Has seiz'd the Court and City, Poor and Rich. (139–70)

The ordered, traditional pattern of family life and the paternal nature of the authority wielded (lines 161–68) are very close to Bolingbroke's view of

Elizabethan England. Indeed, Bolingbroke's account of recent constitutional history given in *On the Study and Use of History* is so close to Pope's version of poetic history that it could easily be the source, particularly when we recall that Pope had the original manuscript from which he made copies to circulate among their intimate friends:

> When you look back three or four generations ago, you will see that the English were a plain, perhaps a rough, but a good-natured hospitable people, jealous of their liberties, and able as well as ready to defend them, with their tongues, their pens, and their swords. The restoration began to turn hospitality into luxury, pleasure into debauch, and country peers and country commoners into courtiers and men of mode. But whilst our luxury was young, it was little more than elegance: the debauch of that age was enlivened with wit, and varnished over with gallantry. The courtiers and the men of mode knew what the constitution was, respected it, and often asserted it. Arts and sciences flourished, and, if we grew more trivial, we were not become either grossly ignorant, or openly profligate. Since the revolution, our kings have been reduced indeed to a seeming annual dependence on parliament; but the business of parliament, which was esteemed in general a duty before, has been exercised in general as a trade since. The trade of parliament, and the trade of funds, have grown universal. Men, who stood forward in the world, have attended to little else. The frequency of parliaments, that increased their importance, and should have increased the respect for them, has taken off from their dignity: and the spirit that prevailed, whilst the service in them was duty, has been debased since it became a trade. Few know, and scarce any respect, the British constitution: that of the Church has been long since derided; that of the State as long neglected; and both have been left at the mercy of the men in power, whoever those men were. Thus the Church, at least the hierarchy, however sacred in its origin or wise in its institution, is become a useless burden on the state: and the state is become, under ancient and known forms, a new and undefinable monster; composed of a king without monarchical splendor, a senate of nobles without aristocratical independency, and a senate of commons without democratical freedom. In the mean time, my lord, the very idea of wit, and all that can be called taste, has been lost among the great; arts and sciences are scarce alive; luxury has been increased but not refined; corruption has been established, and is avowed. When governments are worn out, thus it is: the decay appears in every instance. Public and private virtue, public and private spirit, science and wit, decline all together.[18]

At times, the regressive journey that Pope takes is into his own past history, as in lines 52–71 from *Imit. Hor. Ep.* II.2, which smack so much of anti-Williamite sentiment. At other times, as in the famous lines from the *Epistle to Dr. Arbuthnot*, his father's past represents the state of simple purity that has its analogue in the "state of nature" postulated by the political theorists:

> Born to no Pride, inheriting no Strife,
> Nor marrying Discord in a Noble Wife,
> Stranger to Civil and Religious Rage,
> The good Man walk'd innoxious thro' his Age.
> No Courts he saw, no Suits would ever try,
> Nor dar'd an Oath, nor hazarded a Lye:
> Un-learn'd, he knew no Schoolman's subtle Art,
> No Language, but the Language of the Heart. (392–99)

Yet other historical journeys are into the recent political past, to a time when honest and worthy statesmen still walked the earth, as in *Epilogue to the Satires* 2.74–90:

> But does the Court a worthy Man remove?
> That instant, I declare, he has my Love:
> I shun his Zenith, court his mild Decline;
> Thus SOMMERS once, and HALIFAX were mine.
> Oft in the clear, still Mirrour of Retreat,
> I study'd SHREWSBURY, the wise and great:
> CARLETON'S calm Sense, and STANHOPE'S noble Flame,
> Compar'd, and knew their gen'rous End the same:
> How pleasing ATTERBURY'S softer hour!
> How shin'd the Soul, unconquer'd in the Tow'r!
> How can I PULT'NEY, CHESTERFIELD forget,
> While *Roman* Spirit charms, and *Attic* Wit:
> ARGYLE, the State's whole Thunder born to wield,
> And shake alike the Senate and the Field:
> Or WYNDHAM, just to Freedom and the Throne,
> The Master of our Passions, and his own.
> Names, which I long have lov'd, nor lov'd in vain.

These examples are evidence of a broader commitment to the exemplary function of all history, a commitment that Pope derived from Bolingbroke. In the *Letters on the Study and Use of History*, Bolingbroke produced one of the last manuals on the use of history to expound the exemplary theory. This theory derived from Roman historians, especially Polybius, and centered round the view that the study of history was mandatory training for the man of action, an essential propaedeutic to a career in active politics.[19] What the study of history involved was summed up in Seneca's tag, "longum est iter per praecepta, breve et efficax per exempla,"[20] or in Bolingbroke's well-worn terms, "History is philosophy teaching by examples." The practical utility of history was to furnish examples of human conduct, which, taken in sum, would provide general principles and rules for action. To Bolingbroke, history was applied moral philosophy. Since *moral* referred to both private and public virtue, it embraced both politics and ethics. Pope's understanding of the term *virtue* in a line like "To Virtue

only and her Friends, a Friend" similarly lies in a no-man's-land between
the passive Christian conception of virtue as a state of the soul and an
active, Roman conception of public-spirited action.

Pope of course knew Bolingbroke's *Letters on . . . History* and probably
had it in his hands around the year 1736. He circulated copies to Wyndham, Bathurst, Marchmont, Murray, Lyttelton, and Cornbury, later (in
1738) printing a private edition, a copy of which survives in the Harvard
College Library.[21] Thomas Akstens, in an article to which I am greatly
indebted, has pointed out the similarities between Letter 2 of the *Letters on
. . . History* and the letter written by Pope to Arbuthnot, supposedly on 26
July 1734, in defense of satire, similarities so strong that Pope's letter could
well be a paraphrase.[22] Sherburn expresses doubts about the dating of this
letter, thinking that it was probably a later elaboration of the letter written
on 2 August 1734. Quite possibly, as Akstens suggests, Pope wrote this
letter as a defense of satire sometime in 1736 when he had the manuscript
of the *Letters on . . . History* in front of him. The letter is therefore very good
evidence of the ways in which Bolingbroke's thought represented a suggestible model for Pope's poetic practice. In it, Pope stresses the inefficacy
of general satire without the inclusion of particular examples, which exert
a psychological force on the passions and lead to reformation. This is
precisely Bolingbroke's view of history. Not only does Pope theorize about
satire in Bolingbrokean terms, but he also, like Bolingbroke, provides an
instructive example culled from the history of satire:

> It is certain, much freer Satyrists than I have enjoy'd the encouragement
> and protection of the Princes under whom they lived. Augustus and
> Mecoenas made Horace their companion, tho' he had been in arms on the
> side of Brutus; and allow me to remark it was out of the suff'ring Party too,
> that they favour'd and distinguish'd Virgil . . . it was under the greatest
> Princes and best Ministers, that moral Satyrists were most encouraged;
> and that then Poets exercised the same jurisdiction over the Follies, as
> Historians did over the Vices of men.[23]

This argument has the historian and satirist joint custodians of the nation's
moral and political health, and this was the direction in which Bolingbroke's view of history pointed Pope.

Pope's Satire as Political Theory

It is apparent from the *Epistle to Dr. Arbuthnot* and the correspondence
with the addressee that surrounds it that Pope actually regarded satire as a
kind of politics. The need to defend satire from those who thought it an
illegitimate discourse resulted in an exaggeration of its practical, reformist,
and utilitarian functions. When Arbuthnot asked Pope to be more temper-

ate in his language, the poet's reply makes it clear that he saw satire as a form of applied political theory:

> . . . General Satire in Times of General Vice has no force, & is no Punishment: People have ceas'd to be ashamed of it when so many are joind with them; and tis only by hunting One or two from the Herd that any Examples can be made. If a man writ all his Life against the Collective Body of the Banditti, or against Lawyers, would it do the least Good, or lessen the Body? But if some are hung up, or pilloryed, it may prevent others. And in my low Station, with no other Power than this, I hope to deter, if not to reform.[24]

He believed his writing to be a potent instrument of social and political reform; satire, to Pope, retained some of its aboriginal force as a form of word magic, a direct source of power.

The belief in satire as an instrument of political reform has its modern origins in the Restoration. Among the finest poetic expressions of the poet's public duty is this rousing passage in Marvell's *Tom May's Death:*

> When the Sword glitters ore the Judges head,
> And fear has Coward Churchmen silenced,
> Then is the Poets time, 'tis then he drawes,
> And single fights forsaken Vertues cause.
> He, when the wheel of Empire, whirleth back,
> And though the World's disjointed Axel crack,
> Sings still of ancient Rights and better Times,
> Seeks wretched good, arraigns successful Crimes. (63–70)

The late seventeenth century saw an efflorescence of political verse satire that laid the foundation for the later perfecting of public satirical poetry. The *Poems on Affairs of State* collections both recorded for posterity the political events of the period 1660–1714, and to some extent helped to shape them. Conditions for the writing and distribution of political satire were ideal. A powerful agent of political stability, the widespread belief in divine right, had been destroyed by the logic of events and proved to be no more than a polite fiction; by the 1670s, the king's person was no more immune from criticism than the institution of monarchy had proved to be. Censorship was prosecuted severely enough to be a stimulus to satiric endeavor and not efficiently enough to extirpate it, at least in manuscript form. There was an urban population sufficiently politically educated to read and understand the verse, and the growth of the coffeehouse and club society provided efficient outlets for distribution of the material. Because the radius of political involvement was so short and only those actively engaged in politics were concerned with them, the satires and squibs could be expected to make their mark.

George de F. Lord, editor-in-chief of the recent edition of the *Poems*, is ambivalent about the extent to which the verse satire actually helped to bring about the downfall of James II and to settle the issues of the Protestant succession and the legitimate limitation of monarchical power, but he instances the phenomenal success of Lord Wharton's ballad *Lilliburlero* and the grievous concern shown by Pepys in the *Diary* over the attacks made by Marvell in the Painter poems.[25] Certainly there is sufficient evidence here to support the seventeenth- and eighteenth-century satirist's claim that his art has a practical function, if not the wider claim that he can change the world. Later, in the 1720s, Swift's *Drapier's Letters* provide an unequivocal example of the political commentator's direct influence on government policy in the period.

Many of the poems in the *Poems on Affairs of State* collections express confidence in satire's power to influence events at court. One that Pope certainly knew was Defoe's influential *The True-Born Englishman*, which begins with a passage crediting satire alone with the power to root out the evils of "this discontented land" (lines 27–55). These poems were an important part of Pope's satiric heritage and have never been given their due as an influence on his subsequent poetic habits. Pope owned a copy of the *Poems Relating to State Affairs from Oliver Cromwell to this present Time* published in 1705, and in this copy, still to be found in the British Library, Pope has made extensive marginal comments, including the claim that one of the poems—*On the Death of the Queen and Marshal Luxemburgh*—was his own work.[26]

There are many passages in Pope's own poems and letters in which he offers satire as an alternative to political action, coming into use after the politicians are stymied and when all regular avenues of political reform are clogged by various forms of corruption. In the *Epilogue to the Satires*, Pope makes claims for satire as bold as any made by his contemporaries:

> O sacred Weapon! left for Truth's defence,
> Sole Dread of Folly, Vice, and Insolence!
> To all but Heav'n-directed hands deny'd,
> The Muse may give thee, but the Gods must guide.
> Rev'rent I touch thee! but with honest zeal;
> To rowze the Watchmen of the Publick Weal,
> To Virtue's Work provoke the tardy Hall,
> And goad the Prelate slumb'ring in his Stall. (2.211–19)

Here Pope persuades us that satire is the divinely inspired instrument of "Virtue's Work," the last line of defense of truth and the public good, to be invoked when those officially responsible for upholding these values— "the Watchmen of the Publick Weal"—are asleep in their parliamentary seats. Just as Marvell does in the poem *Tom May's Death*, Pope presents satire as an alternative to political action, and in some sense its highest form. He writes in a postscript to one of Bolingbroke's letters to Swift:

> I pass almost all my time at Dawley and at home; my Lord [Bolingbroke] (of which I partly take the merit to my self) is as much estrang'd from politicks as I am. Let Philosophy be ever so vain, it is less vain now than Politicks, and not quite so vain at present as Divinity: I know nothing that moves strongly but Satire, and those who are asham'd of nothing else, are so of being ridiculous.[27]

The modern reader tends to regard professions like this as hyperbolical or melodramatic. When Pope rises to his full height, as he does in *To Fortescue* to declaim

> Hear this, and tremble! you, who 'scape the Laws.
> Yes, while I live, no rich or noble knave
> Shall walk the World, in credit, to his grave.
> To VIRTUE ONLY and HER FRIENDS, A FRIEND (118–21),

he is regarded as adopting a deliberate posture, that of the Stoic *vir bonus* perhaps—certainly some identifiably rhetorical stance.

In recent years, much work has been done on satire, and critics like Northrop Frye have gone some distance toward providing a typology of the genre.[28] Maynard Mack's pioneering article "The Muse of Satire" notes the gap between the historical figure of the poet and the appreciable degree of "fictionality" that inheres in his poetic persona when figuring in formal verse satire. Mack stresses the distinguishable poetic "voices" heard in Pope's verse and demonstrates that these are satiric strategies, even conventions demanded by the genre.[29] Much as this work has developed our understanding and prevented the egregious silliness of some approaches, especially to Swift, I think that it needs a corrective. The danger is that it can slide into postromantic "man" and "mask" dichotomies that are, on balance, irrelevant to the literature of this period. Everything that we have said so far suggests that Pope really did believe his verse to have the potency he ascribed to it in the *Epilogue to the Satires,* nor do we need to assume that he is posturing or attitudinizing in lines like these:

> So proud, I am no Slave:
> So impudent, I own myself no Knave:
> So odd, my Country's Ruin makes me grave.
> Yes, I am proud; I must be proud to see
> Men not afraid of God, afraid of me:
> Safe from the Bar, the Pulpit, and the Throne,
> Yet touch'd and sham'd by *Ridicule* alone. (2.205–11)

A proximity between satire and political philosophy is established in this period, then, because the two forms of discourse were at an analogous stage in the history of their evolution. The common belief that there were universal and accessible first principles of human nature fully expressed and lived out in a previous historical epoch or "state of nature" is the connecting link between Bolingbroke's style of thought and Pope's, a link greatly strengthened by the initial commitment to ethical reform. This is one aspect of a wider overlap, more nebulous in character but important in its implications. What sets off the Augustan era from later historical epochs, more than any other single factor in my view, is the absence of a sense of relativism, at least in theory. Contract theory, in its various forms the central conception of political obligation, is based upon a view of the permanent and universal features of human nature, which dictate the terms of the contract. The study of anthropology, which would irreparably damage such assumptions, was still in its infancy. And we find in satire, particularly in the satire of Alexander Pope, an equally sanguine expression of the conviction that there is a proper way to behave, that moral beliefs held by two men can only conflict if one of them is depraved. For readers fresh to Pope's work, the experience of reading, say, the *Moral Essays* is bewildering precisely because of the confidence these poems manifest in their own rightness. In the *Epistle to Bathurst*, a passage like lines 219–28 can be perplexing to the reader brought up to believe in a plurality of ethical principles because it implies that there are right ways and wrong ways:

> The Sense to value Riches, with the Art
> T'enjoy them, and the Virtue to impart,
> Not meanly, nor ambitiously pursu'd,
> Not sunk by sloth, nor rais'd by servitude;
> To balance Fortune by a just expence,
> Join with Oeconomy, Magnificence;
> With Splendour, Charity; with Plenty, Health;
> Oh teach us, BATHURST! yet unspoil'd by wealth!
> That secret rare, between th' extremes to move
> Of mad Good-nature, and of mean Self-love.

And the *Epistle to Burlington* is even more puzzling because it will not admit, even in aesthetic matters, that *de gustibus non est disputandum*. The reader wonders how it is that Pope can pick his way so deftly through the estates of Villario, Sabinus, and Timon, always knowing that his taste is superior in precise respects to theirs. The *Moral Essays* are unnerving for the reader who is always measuring himself by Pope's exacting standards; and I am sure that I do not speak for myself alone in finding many tests that I could not pass.

This monolithic quality, this belief that there are normative standards of behavior as universal, simple, and available as the law of nature itself is also an attribute of political theory. The political system devised by Locke is presented as an institutionalization of rights held by subjects under the law of nature. The "positive" laws of artificial society are nothing more than the laws of reason given official backing. Therefore, there is a single *correct* form of government.

It is this assumption that Bolingbroke's later political theory takes to unprecedented lengths. As his political career progressed and his hopes of regaining office receded, Bolingbroke's thought became increasingly naive. Particularly in works like *The Idea of a Patriot King*, he professed belief in what Edmund Burke called the "supernatural virtue" of a king who would realize in his governing the "spirit of patriotism." What Bolingbroke was calling for was, in truth, ethical reform. Quite simply, he wanted kings to be better people and saw no difficulty in determining the nature of goodness. Neither did Pope. His satire also bristles with confidence about how goodness is to be defined, and he assumes, usually at least, that if a politician is once made aware that he is vicious and corrupt, the conditions are created for his reform. Pope and Bolingbroke shared an ethical approach to political change, a mutual commitment to the ideal of virtue and to the possibility of ethical revolution. This commitment is partly sanctioned by the very nature of political thought in the period. Hidden somewhere in the ecology of this terrain lies the secret of the age that is referred to in literary history as the Augustan era.

Notes

In the dating of all letters, 1 January is assumed to be New Year's Day. Dates of letters are given in note references when they are not clearly indicated in the text. In all note and bibliographical references, place of publication is assumed to be London unless specified otherwise.

Abbreviations Used in the Notes

Corr.—*The Correspondence of Alexander Pope*. Edited by George Sherburn. 5 vols. Oxford, 1956.

Craftsman—*The Craftsman*.1726–1736. Collected edition published in 14 vols. Vols. 1–7, 1731; vols. 8–14, 1737.

Guerinot—J. V. Guerinot. *Pamphlet Attacks on Alexander Pope, 1711–1744: A Descriptive Bibliography*. 1969.

Spence—*Observations, Anecdotes and Characters of Books and Men: Collected from Conversation by Joseph Spence*. Edited by James M. Osborn. 2 vols. Oxford, 1966. References to this work are given as item numbers.

TE—*The Twickenham Edition of the Poems of Alexander Pope*. 10 vols. 1939–1967.

Williams—*The Correspondence of Jonathan Swift*. Edited by Harold Williams. 5 vols. 1963.

Works—*The Works of Lord Bolingbroke*. 4 vols. Philadelphia, 1841; rpt. 1969.

Notes to Introduction

1. Williams, 2:314 (Bolingbroke to Swift, 17 March 1719).
2. William Warburton, *A Letter to the Editor of the Letters on the Spirit of Patriotism*, pp. 12–13.
3. Spence, 274, 275.
4. TE, 3, pt. 1:xxix–xxxi.
5. Maynard Mack, *The Garden and the City*.
6. See also Pat Rogers, *Grub Street* and *Hacks and Dunces*; and Howard D. Weinbrot, *Augustus Caesar in "Augustan" England*.
7. James Boswell, *Life of Johnson*, edited by G. B. Hill and revised by L. F. Powell, 1:268–69.

8. Leslie Stephen, *English Thought in the Eighteenth Century*, 1:177–78.
9: D. G. James, *The Life of Reason*, p. 238.
10. Isaac Kramnick, *Bolingbroke and His Circle*, p. 3.
11. Louis I. Bredvold, "The Gloom of the Tory Satirists."
12. See Hugo M. Reichard, "The Independence of Pope as a Political Satirist."
13. Kramnick, *Bolingbroke and His Circle*, p. 219.

Notes to Chapter One: "A Freemasonry of Two"

1. *Corr.*, 3:326 (Pope to Jonathan Richardson, October 1732).
2. Ibid., 4:150 (Kent to Lord Burlington, 28 November 1738).
3. See Morris R. Brownell, *Alexander Pope's Villa*, p. 22; and John Riely and W. K. Wimsatt, "A Supplement to *The Portraits of Alexander Pope*."
4. W. K. Wimsatt, *The Portraits of Alexander Pope*, p. 144n.
5. Ibid., pp. 150–51.
6. *Corr.*, 4:125–26 (Pope to William Fortescue, 8 September 1738).
7. Spence, 646.
8. James Reeves, *The Reputation and Writings of Alexander Pope*, p. 229.
9. H. T. Dickinson, *Bolingbroke*, p. 312.
10. Spence, 280.
11. Frederick M. Keener, *An Essay on Pope*, p. 137.
12. *Works*, 3:42–43.
13. Dustin H. Griffin, *Alexander Pope*, pp. 60–65.
14. *Corr.*, 4:339; *Works*, 4:373.
15. Jonathan Swift, *Journal to Stella*, ed. Harold Williams, 2:401.

16. *The Letters of Philip Dormer Stanhope, Fourth Earl of Chesterfield*, ed. Bonamy Dobrée, 1:441.

17. TE, 3, pt. 1:xxix.

18. *Works*, 3:40.

19. Ibid., 4:111.

20. Ibid., 3:138.

21. Spence, 288.

22. *Works*, 4:447.

23. Ibid., 3:209.

24. Ibid., 3:241.

25. Ibid., 3:242.

26. See Rachel Trickett, *The Honest Muse*, chap. 4.

27. *Works*, 3:481.

28. Ibid., 4:327.

29. Ibid., 4:328.

30. Ibid., 4:329.

Notes to Chapter Two:
The Early Days

1. Spence, 150.

2. Jonathan Swift, *Journal to Stella*, ed. Harold Williams, 1:91–92.

3. *The Poetical Works of Alexander Pope*, ed. Adolphus William Ward, p. xxv.

4. *Corr.*, 1:201.

5. H.M.C., *Downshire* MSS, I, 786, 792, 785.

6. Ibid., I, 804–5.

7. Ibid., I, 812.

8. Ibid., I, 836.

9. Ibid., I, 888.

10. MS English Letters d.59. George Sherburn transcribed this manuscript material in two articles: "New Anecdotes about Alexander Pope" and "Letters of Alexander Pope, Chiefly to Sir William Trumbull," along with the material from the Downshire manuscripts in the Berkshire Record Office. See also Sherburn, "Pope on the Threshold of His Career," for a summary of his findings.

11. Spence, 71.

12. Sherburn, "Pope on the Threshold," p. 46.

13. *Corr.*, 1:45 (Sir William Trumbull to Pope, 9 April 1708); Sherburn, "Letters of Pope," p. 398.

14. Sherburn, "New Anecdotes about Pope," p. 344.

15. Ibid., p. 343.

16. Ibid., p. 344.

17. H.M.C., *Downshire* MSS, I, 782. Pomponius Atticus refused to seek any office of state; instead he left Rome for Athens to assume a life of retirement and study. This would be a stock classical exemplum in the eighteenth century, but the disparity between Pope's and Bolingbroke's attitudes toward him is striking.

18. Sherburn, "New Anecdotes about Pope," p. 347. See also James Osborn's remarks in Spence, 616–18.

19. See Kathleen M. Lynch, *Jacob Tonson*, chap. 3, for the dating of Pope's Kit-Cat activity.

20. Joseph Addison, *Spectator*, ed. Donald F. Bond, no. 555. In the introduction to this edition (pp. xlviii–xlix), Bond challenges Norman Ault's suggestion that Pope contributed substantially to the *Spectator*. In *The Prose Works of Alexander Pope* (Oxford, 1936), Ault included numerous *Spectator* essays as being by Pope, arguing the case in pp. xxxiii–lv.

21. J. M. Aden, *Pope's Once and Future Kings*, pp. 82–90.

22. Owen Ruffhead, *The Life of Alexander Pope*, proof copy, Bodleian Library (1767), p. 140n. See also Spence, 153.

23. *Corr.*, 1:175.

24. *The Letters of John Gay*, ed. C. F. Burgess, pp. 2–3 (Gay to Maurice Johnson, Jr., 23 April 1713).

25. Peter Smithers, *The Life of Joseph Addison*, p. 265.

26. Sherburn, "Letters of Pope," p. 396.

27. Swift, *Journal to Stella*, 2:550.

28. Sherburn, "New Anecdotes about Pope," p. 345.

29. Irvin Ehrenpreis, *Swift*, 2:593.

30. Adina Forsgren, *John Gay*, 2:95.

31. Spence, 135; see also 218.

32. *Corr.*, 1:195.

33. *The Memoirs of Martinus Scriblerus*, ed. Charles Kerby-Miller, p. 23.

34. H. T. Dickinson, *Bolingbroke*, p. 11.

35. Swift, *Journal to Stella*, 1:237, 240.

36. See *The Letters and Correspondence of Henry St. John, Lord Viscount Bolingbroke, 1710–1714*, ed. Gilbert Parke, 4:112–13, 158.

37. *Corr.*, 1:275 (Pope to Congreve, 16 January 1715).

38. TE, 7:24.

39. Williams, 2:176–77 (Swift to Pope, 28 June 1715).

40. A good example of the contiguity in intellectual debate is the discussion in both countries of the relative merits of Newtonian and Cartesian physics. Two of Bolingbroke's close friends came out on opposite sides of the question. See Marjorie Hope Nicolson, "Newton Demands the Muse"; and Dennis J. Fletcher, "Bolingbroke and the Diffusion of Newtonianism in France."

41. See Paul Mazon, "Madame Dacier et les traductions d'Homère en France."

42. TE, 7:13–14.

43. Catalogue of the Collection of Autograph Letters and Historical Documents Formed between 1865 and 1882 by A. Morrison, 2d ser., 1:316.

44. Dennis J. Fletcher, "The Intellectual Relations of Lord Bolingbroke with France," pt. 1, chap. 3.

45. Ibid. Conti translated the Rape of the Lock and the Essay on Man into Italian.

46. Anne Dacier, L'Iliade d'Homère . . . avec quelques reflexions sur la préface angloise de M. Pope, 3:685–86.

47. Corr., 2:157.

48. Ibid., 2:157–58. Presumably it was the letter written by Buckingham on the Dacier–de la Motte dispute, which was brought to Pope's attention while he was editing Buckingham's works, that reminded Pope of Mme Dacier's tract.

49. See TE, 7:xliii–xliv; Guerinot, pp. 78, 86–88.

50. Aden, Pope's Once and Future Kings, pp. 157–59.

51. See Williams, 2:175 (Swift to Knightly Chetwode, 28 June 1715).

52. The best biographical account of Ford is in The Letters of Jonathan Swift to Charles Ford, ed. David Nichol Smith.

53. Corr., 2:27.

54. Letters of Swift, p. 235 (Bolingbroke to Ford, 29 January 1720).

55. Aden, Pope's Once and Future Kings, pp. 169–70.

56. Corr., 2:175 (Pope to Viscount Harcourt, 21 June 1723).

57. Ibid., 2:218.

Notes to Chapter Three: Bolingbroke and Pope, 1723–1730

1. Corr., 2:403 (Bolingbroke to Swift, 22 September 1726).

2. Ibid., 2:184 (Pope to Swift, August 1723).

3. Ibid., 2:220 (Bolingbroke to Pope).

4. Spence, 294, 301.

5. Corr., 2:199 (Swift to Pope, 20 September 1723).

6. TE, 7:ccxxxiii–ccxxxiv; J. M. Aden, Pope's Once and Future Kings, p. 171.

7. Corr., 2:368 (Pope to Fortescue, 17 February 1726).

8. Ibid., 2:380 (Pope to Caryll, 1726).

9. Ibid., 2:403; see also 2:393–400, 401.

10. Bertrand A. Goldgar, Walpole and the Wits, p. 43.

11. Simon R. Varey, "John Gay"; see also Varey, "The Craftsman, 1726–1752," pp. 298–305.

12. Corr., 2:395 (Pope to Swift, 3 September 1726).

13. Ibid., 2:412–13.

14. See the fine account of this in Morris R. Brownell, Alexander Pope and the Arts of Georgian England, pp. 71–249.

15. Corr., 2:328.

16. Maynard Mack, The Garden and the City, p. 28.

17. Corr., 2:236–40.

18. See Peter E. Martin, "Intimations of the New Gardening." This wholly convincing article argues that Digby's Sherborne was a formative influence on Pope as gardener. Sherborne was a pictorial garden, a garden of romantic prospects, and an iconographical monument to Digby family history. Digby shared Pope's reverential sense of filial duty and his respect for family household gods.

19. Brook Taylor, Contemplatio Philosophica, pp. 31–32.

20. Works, 2:349.

21. John Dixon Hunt, The Figure in the Landscape, p. 58. Hunt erroneously cites the earlier work Of the Study and Use of History as the source of this quotation.

22. Williams, 2:398.

23. These Latin inscriptions are conveniently translated by M. R. Hopkinson

in her *Married to Mercury*, bk. 2, chap. 2. The inscription in Bolingbroke's temple, placed over the sculpture of a river-god, reads:

By the frenzies of an outrageous faction,
On account of his unstained fidelity to his queen,
And his strenuous endeavour to accomplish a general peace
Having been forced to seek a new country
Here, at the source of this sacred fountain
Henry of Bolingbroke
Unjustly banished,
Lived pleasantly.

And near the house:

If my country recovers from her madness,
Let her restore me to my native land,
If not, where better than among these people,
To found and adorn this villa:
Hence as from a harbour
It is sweet to gaze on the misfortunes of others
And the insolent sport of Fortune.
Here,
Neither desiring nor fearing death
I enjoy that immovable tranquillity
Which springs from a happy mind,
The time that remains to me of exile
Or of life.

24. *Georgics*, 2.149; *Epistles*, 1.18, 103.
25. Kenneth Woodbridge, "Bolingbroke's Château of La Source," p. 58. Pope's lines to Edward Blount, which first appeared in a letter dated 2 June 1725, now decorate Stourhead, and read as follows:

Nymph of the Grot, these sacred Springs I keep,
And to the Murmur of these Waters sleep,
Ah spare my Slumbers, gently tread the Cave!
And drink in silence, or in silence lave!

26. *Corr.*, 2:229. Another example of Pope's interest in the haunting of a location by spirits of living men is found in *Corr.*, 2:387–88 (Pope to Swift, 22 August 1726). Here he turns Swift into a *genius loci*—a phantom haunting the places he and Swift visited together while the latter was in England. Without Swift's informing presence, Lord Cobham's Stowe and Bathurst's woods at Cirencester Park lose significance. Pope's delight in the dream vision and the fantastic is an aspect of his gardening and a much-neglected aspect of his verse.
27. Ibid., 4:34 (Pope to Fortescue, 21 September 1736).
28. Brownell, *Pope and the Arts*, pp. 225–29.
29. *Corr.*, 2:325, 343.
30. *Lettres Historiques, Politiques, Philosophiques . . . de Bolingbroke*, ed. P. H. Grimoard, 2:429. H. T. Dickinson has either misunderstood or mistranslated this letter. Citing it as evidence, he says that Bolingbroke "even claimed he had lost all political ambition and that he would be happy to live in peaceful obscurity" (*Bolingbroke*, p. 138). Clearly, Bolingbroke is saying the reverse.
31. Sheila Biddle, *Bolingbroke and Harley*, p. 87.
32. B.L. Add. MS. 27, 732, f. 135 and v. Bolingbroke's correspondence with Lord Essex shows a deterioration in the relationship, perhaps because Essex grew impatient at this kind of protestation; see ibid., f. 181.
33. John Dixon Hunt, *The Figure in the Landscape*, p. 75.
34. *Corr.*, 2:331–32.
35. University of London Institute of Historical Research, *The Victoria History of the Counties of England*, ed. R. B. Pugh et al., 3:265.
36. David Jacques, "The Art and Sense of the Scriblerus Club in England, 1715–35."
37. *Corr.*, 2:503.
38. Ibid., 2:441.
39. Ibid., 3:11–12 (Pope to Fortescue, 1729).

40. Ibid., 3:26 (Pope to Oxford, 13 March 1729).

41. Ibid., 3:53.

42. Ibid., 3:91 (Pope to Fortescue, 20 February 1730).

43. Ibid., 2:525 (Pope to Bathurst, 7 November [1728]).

44. Ibid., 2:527 (Pope to James Stopford, 20 November 1728).

45. *Craftsman*, nos. 22, 16, and 61.

46. Ibid., no. 40.

47. See Romney Sedgwick, ed., *The History of Parliament*, 1:36–37; and *Craftsman*, no. 23.

48. *Corr.*, 2:426–27.

49. Aubrey Williams, *Pope's "Dunciad,"* p. 41.

50. *Craftsman*, no. 20.

51. Ibid., no. 29.

52. Ibid., no. 74.

53. TE, 5:132n.

54. *Craftsman*, no. 7.

55. *Hyp Doctor*, 2–9 November 1731; see also Graham Midgley, *The Life of Orator Henley*, pp. 170–84.

56. Williams, 3:278.

57. *Corr.*, 2:453–54 (Pope to Gay, 16 October 1727).

58. Bertrand A. Goldgar, "Pope and the *Grub-street Journal.*"

59. Ibid., p. 372.

60. Ibid., p. 375.

61. James T. Hillhouse, *The "Grub-street Journal,"* pp. 25–39. See also the discussion in Thomas R. Lounsbury, *The Text of Shakespeare*, chap. 19.

62. Goldgar, *Walpole and the Wits*, chap. 4.

Notes to Chapter Four: Bolingbroke and Pope, 1731–1735

1. *Corr.*, 3:163 (Bolingbroke to Swift, January 1731).

2. G. S. Rousseau and Marjorie Hope Nicolson, *"This Long Disease, My Life,"* chap. 1, sec. 5. George Sherburn's dates for the relevant letters are not reliable.

3. *Corr.*, 3:193 (Pope to Oxford, 22 April 1731).

4. Rousseau and Nicolson, *"This Long Disease, My Life,"* p. 47.

5. *Corr.*, 3:211.

6. Patrick Delany, *Revelation Examin'd with Candour . . .*, 1:xxviii.

7. See Chap. 5: "Bolingbroke, Pope, and the *Essay on Man* Revisited."

8. *Craftsman*, no. 238 (23 January 1731).

9. *Corr.*, 3:199 (Pope to Oxford, 21 May 1731).

10. Ibid., 3:236 (Pope to Oxford, 31 October 1731).

11. See Malcolm Goldstein, *Pope and the Augustan Stage*, pp. 48–51.

12. *Corr.*, 3:158.

13. Ibid., 3:177 (Pope to Mallet, 18 February 1731?).

14. The *Craftsman* regularly carried allegorical "Advertisements," designed to cure such allegorical ailments as "the Murmurs of a *grumbling Conscience.*" Interestingly, no. 39 purports to be by the celebrated Dr. John Moore, who invented worm powders. It quotes two stanzas of Pope's poem "To Mr. John Moore, Author of the Celebrated Worm-Powder," which was first published by Curll in 1726 but was later reprinted in vol. 3 of the 1727 *Miscellanies.* The two lines of Swift's poem that precede those quoted allude to *Craftsman* no. 16, "The First Vision of Camilick."

15. Most critics now accept that the Duke of Chandos was not intended; George Sherburn's article " 'Timon's Villa' and Cannons" is convincing. But F. W. Bateson's liberal view that "it is morally certain that 'Timon' was not intended to caricature the Duke of Chandos, or indeed anybody in particular" (TE, 3, pt. 2:xxvi–xxvii) need not prevail. Houghton and Blenheim remain possibilities; see Morris R. Brownell, *Alexander Pope and the Arts of Georgian England*, pp. 309–17 and app. C.

16. Kathleen Mahaffey, "Timon's Villa." See also Maynard Mack, *The Garden and the City*, pp. 122–23, 272–78.

17. TE, 3, pt. 2, reproduces this interesting pamphlet on pp. 176–88. See pp. 186–87 for the mention of Houghton.

18. This is a much earlier date than is usually suggested for Pope's coming out into the open. R. W. Rogers suggests 1733 as the year in which "Pope began to give up his carefully preserved detachment from the political strife of the day" (*The*

Major Satires of Alexander Pope, p. 73).
Maynard Mack also favors 1733 as the date
for Pope's becoming "spiritual patron of
the opposition" (*The Garden and the City*, p.
172). Recently, Bertrand A. Goldgar has
argued for the very late date of 1738 as
being significant in Pope's move toward
politics (*Walpole and the Wits*, p. 178). Goldgar's criterion for what is a "political
poem" appears to be whether it was
attacked on political grounds in government journals and newspapers; that criterion is eccentric. Alternative explanations
for the government's failure to notice
Pope's Imitations include the following:
the poems appeared sporadically and
were not taken as seriously as Pope's original works were; Pope had a privileged
status, rather as famous Soviet dissidents
now have; and the poems are not easily
understood and therefore do not make
simple targets. In any event, Howard D.
Weinbrot, in a review of *Walpole and the
Wits*, made the obvious point that even
with Goldgar's criterion, 1733 is a more
accurate date, as much notice *had* been
taken of Pope's poems by then. Indeed,
the newspapers connected Pope with
Bolingbroke much earlier than this: in the
Weekly Journal for 10 February 1728, for
example, the following song appears:

> I Sing a noble Ditty
> Of *London*'s noble City,
> Whose Wits are all so witty
>   That common Sense can't reach
>   'em
> There's *D'Anvers, S——*, and
> *P———* Sir,
> With whom no Men can cope Sir,
> And if they cou'd, we hope, Sir,
>   They'll yield to *Polly Peachum*.

> The Dean's a fine *Mercator*,
> And *P———* a fine Translator,
> The *Squire* a Calculator,
>   And *Poll* too has her Talent.
> To know what Trade and Coin is
> No Man like the Divine is,
> And *Sawny*'s Wit as fine is
>   As *Polly*'s *Gay* and Gallant.

> Squire *D'Anvers* has his Merits,
> He *Roger*'s Gifts inherits

> And gives his Masters Spirits,
>   When *Polly* scarce can raise 'em.
> These four in strict Alliance
> Most bravely bid Defiance
> To Virtue, Sense and Science;
>   And who but needs must praise
>   'em!

> The Dean his Tales rehearses,
> The Poet taggs his Verses,
> The Squire his Flams disperses
>   And *Poli* her Parts has shewn;
> They thus all Humours hit, Sir,
> The Courtier, and the Cit, Sir,
> And they are both so bit, Sir,
>   The like was never known.

19. *Works*, 3:42.
20. *Corr.*, 3:290–91; *Epistle to Bathurst*, 249–74.
21. For the Parliamentary Report on the Charitable Corporation, see William Cob-bett, *Parliamentary History of England*, 8(1811), paragraphs 1077–1167.
22. *Corr.*, 3:282–83.
23. Ibid., 3:280 (Pope to Oxford, 28 April 1732).
24. Ibid., 3:319–20 (Swift to Gay, 3 October 1732).
25. Ibid., 3:318, 322.
26. Ibid., 3:276.
27. Ibid., 3:295 (Pope to Bathurst, 9 July 1732).
28. Ibid., 3:326 (Pope to Jonathan Richardson, October 1732?).
29. Spence, 321a.
30. Howard Erskine-Hill is rather uncri-tical of Pope and his circle's respect for landownership (*The Social Milieu of Alexan-der Pope*, pp. 266–67). Landlordism was not important to them only because it allowed them to protect the community's interests. On the other hand, Isaac Kram-nick tends to emphasize only the self-interested aspects of their attack on money, which posed a threat to the land-based power structure (*Bolingbroke and His Circle*, pp. 220–23).
31. That these views are identifiable parts of Tory ideology can be seen in H. T. Dickinson, *Liberty and Property*, pp. 51–56.
32. *Lady Mary Wortley Montagu*, ed. Robert Halsband and Isobel Grundy, p. 282. Another version of this poem exists in

B.L. Add. MS. 35, 335, which is not mentioned in the new edition.

33. Guerinot, p. 253.

34. H. T. Dickinson, *Bolingbroke,* p. 243.

35. Paul Langford, *The Excise Crisis,* pp. 106–8.

36. Dickinson, *Bolingbroke,* pp. 230–42.

37. Quoted in Robert Halsband, *Lord Hervey,* p. 109. See his account of the quarrel, pp. 107–20.

38. See Ronald Paulson, *The Fictions of Satire,* pp. 120–28; and Erskine-Hill, *Social Milieu of Pope,* p. 270.

39. His habit of rambling developed much earlier; see the interesting account in Pat Rogers, "Pope's Rambles."

40. *Corr.,* 3:444 (Pope to Swift, 19 December 1734).

41. Ibid., 3:414 (Bolingbroke to Swift, 27 June–6 July 1734).

Notes to Chapter Five: The *Essay on Man* Revisited

1. John Barnard, ed., *Pope,* p. 21.

2. Owen Ruffhead, *The Life of Alexander Pope,* proof copy, Bodleian Library (1767), p. 263. For interesting comment on this biography, see Robert M. Ryley, "Warburton, Warton and Ruffhead's *Life of Pope.*"

3. *The Works of Alexander Pope,* ed. Joseph Warton, 1:lxxii.

4. *The Poetical Works of Alexander Pope,* ed. Adolphus William Ward, p. xxxviii.

5. *The Works of Alexander Pope,* ed. Whitwell Elwin and W. J. Courthope, 5:252.

6. Walter Sichel, *Bolingbroke and His Times,* 2:326; TE, 3, pt. 1:xxix–xxxi.

7. *The Works of Alexander Pope,* ed. William Roscoe, 1:397.

8. TE, 3, pt. 1:xxx.

9. Ibid., p. xxxi.

10. Douglas H. White, *Pope and the Context of Controversy.*

11. TE, 3, pt. 1:xxix.

12. G. S. Rousseau and Marjorie Hope Nicolson, *"This Long Disease, My Life,"* p. 40.

13. Miriam Leranbaum, *Alexander Pope's "Opus Magnum," 1729–1744,* pp. 61–62.

14. John Joerg, "Bolingbroke's Philosophical Writings."

15. The references are *Works,* 3:71, 314, 323, 455; 4:152.

16. See Spence, app. B, 310.

17. Spence, 340.

18. *Corr.,* 3:249.

19. Ibid., 3:275.

20. Ibid., 3:433.

21. *Works,* 4:111.

22. Ibid., 3:127.

23. The exact quotation reads: ". . . Thus much, at least, will here be found, not taken for granted, but proved, that any reasonable Man . . . may be as much assured, as he is of his own Being, however, it is not so clear a Case, that there is nothing in it [Christianity]."

24. W. H. Wilkins, *Caroline the Illustrious,* 2:229.

25. Ernst Campbell Mossner, *Bishop Butler and the Age of Reason,* p. 4.

26. TE, 3, pt. 1:169.

27. Alexander Pope, *Essay on Man,* Pierpont Morgan and Houghton MSS, ed. Maynard Mack, p. xvii.

28. Leranbaum, *Pope's "Opus Magnum,"* p. 20; see also Spence, 310.

29. George Sherburn, "Pope at Work."

30. James Boswell, *Life of Johnson,* 3:402.

31. George Sherburn, "Two Notes on the *Essay on Man,*" p. 402.

32. Joseph Warton, *An Essay on the Genius and Writings of Pope,* 2:62.

33. Boswell, *Life of Johnson,* 3:403–4.

34. See Giles G. Barber, "Bolingbroke, Pope and the *Patriot King.*" I am also indebted to Barber, "A Bibliography of Henry St. John, Viscount Bolingbroke."

35. See David Mallet, *Ballads and Songs,* ed. Frederick Dinsdale, p. 35. Dinsdale thinks Mallet also wrote the *Familiar Epistle* and the offending Advertisement itself. Almost certainly, however, Bolingbroke wrote the latter piece.

36. Henry St. John, Viscount Bolingbroke, *To the Author of a Libel . . . ,* p. 8.

37. *Corr.,* 4:6.

38. Bolingbroke, *To the Author . . . ,* pp. 20–22.

39. Unfortunately, the story is not confirmed by William King in his *Political and Literary Anecdotes of His Own Times.*

40. Barber, "A Bibliography of Henry St. John, Viscount Bolingbroke," pp. 261–62.

41. Reuben Brower, *Alexander Pope*, p. 239.

42. Ibid., pp. 238–39.

43. Leranbaum, *Pope's "Opus Magnum,"* p. 39.

44. Bernard Fabian, "Pope and Lucretius," p. 536.

45. See Margaret C. Jacob, *The Newtonians and the English Revolution 1689–1720.*

46. Fabian, "Pope and Lucretius," p. 528.

47. See Maynard Mack, "Pope's Books."

48. Richard Levin, *New Readings vs. Old Plays*, pp. 209–29.

49. Fabian, "Pope and Lucretius," p. 531.

50. Pope certainly knew Creech's translation, but he did not fully approve of it. On the other hand, he knew the original extremely well. Is Fabian justified in supporting his points by reference to the poem in translation? See Spence, 479, 532.

51. *Works*, 3:44.

52. Fabian, "Pope and Lucretius," p. 526.

53. TE, 3, pt. 1:15n.

54. Fabian, "Pope and Lucretius," p. 536.

55. *Works*, 4:322.

56. Walter Sichel, *Bolingbroke and His Times*, 2:316–30.

57. *Works*, 4:371.

58. Pope was uneasy about these lines; see TE, 3, pt. 1:123–24, app. B.

59. *Works*, 4:182.

60. Alexander Pope, "A Discourse on Pastoral Poetry," *The Prose Works*, p. 298.

61. *Works*, 4:245.

62. Ibid., 3:42.

63. See, for instance, *Fragments* 44; the view is pervasive in Bolingbroke's writings.

64. *Works*, 4:327. See also Brean S. Hammond, " 'Know Then Thyself' and John Gay."

65. Spence, 311.

Notes to Chapter Six: The Last Phase, 1736–1744

1. *Corr.*, 3:427.

2. Spence, 325; see also 506.

3. *Corr.*, 3:277 (Gay to Swift, 13 March 1732).

4. TE, 3, pt. 2, app. A, pp. 159–70.

5. Romney Sedgwick, ed., *The History of Parliament*, p. 107.

6. Howard Erskine-Hill, *The Social Milieu of Alexander Pope*, pp. 96–97.

7. See Pat Rogers, "A Pope Family Scandal"; and E. P. Thompson, "Alexander Pope and the Windsor Blacks." This fascinating exchange revolves around the involvement of Pope's brother-in-law, Charles Rackett, and his son Michael, in an outbreak of social unrest in Windsor Forest between 1722 and 1723. Many of the "Blacks" who took part in attacks on the king's deer and on his foresters were Tory in outlook and resented royal encroachment on the traditional economics of the forest. Some of them, including Rackett, were suspected Jacobites. Thompson convincingly argues that Pope would have been out of sympathy with the reintroduction of "savage laws" to bolster the privileged courtiers against the local inhabitants of Windsor Forest. Perhaps he was responsible for protecting Rackett from prosecution. At all events, Windsor Forest in 1723 came to resemble Pope's picture of it as it had been under "sportive Tyrants" in the 1713 poem *Windsor Forest*.

8. In a seminar paper given at the University of Liverpool in February 1978, Dr. Howard Erskine-Hill argued that the *Rape of the Lock* has a level of political allegory, "rape" referring to William III's unlawful seizure of the crown. This interpretation deserves careful attention. Another piece of evidence in favor of the constancy of Pope's Stuart commitment is furnished in G. E. Jones, "The Jacobites, Charles Molloy and *Common Sense*." This article shows the original inspiration of Charles Molloy's antigovernment periodical *Common Sense*, begun in 1737, to have derived from the Pretender and provides evidence that Pope was connected with it in the early days.

9. *Corr.*, 4:446 (Pope to Bethel, 20 March 1743).

10. Ibid., 3:500–501 (Pope to Bathurst, 8 October 1735).

11. Ibid., 4:6.

12. *Works*, 2:177.

13. Erskine-Hill, *Social Milieu of Pope*, pp. 204–40.

14. *Corr.*, 4:13.

15. Ibid., 4:27–28 (Pope to Swift, 17 August 1736).

16. Williams, 4:437–38.

17. *Works*, 2:359–60.

18. *Corr.*, 4:50–51.

19. See the poems of Lyttelton in *The British Poets*, 56:68.

20. *Corr.*, 4:138–39.

21. Ibid., 4:143–44.

22. Ibid., 4:169.

23. Petworth House Archives 19, f. 102–4 (Bolingbroke to Wyndham, 3 February 1738).

24. *Corr.*, 4:149 (Pope to Bathurst, 23 November 1738).

25. Mable Hessler Cable, "The Idea of a Patriot King in the Propaganda of the Opposition to Walpole, 1735–39."

26. Malcolm Goldstein, *Pope and the Augustan Stage*, pp. 56–64.

27. See especially *Corr.*, 4:126–27 (Pope to Hill, 12 September 1738); and *The Works of Aaron Hill*, 2:17.

28. Goldstein, *Pope and the Augustan Stage*, p. 61. He appears to know practically nothing about the political activity of the period.

29. *Corr.*, 4:136 (Pope to Orrery, 19 October 1738). See Pope's satire on "Vanmuck" in *Epistle* II.2.229.

30. Howard D. Weinbrot, *Augustus Caesar in "Augustan" England*, especially chap. 6.

31. TE, 4:xxxvii–xxxviii.

32. As one example, we might take lines 89–92 of the poem. What, finally, is the judgment on Cibber's play *The Careless Husband?*

33. See especially *Daily Gazeteer*, 6 April 1738.

34. *Corr.*, 4:108–9 (Pope to Allen, 6 July 1738).

35. Ibid., 4:178 (Pope to Swift, 17–19 May 1738).

36. See Robert W. Rogers, *The Major Satires of Alexander Pope*, pp. 74–75.

37. *Corr.*, 4:271–73 (Pope to Marchmont, October 1740). See also *A Selection from the Papers of the Earls of Marchmont*, ed.

G. H. Rose, 2:177–387 passim for correspondence between Marchmont and Bolingbroke. By this time, Bolingbroke was in France again. Marchmont visited him early in 1740, probably bringing letters from Pope that do not survive.

38. *Corr.*, 4:261.

39. I have quoted the version of TE, 6:382–83, which differs slightly from that sent to Bolingbroke.

40. *Corr.*, 4:369.

41. TE, 3, pt. 1:xv–xxii.

42. Margaret C. Jacob, *The Newtonians and the English Revolution 1689–1720*, chap. 6.

43. *Corr.*, 4:171–72 (Pope to Warburton, 11 April 1739).

44. Ibid., 4:199.

45. Ibid., 4:207 (Pope to Henry Brooke, 1 December 1739).

46. *The Works of the Right Reverend William Warburton*, ed. Richard Hurd, 1:211.

47. *Corr.*, 4:251 (Pope to Warburton, 24 June 1740).

48. Ibid., 4:402 (Pope to Warburton, 18 June 1742).

49. Rogers, *The Major Satires*, chap. 5.

50. *Corr.*, 4:434 (Pope to Warburton, 28 December 1742).

51. Erskine-Hill, *Social Milieu of Pope*, pp. 234–35.

52. *Corr.*, 4:464 (Pope to Martha Blount, early August 1743).

53. Rogers, *The Major Satires*, pp. 97–98.

54. Spence, 290.

55. *Works of Warburton*, ed. Richard Hurd, 12:334–40.

56. *Corr.*, 4:504 (Pope to Allen, 6 March 1744), 4:515–16 (Pope to Warburton, ? April 1744).

57. Owen Ruffhead, *The Life of Alexander Pope*, proof copy, Bodleian Library (1767), p. 219.

58. Spence, 647, 653.

59. H. T. Dickinson, *Bolingbroke*, chap. 14; Fannie E. Ratchford, "Pope and the Patriot King"; Giles G. Barber, "Bolingbroke, Pope and the *Patriot King.*"

60. See especially [Warburton], *A Letter to the Editor of the Letters on the Spirit of Patriotism . . .* (1749); and [Bolingbroke], *To the Author of a Libel . . .* (1749).

Notes to Chapter Seven: The *Epistle to Bolingbroke*

1. *The Wentworth Papers, 1705–1739*, ed. James J. Cartwright, p. 395.

2. There are a number of recent articles on Pope's Erasmianism, with all of which I tend to disagree in that I regard Pope's invocation of Erasmus as a tactical maneuver rather than a sincere belief. See Patrick Cruttwell, "Pope and His Church"; Edwin Nierenberg, "Pope and God at Twickenham"; G. Douglas Atkins, "Pope and Deism"; and Chester Chapin, "Alexander Pope."

3. Atkins, *Pope and Deism*, p. 278. Discussions of Pope's deistic tendencies are bedeviled by the difficulty in defining what exactly was meant by the term in eighteenth-century usage, but the general trend among recent critics is to deny that he was influenced in that direction; see John Laird, *Philosophical Incursions into English Literature*, chap. 3; Arthur Friedman, "Pope and Deism"; Nancy K. Lawlor, "Pope's *Essay on Man*"; Douglas H. White, *Pope and the Context of Controversy*; G. Douglas Atkins, "Pope and Deism"; and Bernard Fabian, "Pope and Lucretius." The eighteenth-century theologian Samuel Clarke gives an excellently clear definition of deism in his *Evidences of Natural and Revealed Religion*, stating that the crucial points are the nonacceptance of the doctrine of a future state beyond the grave and the rejection of revealed religion as the means of discovering the deity's true nature. Pope's *Essay on Man* does seem to me to warrant the description *deist* on these grounds. Pope goes no further, in lines 73–112, than to *hope* that there is such a future state, and there is no mention of revelation in the poem, or indeed of Christ as a living presence. Clearly, however, Pope would not go as far along the deist road as did Bolingbroke; see *Corr.*, 3:213 (Bolingbroke to Swift, 2 August 1731).

4. Pope was profoundly uncertain from the outset about the *Essay on Man*'s reception. To test the ground, he pretended to his orthodox Catholic friend John Caryll that he was not its author. An even more strenuous attempt to ensure its orthodoxy was blocked by Bishop Berkeley; Pope had intended to begin the poem with an invocation to "our Saviour" based on Lucretius's invocation to Epicurus in *De Rerum Natura* (see Spence, 305).

5. Thomas E. Maresca, *Pope's Horatian Poems*, chap. 5. Parenthetical references throughout the following paragraph are to this work.

6. Peter Dixon arrives at a similar view in *The World of Pope's Satires*, chap. 9. Barbara Lauren takes issue with Maresca's assumption that retirement is Pope's escape from the world, arguing that retirement is itself an aspect of committed political satire. I dispute her assumption that "Pope's concerns in this poem are above all political" ("Pope's *Epistle to Bolingbroke*," p. 419).

7. See, for example, *Craftsman*, no. 66, 9 October 1727, where Barnard is defended against charges made by James Pit that he is a high-church Tory and an enemy of dissent.

8. That Pope's use of exemplary history derives from Bolingbroke is supported by Thomas Akstens, "Pope and Bolingbroke on 'Examples.' " Bolingbroke's influential theory of the virtuous monarch is present in *The Idea of a Patriot King*, which probably was composed shortly after Pope's poem.

9. "Operas and masquerades, with all the politer elegancies of a wanton age, are much less to be regarded for their expense (great as it is) than for the tendency which they have to deprave our manners" (*Works*, 1:476; originally printed as *Craftsman*, no. 29).

10. Lines 106–8. All quotations from Horace are from the Loeb translation of Horace, *Satires, Epistles and Ars Poetica*, ed. and trans. by H. Rushton Fairclough.

11. This point can be made in general about Pope's manipulation of Horace. George K. Hunter speaks of Pope's introduction of "the injured Byronic sensibility of the individual" into *To Fortescue* ("The Romanticism of Pope's Horace," p. 403). This article is important in that it challenges the Augustan/romantic polarity, as I also wish to do.

12. The most recent discussion of the relationship between Pope's and Horace's

poems also concludes that "the key to the difference between them . . . lies in the intensity of Pope's feelings for Bolingbroke." See Frank Stack, "Pope's *Epistle to Bolingbroke* and *Epistle* I.i," p. 187.

13. Williams, 2:316 (Bolingbroke to Swift, 17 March 1718–1719). The lines read:

> Survey mankind, observe what risks they run,
> What fancy'd ills, thro' real dangers, shun,
> Those fancy'd ills, so dreadful to the great,
> A lost election, or impair'd Estate.
> Observe the merchant, who, intent on Gain
> Affronts the terrors of the Indian main,
> Tho' storms arise, and broken Rocks appear,
> He flys from poverty, and knows no other fear.
> Vain Men! who might arrive, with toil far less,
> By smoother paths, att greater happiness;
> For 'tis superior bliss not to desire
> That trifling good, which fondly you admire,
> Possess precarious, and too dear acquire.

14. Griffin, *Alexander Pope*, p. 205.

15. Maresca, *Pope's Horatian Poems*, pp. 178–81.

16. For Montaigne's skepticism, see *Works*, 4:178–80, 328–29; for Locke's gullibility, see *Works*, 3:404–5.

17. I can find little justification for John Butt's supposition that "Aristippus was Bolingbroke's favourite philosopher" (TE, 4:281n). Given the extreme dearth of knowledge about Aristippus—presumably, everything Bolingbroke knew about him came from Diogenes Laertius—this is not a very intelligible claim. Swift calls Bolingbroke "Aristippus" in a letter dated 5 April 1729 (*Corr.*, 3:29) as a gibe at his extravagance. The name was a private joke.

18. See especially *Works*, 3:420–28.

19. Yasmine Gooneratne, *Alexander Pope*, p. 7.

20. See, for instance, Reuben Brower, *Alexander Pope*; John M. Aden, *Something Like Horace*; and Howard D. Weinbrot, *The Formal Strain*.

21. Elder Olson, "Rhetoric and the Appreciation of Pope."

22. Maynard Mack, "The Muse of Satire."

23. See Irvin Ehrenpreis, *Literary Meaning and Augustan Values*, pp. 49–60.

24. The point is made explicitly by Dustin Griffin: "Self-revelation . . . is almost always a carefully calculated performance, acted out in a public arena and designed to persuade an audience . . . Pope, though always personal, is never private" (*Alexander Pope*, p. 12). Griffin's book belongs to the class of those who regard Pope as a role-player but argue for an intimate relationship between true self and role.

Notes to Chapter Eight: The Common Language

1. P. G. M. Dickson, *The Financial Revolution in England*, p. 203.

2. B. W. Hill, *The Growth of Parliamentary Parties, 1689–1742*, p. 210.

3. Quentin Skinner, "The Principles and Practice of Opposition."

4. See Jeffrey Hart, *Viscount Bolingbroke*; Harvey C. Mansfield, *Statesmanship and Party Government*; Isaac Kramnick, *Bolingbroke and His Circle*; and J. H. Grainger, "The Deviations of Lord Bolingbroke."

5. J. P. Kenyon, *Revolution Principles*, pp. 203–4.

6. Kramnick, *Bolingbroke and His Circle*, p. 111.

7. J. H. Plumb, *The Growth of Political Stability in England, 1675–1725*.

8. Annual sessions of Parliament were secured indirectly by the financial requirements of the executive, which ensured frequent recourse to Parliament for revenue.

9. H. T. Dickinson, *Liberty and Property*, chap. 4.

10. Plumb, *Growth of Political Stability*, p. 129.

11. The *Remarks* and the *Dissertation* first appeared as *Craftsman* essays between 1730–1731 and 1733–1734 respectively. It is not certain when the *Patriot King* was written, but I think it was written in 1738–1739. Pope had read it before he died, though it remained unpublished until 1749.

12. *Works*, 2:140. Bolingbroke oscillated between the Lockean prehistoric contract and the "ancient constitution" view in his thinking about political origins.

13. Arbitrary power remained a bogey for a considerable time, especially in literature. See James T. Boulton, "Arbitrary Power."

14. See Pat Rogers, "Swift and Bolingbroke on Faction."

15. *Works*, 2:118.

16. H. T. Dickinson, *Bolingbroke*, p. 252.

17. The *Craftsman* kept before its readers' attention a whole series of wicked ministers in history, whose dealings with their monarchs were represented as analogous to Walpole's—Wolsey, Sejanus, Mortimer. Especially in its reviews of plays it sought possibilities of drawing parallels to Walpole.

18. *Works*, 2:151–52.

19. Kramnick, *Bolingbroke and His Circle*, p. 78.

20. See J. G. A. Pocock, *Politics, Language and Time*, chap. 4; Skinner, "The Principles and Practice of Opposition"; Kramnick, *Bolingbroke and His Circle*, chap. 9; and Dickinson, *Bolingbroke*, chap. 12.

21. Pocock, *Politics, Language and Time*, pp. 124–47.

22. See F. W. Walbank, *Polybius*, pp. 130–37.

23. See Herbert Butterfield, *The Statecraft of Machiavelli*, and Hart, *Viscount Bolingbroke*, for discussions of Bolingbroke's debt to Machiavelli.

24. *Works*, 2:426.

25. Ibid., 2:401.

26. Ralf Dahrendorf, "Out of Utopia."

27. See, for instance, the *London Journal*, nos. 558, 570, 571, 581, and 765.

28. Edmund Burke, *A Vindication of Natural Society* . . . .

29. Ibid., p. 67.

30. *Works*, 2:412, 373, 374, 396–97.

31. Ronald C. Paulson, *The Fictions of Satire*, pp. 120–28.

32. The *Craftsman* was largely responsible for generating and perpetuating this mythology.

33. Burke, *Vindication of Natural Society*, pp. 69–70.

34. *Corr.*, 1:126 (Pope to Caryll, 19 July 1711).

35. Ibid., 1:454.

36. See Chapter 7, note 2; in addition to the studies listed there, see also James King, "Pope and Erasmus' 'Great Injur'd Name.' "

37. See, for instance, F. B. Thornton, *Alexander Pope*, for an account of Pope's religious observance.

38. Simon R. Varey, "The *Craftsman*, 1726–1752."

39. *Craftsman*, no. 297.

40. Ibid., pp. 51, 52, 55.

41. Erskine-Hill, *The Social Milieu of Alexander Pope*, pt. 3, chap. 8.

42. It has been argued that Gay's second series *Fables* was inspired by the *Craftsman*; see Edwin Graham, "John Gay's Second Series."

43. James M. Osborn, "Pope, the Byzantine Empress, and Walpole's Whore."

44. See *Epistle to Bathurst*, 135–37; *Epistle to Arbuthnot*, 327; and *Epistle to Augustus*, 251.

Notes to Chapter Nine: Satire and Political Theory

1. Bertrand A. Goldgar, *Walpole and the Wits*.

2. Benedict de Spinoza, *Tractatus Politicus*, in his *Political Works*, ed. by A. G. Wernham, p. 261.

3. See Anthony Quinton, ed., *Political Philosophy*, pp. 1–18.

4. Sheldon S. Wolin, *Politics and Vision*, pp. 17–21.

5. Thomas Hobbes, *Leviathan*, ed. C. B. Macpherson, pp. 185–86.

6. C. B. Macpherson, *The Political Theory of Possessive Individualism*, p. 20.

7. Wolin, *Politics and Vision*, pp. 262–65.

8. Northrop Frye, "Varieties of Literary Utopias," p. 109.

9. Peter Laslett, in his edition of Locke's *Two Treatises of Government*, pp. 58-79, demonstrates that much of the second treatise was actually composed *after* 1689.

10. See H. T. Dickinson, *Liberty and Property*, chap. 2, and J. P. Kenyon, *Revolution Principles*.

11. Dickinson, *Liberty and Property*, chap. 2.

12. *Works*, 4:196.

13. Isaac Kramnick, *Bolingbroke and His Circle*, p. 98. See also Isaac Kramnick, "An Augustan Reply to Locke," p. 585.

14. Kramnick probably exaggerates also the extent to which Locke's ideas were a *deliberate* sponsorship of the moneyed interest. He was more directly concerned with defending the landed interest, although his political views could accommodate forms of property other than real estate more easily than could his opponents' views.

15. *Works*, 4:160.

16. P. K. Elkin, *The Augustan Defence of Satire*, chap. 4.

17. John Dryden, *A Discourse . . . concerning the Original and Progress of Satire*, 2:137.

18. *Works*, 2:332–33.

19. G. H. Nadel, "Philosophy of History before Historicism."

20. Quoted by Bolingbroke, *Works*, 2:178.

21. G. H. Nadel, "New Light on Bolingbroke's *Letters on History*."

22. Thomas Akstens, "Pope and Bolingbroke on 'Examples.' "

23. *Corr.*, 3:420 (Pope to Arbuthnot, 26 July 1734).

24. Ibid., 3:423.

25. George de F. Lord, ed., *Poems on Affairs of State*, 1:xlix.

26. Maynard Mack, "Pope's Books," p. 288.

27. *Corr.*, 3:276 (Bolingbroke and Pope to Swift, March 1732).

28. Northrop Frye, *The Anatomy of Criticism*, pp. 223–39. See also Alvin B. Kernan, *The Cankered Muse* and *The Plot of Satire*.

29. Maynard Mack, "The Muse of Satire."

Bibliography

Primary Sources

Addison, Joseph. *The Spectator.* Edited by Donald F. Bond. 5 vols. Oxford, 1965.

Additional MSS. 27, 732–5 (Essex MSS); 35, 335 (British Library).

Arbuthnot, John. *The Life and Works of John Arbuthnot.* Edited by G. A. Aitken. 8 vols. 1892.

Bentley, Thomas. *A Letter to Mr. Pope.* 1735.

Henry St. John, Viscount Bolingbroke. *A Familiar Epistle to the Most Impudent Man Living.* 1749.

———. *The Letters and Correspondence of Henry St. John, Lord Viscount Bolingbroke, 1710–1714.* Edited by Gilbert Parke. 4 vols. 1798.

———. *Lettres Historiques, Politiques, Philosophiques . . . de Bolingbroke.* Edited by P. H. Grimoard. 3 vols. Paris, 1808.

———. *The Philosophical Works.* Edited by David Mallet. 5 vols. 1754–1776.

———. *To the Author of a Libel . . . .* 1749.

———. *The Works of Lord Bolingbroke.* 4 vols. 1841. Reprint. Philadelphia, 1969.

Burke, Edmund. *A Vindication of Natural Society . . . .* 1756.

Butler, Joseph. *The Analogy of Religion . . . to the Constitution and Course of Nature.* 1736.

Clarke, Samuel. *Evidences of Natural and Revealed Religion.* 4th ed. 1716.

The Craftsman. 1726–1736.

de Crousaz, J. P. *An Examination of Mr. Pope's Essay on Man.* Translated by Elizabeth Carter. 1739.

[Curll, Edmund.] *The Popiad . . . .* Bound with "Madame Dacier's Reflections upon Mr. Pope's Account of Homer." 1728.

Dacier, Anne. *L'Iliade d'Homère . . . avec quelques reflexions sur la préface angloise de M. Pope.* 3 vols. Paris, 1719.

Daily Gazeteer. 1737.

Delany, Patrick. *Revelation Examin'd with Candour . . . .* 2 vols. 1732.

Dennis, John. *A True Character of Mr. Pope . . . .* 2d ed. 1717.

Dryden, John. *A Discourse . . . concerning the Original and Progress of Satire.* 1693. In *Dryden: Of Dramatic Poesy.* Edited by George Watson. 2 vols. 1962. Reprint. 1968.

Fielding, Henry. *A Fragment of a Comment on Bolingbroke's Essays.* In *The Journal of a Voyage to Lisbon.* Edited by Austin Dobson. 1892.

Gay, John. *The Letters of John Gay.* Edited by C. F. Burgess. Oxford, 1966.

———. *The Poetry and Prose of John Gay.* Edited by Vinton A. Dearing. 2 vols. Oxford, 1974.

The Gentleman's Magazine. 1731–1833.

Hervey, John, Lord. *Sedition and Defamation Display'd.* 1731.

Hill, Aaron. *The Works of Aaron Hill.* 4 vols. 1753.

Historical Manuscripts Commission (H.M.C.), *Downshire MSS.*, I.

179

Horace, Quintus Flaccus. *Satires, Epistles and Ars Poetica*. Edited and translated by H. Rushton Fairclough. 1929.

The Hyp Doctor. 1730–1739.

Leland, John. *A View of the Principal Deistical Writers of the Last and Present Century*. 2 vols. 1755.

The London Journal. 1720–1734.

Lord, George de F., ed. *Poems on Affairs of State: Augustan Satirical Verse, 1660–1714*. 7 vols. New Haven, Conn., 1963–1975.

Lyttelton, George. *The Persian Letters*. 1735.

———. Poems. In *The British Poets*. 100 vols. Chiswick, 1822. Vol. 56.

Mallet, David. *Ballads and Songs*. Edited by Frederick Dinsdale. 1857.

Mandeville, Bernard. *The Fable of the Bees*. Edited by F. B. Kaye. 2 vols. Oxford, 1924.

Marchmont, Earls of. *A Selection from the Papers of the Earls of Marchmont*. Edited by G. H. Rose. 3 vols. 1831.

The Memoirs of Martinus Scriblerus. Edited by Charles Kerby-Miller. New Haven, Conn., 1950.

Montagu, Lady Mary Wortley. *The Complete Letters of Lady Mary Wortley Montagu*. Edited by Robert Halsband. 3 vols. Oxford, 1965–1967.

———. *Lady Mary Wortley Montagu: Essays and Poems . . . .* Edited by Robert Halsband and Isobel Grundy. Oxford, 1977.

The Monthly Review. 1749–1789.

Morrison, Alfred. *Catalogue of the Collection of Autograph Letters and Historical Documents Formed between 1865 and 1882*. Compiled and annotated under the direction of A. W. Thibaudeau. 6 vols. 1883–1892. 2d series. 3 vols. 1882–1893. (Printed for private circulation.)

MS. Eng. Lett. d.59. Bodleian Library, Oxford.

Oldmixon, John. *The Catholick Poet . . . .* 1716.

Orrery, John, Earl of. *Remarks on the Life and Writings of Dr. Swift*. 1752.

Parnell, Thomas. *An Essay on the Different Stiles of Poetry*. 1713.

———. *The Poetical Works of Thomas Parnell*. Edited by G. A. Aitken. 1894.

Pasquin. 1722–1724.

Petworth House Archives 19; Egremont MSS (Bolingbroke/Wyndham correspondence).

Philips, Ambrose. *Pastorals, Epistles, Odes and Other Original Poems*. 1748. Reprint, 1973.

Pope, Alexander. *The Correspondence of Alexander Pope*. Edited by George Sherburn. 5 vols. Oxford, 1956.

———. *An Essay on Man*. Pierpont Morgan and Houghton MSS. Edited by Maynard Mack. Roxburghe Club. Oxford, 1962.

———. *The Poetical Works of Alexander Pope*. Edited by Adolphus William Ward. 1869.

———. *The Prose Works of Alexander Pope: The Earlier Works, 1711–1720*. Edited by Norman Ault. 1936. Reprint. Oxford, 1968.

———. *The Twickenham Edition of the Poems of Alexander Pope*. Edited by John Butt et al. 10 vols. 1939–1967.

———. *The Works of Alexander Pope*. Edited by Whitwell Elwin and W. J. Courthope. 10 vols. 1871–1889.

———. *The Works of Alexander Pope*. Edited by William Roscoe. 10 vols. 1824.

———. *The Works of Alexander Pope*. Edited by Joseph Warton. 9 vols. 1797.

Ruffhead, Owen. *The Life of Alexander Pope*. Proof copy, Bodleian Library, 1767. 1st ed., 1769.

Sedgwick, Romney, ed. *The History of Parliament: The House of Commons, 1715–1754*. 2 vols. 1970.

Sherburn, George. "Letters of Alexander Pope, Chiefly to Sir William Trumbull." *Review of English Studies* 9(1958): 388–406.

———. "New Anecdotes about Alexander Pope." *Notes and Queries* 203(1958): 343–49.

Spence, Joseph. *Observations, Anecdotes and Characters of Books and Men: Collected from Conversation by Joseph Spence*. Edited by James M. Osborn. 2 vols. Oxford, 1966.

de Spinoza, Benedict. *Political Works*. Edited by A. G. Wernham. Oxford, 1958.

Swift, Jonathan. *The Correspondence of Jonathan Swift*. Edited by Harold Williams. 5 vols. 1963.

———. *Journal to Stella*. Edited by Harold Williams. 2 vols. Oxford, 1948.

———. *The Letters of Jonathan Swift to Charles Ford*. Edited by David Nichol Smith. Oxford, 1935.

———. *The Poems of Jonathan Swift*. 2d ed. Edited by Harold Williams. 3 vols. Oxford, 1958.

———. *The Prose Works of Jonathan Swift*. Edited by Herbert Davis. 13 vols. Oxford, 1939–1964.

Taylor, Brook. *Contemplatio Philosophica*. Edited by Sir William Young. 1793.

Trapp, Joseph. *Peace*. 1713.

Warburton, William. *A Letter to the Editor of the Letters on the Spirit of Patriotism . . . Occasioned by the Editor's Advertisement*. 1749.

———. *A View of Lord Bolingbroke's Philosophy*. 1754.

———. *A Vindication of Mr. Pope's "Essay on Man" from the Misrepresentations of M. de Crousaz: In Six Letters*. 1740.

———. *The Works of the Right Reverend William Warburton*. Edited by Richard Hurd. 14 vols. 1811.

Warton, Joseph. *An Essay on the Genius and Writings of Pope*. 4th ed. 2 vols. 1782.

The Weekly Journal. 1717–1725.

The Wentworth Papers, 1705–1739. Edited by James J. Cartwright. 1883.

Wollaston, William. *The Religion of Nature Delineated*. 1722.

Secondary Sources

Aden, John M. *Pope's Once and Future Kings: Satire and Politics in the Early Career*. Knoxville, Tenn., 1978.

———. *Something Like Horace: Studies in the Art and Allusion of Pope's Horatian Satires*. Nashville, 1969.

Akstens, Thomas. "Pope and Bolingbroke on 'Examples': An Echo of the *Letters on History* in Pope's *Correspondence*." *Philological Quarterly* 52 (1973): 232–38.

Allen, Robert J. *The Clubs of Augustan London*. Cambridge, Mass., 1933.

Atkins, G. Douglas. "Pope and Deism: A New Analysis." *Huntington Library Quarterly* 35 (1971–1972): 257–78.

Audra, Emile. *L'Influence française dans l'oeuvre de Pope*. Paris, 1931.

———. *Les Traductions françaises de Pope, 1717–1825*. Paris, 1931.

Barber, Giles G. "A Bibliography of Henry St. John, Viscount Bolingbroke." B.Litt. diss., University of Oxford, 1963.

———. "Bolingbroke, Pope and the *Patriot King*." *The Library* 19 (1964): 67–89.

Barnard, John, ed. *Pope: The Critical Heritage*.1973.

Biddle, Sheila. *Bolingbroke and Harley.* 1975.

Boswell, James. *Life of Johnson.* Edited by G. B. Hill and revised by L. F. Powell. 6 vols. Oxford, 1971.

Boulton, James T. "Arbitrary Power: An Eighteenth Century Obsession." University of Nottingham Inaugural Address (November 1966), pp. 3–24.

Bredvold, Louis I. "The Gloom of the Tory Satirists." In *Eighteenth Century English Literature,* edited by James L. Clifford, pp. 3–20. Oxford, 1959.

Brower, Reuben. *Alexander Pope: The Poetry of Allusion.* Oxford, 1959. Reprint. 1968.

Brownell, Morris R. *Alexander Pope and the Arts of Georgian England.* Oxford, 1978.

———. *Alexander Pope's Villa.* Exhibition catalogue for the Greater London Council's exhibition "Views of Pope's Villa, Grotto and Garden: A Microcosm of English Landscape." 1980.

Butterfield, Herbert. *The Statecraft of Machiavelli.* 1940.

Cable, Mable Hessler. "The Idea of a Patriot King in the Propaganda of the Opposition to Walpole, 1735–39." *Philological Quarterly* 18 (1939): 119–30.

Chapin, Chester. "Alexander Pope: Erasmian Catholic." *Eighteenth Century Studies* 6 (1972–1973): 411–30.

Chesterfield, Philip Dormer Stanhope, Earl of. *Letters of Philip Dormer Stanhope, Fourth Earl of Chesterfield.* Edited by Bonamy Dobrée. 6 vols. 1932.

Cobbett, William. *Parliamentary History of England.* 36 vols. 1806–1820.

Cruttwell, Patrick. "Pope and His Church." *Hudson Review* 13 (1960): 392–405.

Dahrendorf, Ralf. "Out of Utopia: Towards a Reorientation of Sociological Analysis." *American Journal of Sociology* 64, no. 2 (September 1958): 115–27.

Dickinson, H. T. *Bolingbroke.* 1970.

———. "Henry St. John and the Struggle for Leadership of the Tory Party." Ph.D. diss., University of Newcastle, 1967.

———. *Liberty and Property.* 1977.

Dickson, P. G. M. *The Financial Revolution in England.* 1967.

Dixon, Peter. *The World of Pope's Satires.* 1968.

Earle, Peter. *The World of Defoe.* 1976.

Ehrenpreis, Irvin. *Literary Meaning and Augustan Values.* Charlottesville, Va., 1974.

———. *Swift: The Man, His Works, and the Age.* 3 vols. 1962–1983.

Elkin, P. K. *The Augustan Defence of Satire.* Oxford, 1973.

Elliott, R. C. *The Power of Satire.* Princeton, 1960.

Erskine-Hill, Howard H. *The Social Milieu of Alexander Pope.* New Haven, Conn., 1975.

Evans, A. W. *Warburton and the Warburtonians.* 1932.

Fabian, Bernard. "Pope and Lucretius: Observations on 'An Essay on Man.' " *Modern Language Review* 74 (1979): 524–37.

Fletcher, Dennis J. "Bolingbroke and the Diffusion of Newtonianism in France." *Studies in Voltaire and the Eighteenth Century* 53 (1967): 29–46.

———. "The Intellectual Relations of Lord Bolingbroke with France." Master's diss., University of Wales, 1953.

Forsgren, Adina. *John Gay: Poet "of a Lower Order."* 2 vols. Stockholm, 1964–1971.

Foxon, D. F. *English Verse 1701–1750: A Catalogue of Separately Printed Poems.* 2 vols. Cambridge, 1975.

Friedman, Arthur. "Pope and Deism." In *Pope and His Contemporaries: Essays Presented to George Sherburn,* edited by James L. Clifford and Louis Landa, pp. 89–95. Oxford, 1949.

Frye, Northrop. *The Anatomy of Criticism.* 1957. Reprint. Princeton, N.J., 1973.

———. "Varieties of Literary Utopias." In *The Stubborn Structure: Essays on Criticism and Society*, pp. 109–34. 1970.

Goldgar, Bertrand A. "Pope and the *Grub-street Journal*." *Modern Philology* 74(1976–1977): 366–80.

———. *Walpole and the Wits: The Relation of Politics to Literature, 1722–1742*. Lincoln, Neb., 1976.

Goldstein, Malcolm. *Pope and the Augustan Stage*. Stanford, 1958.

Gooneratne, Yasmine. *Alexander Pope*. Cambridge, 1976.

Graham, Edwin. "John Gay's Second Series: The *Craftsman* in Fables." *Papers in English Language and Literature* 5, no. 1 (Winter 1969): 17–25.

Grainger, J. H. "The Deviations of Lord Bolingbroke." *Australian Journal of Politics and History* 15 (1969): 41–59.

Griffin, Dustin H. *Alexander Pope: The Poet in the Poems*. Princeton, N.J., 1978.

Guerinot, J. V. *Pamphlet Attacks on Alexander Pope, 1711–1744: A Descriptive Bibliography*. 1969.

Halsband, Robert. *Lord Hervey: Eighteenth Century Courtier*. Oxford, 1973.

Hammond, Brean S. " 'Know Then Thyself' and John Gay." *Notes and Queries*, n.s. 23, no. 8 (August 1976): 348.

Hart, Jeffrey. *Viscount Bolingbroke: Tory Humanist*. 1965.

Hervey, John, Lord. *Some Materials towards Memoirs of the Reign of King George II, by John, Lord Hervey*. Edited by Romney Sedgwick. 3 vols. 1931.

Hill, B. W. *The Growth of Parliamentary Parties, 1689–1742*. 1976.

Hillhouse, James T. *The "Grub-street Journal."* Durham, N.C., 1928.

Hobbes, Thomas. *Leviathan*. Edited by C. B. Macpherson. 1968. Reprint. Harmondsworth, Middlesex, 1974.

Hodgart, Matthew. *Satire*. 1969.

Hopkinson, M. R. *Married to Mercury*. 1936.

Hunt, John Dixon. *The Figure in the Landscape: Poetry, Painting, and Gardening during the Eighteenth Century*. Baltimore, 1976.

Hunter, George K. "The Romanticism of Pope's Horace." *Essays in Criticism* 10 (1960) : 390–404.

Jacob, Margaret C. *The Newtonians and the English Revolution 1689–1720*. Sussex, 1976.

Jacques, David. "The Art and Sense of the Scriblerus Club in England, 1715–35." *Garden History* 4 (Spring 1976): 30–53.

James, D. G. *The Life of Reason: Hobbes, Locke, Bolingbroke*. 1949.

Joerg, John. "Bolingbroke's Philosophical Writings: The Probable Date of Composition: After 1734." *Notes and Queries* 214 (May 1969): 184.

Jones, G. E. "The Jacobites, Charles Molloy and *Common Sense*." *Review of English Studies* 4 (1953): 144–47.

Keener, Frederick M. *An Essay on Pope*. New York, 1974.

Kenyon, J. P. *Revolution Principles: The Politics of Party, 1689–1720*. Cambridge, 1977.

Kernan, Alvin B. *The Cankered Muse*. New Haven, Conn., 1959.

———. *The Plot of Satire*. New Haven, Conn., 1965.

King, James. "Pope and Erasmus' 'Great, Injur'd Name.' " *English Studies* 55 (1974): 424–27.

King, William. *Political and Literary Anecdotes of His Own Times*. 1818.

Kramnick, Isaac. "An Augustan Reply to Locke: Bolingbroke on Natural Law and the Origin of Government." *Political Science Quarterly* 82 (1967): 571–94.

———. *Bolingbroke and His Circle: The Politics of Nostalgia in the Age of Walpole*. Cambridge, Mass., 1968.

Laird, John. *Philosophical Incursions into English Literature*. Cambridge, 1946.

Langford, Paul. *The Excise Crisis: Society and Politics in the Age of Walpole*. Oxford, 1975.

Lauren, Barbara. "Pope's *Epistle to Bolingbroke:* Satire from the Vantage of Retirement." *Studies in English Literature* 15 (1975): 419–30.

Lawlor, Nancy K. "Pope's *Essay on Man:* Oblique Light for a False Mirror." *Modern Language Quarterly* 28 (1967): 305–16.

Leranbaum, Miriam. *Alexander Pope's "Opus Magnum," 1729–1744*. Oxford, 1977.

Levin, Richard. *New Readings vs. Old Plays*. Chicago, 1979.

Locke, John. *Two Treatises of Government*. Edited by Peter Laslett. 1960. Rev. ed. New York, 1965.

Lounsbury, Thomas R. *The Text of Shakespeare*. 1906.

Lynch, Kathleen M. *Jacob Tonson: Kit-Cat Publisher*. Knoxville, Tenn., 1971.

Mack, Maynard. *The Garden and the City: Retirement and Politics in the Later Poetry of Pope, 1731–1743*. 1969.

———. "The Muse of Satire." *Yale Review* 41 (1951): 80–92.

———. "Pope's Books: A Biographical Survey with a Finding List." In *English Literature in the Age of Disguise*, edited by Maximilian E. Novak, pp. 209–305. Berkeley, 1977.

Macpherson, C. B. *The Political Theory of Possessive Individualism: Hobbes to Locke*. 1962. Reprint. Oxford, 1972.

Mahaffey, Kathleen. "Timon's Villa: Walpole's Houghton." *Texas Studies in Language and Literature* 9 (1969): 193–222.

Mannheim, Karl. *Ideology and Utopia: An Introduction to the Sociology of Knowledge*. Translated by Louis Wirth and Edward Shils. 1936. Reprint. 1972.

Mansfield, Harvey C. *Statesmanship and Party Government: A Study in Burke and Bolingbroke*. Chicago, 1965.

Maresca, Thomas E. *Pope's Horatian Poems*. Columbus, Ohio, 1966.

Martin, Peter E. "Intimations of the New Gardening: Alexander Pope's Reaction to the 'Uncommon' Landscape at Sherborne." *Garden History* 4 (Spring 1976): 57–87.

Mazon, Paul. "Madame Dacier et les traductions d'Homère en France." In *The Zaharoff Lectures, 1924–1938*. 1935. Reprint. Oxford, 1939.

Midgley, Graham. *The Life of Orator Henley*. Oxford, 1973.

Mossner, Ernst Campbell. *Bishop Butler and the Age of Reason*. New York, 1936.

Nadel, G. H. "New Light on Bolingbroke's *Letters on History*." *Journal of the History of Ideas* 23 (1962): 550–57.

———. "Philosophy of History before Historicism." *History and Theory* 3 (1964): 291–315.

Nicolson, Marjorie Hope. *"Newton Demands the Muse": Newton's "Opticks" and the Eighteenth Century Poets*. Princeton, N.J., 1946.

Nierenberg, Edwin. "Pope and God at Twickenham." *Personalist* 44 (1963): 472–89.

Olson, Elder. "Rhetoric and the Appreciation of Pope." *Modern Philology* 37 (1939): 13–35.

Osborn, James M. "Pope, the Byzantine Empress, and Walpole's Whore." *Review of English Studies* 6 (1955): 372–82.

Paulson, Ronald C. *The Fictions of Satire*. Baltimore, 1967.

Plumb, J. H. *The Growth of Political Stability in England, 1675–1725*. 1967.

———. *Sir Robert Walpole*. 2 vols. 1956–1960.

Pocock, J. G. A. *Politics, Language and Time: Essays on Political Thought and History*. 1972.

Quinton, Anthony, ed. *Political Philosophy.* 1967. Reprint. Oxford, 1973.

Ratchford, Fannie E. "Pope and the *Patriot King.*" *Texas Studies in English* 6 (1926): 157–77.

Reeves, James. *The Reputation and Writings of Alexander Pope.* 1976.

Reichard, Hugo M. "The Independence of Pope as a Political Satirist." *Journal of English and Germanic Philology* 54 (1955): 309–17.

Riely, John, and W. K. Wimsatt. "A Supplement to *The Portraits of Alexander Pope.*" In *Evidence in Literary Scholarship: Essays in Memory of James Marshall Osborn,* edited by René Wellek and Alvaro Ribeiro, pp. 141–44. Oxford, 1979.

Rogers, Pat. *Grub Street: Studies in a Subculture.* 1972.

———. *Hacks and Dunces: Pope, Swift, and Grub Street.* 1980.

———. "A Pope Family Scandal." *TLS,* 31 August 1973, p. 1005.

———. "Pope's Rambles." In *Augustan Worlds: Essays in Honour of A. R. Humphreys.* Edited by J. C. Hilson, M. M. B. Jones, and J. R. Watson, pp. 107–18. Leicester, 1978.

———. "Swift and Bolingbroke on Faction." *Journal of British Studies* 9 (1970): 71–101.

Rogers, Robert W. "Alexander Pope's 'Universal Prayer.' " *Journal of English and Germanic Philology* 54 (1955): 612–24.

———. *The Major Satires of Alexander Pope.* Urbana, Ill., 1955.

Rousseau, G. S., and Marjorie Hope Nicolson. *"This Long Disease, My Life": Alexander Pope and the Sciences.* Princeton, 1968.

Ryley, Robert M. "Warburton, Warton and Ruffhead's *Life of Pope.*" *Papers in English Language and Literature* 4 (1968): 51–62.

Sherburn, George. "Pope at Work." In *Essays on the Eighteenth Century Presented to David Nichol Smith.* Edited by James Sutherland and F. P. Wilson, pp. 49–64. Oxford, 1945.

———. "Pope on the Threshold of His Career." *Harvard Library Bulletin* 13 (1959): 29–46.

———. " 'Timon's Villa' and Cannons." *Huntington Library Bulletin* 8 (1935): 131–52.

———. "Two Notes on the *Essay on Man.*" *Philological Quarterly* 12 (1933): 402–3.

Sichel, Walter. *Bolingbroke and His Times.* 2 vols. 1901–1902.

Skinner, Quentin. "The Principles and Practice of Opposition: The Case of Bolingbroke versus Walpole." In *Historical Perspectives: Studies in English Thought and Society in Honour of J. H. Plumb,* edited by Neil McKendrick, pp. 93–128. 1974.

Smithers, Peter. *The Life of Joseph Addison.* Oxford, 1968.

Stack, Frank. "Pope's *Epistle to Bolingbroke* and *Epistle* I.i." In *The Art of Alexander Pope,* edited by Anne Smith and Howard Erskine-Hill, pp. 169–91. 1979.

Stephen, Leslie. *English Thought in the Eighteenth Century.* 2 vols. 1876.

Thompson, E. P. "Alexander Pope and the Windsor Blacks." *TLS,* 7 September 1973, pp. 1031–33.

Thornton, F. B. *Alexander Pope: Catholic Poet.* New York, 1952.

Trickett, Rachel. *The Honest Muse: A Study in Augustan Verse.* Oxford, 1967.

University of London Institute of Historical Research. *The Victoria History of the Counties of England: A History of Middlesex.* Edited by R. B. Pugh et al. Vol. 3. 1962.

Varey, Simon R. "John Gay: A Contribution to *The Craftsman.*" *Etudes Anglaises* 29 (September–December 1976): 579–82.

———. "*The Craftsman,* 1726–1752: A Historical and Critical Account." Ph.D.

diss., University of Cambridge, 1976.

Walbank, F. W. *Polybius.* Sather Classical Lectures, vol. 42, no. 7. Berkeley, 1972.

Weinbrot, Howard D. *Augustus Caesar in "Augustan" England: The Decline of a Classical Norm.* Princeton, N.J., 1978.

———. *The Formal Strain: Studies in Augustan Imitation and Satire.* Chicago, 1969.

———. Review of *Walpole and the Wits,* by Bertrand A. Goldgar. *Eighteenth Century Studies* 11 (1977–1978): 263–68.

White, Douglas H. *Pope and the Context of Controversy: The Manipulation of Ideas in "An Essay on Man."* Chicago, 1970.

Wilkins, W. H. *Caroline the Illustrious: Queen-Consort of George II.* 2 vols. 1901.

Williams, Aubrey. *Pope's "Dunciad."* 1955.

Wimsatt, W. K. *The Portraits of Alexander Pope.* New Haven, Conn., 1965.

Wolin, Sheldon S. *Politics and Vision: Continuity and Innovation in Western Political Thought.* 1960.

Woodbridge, Kenneth. "Bolingbroke's Château of La Source." *Garden History* 4 (Autumn 1976): 50–64.

Index